Cornerstones

*Daily Meditations for the Journey
into Manhood and Recovery*

VICTOR LA CERVA, MD

Hazelden
Publishing

Hazelden Publishing
Center City, Minnesota 55012
hazelden.org/bookstore

Library of Congress Cataloging-in-Publication Data

Names: La Cerva, Victor, author.
Title: Cornerstones : meditations for the journey into manhood and recovery / Victor La Cerva.
Description: Center City, Minnesota : Hazelden Publishing, 2018. | Series: Hazelden meditations
Identifiers: LCCN 2018020671 (print) | LCCN 2018034074 (ebook) | ISBN 9781616497637 () | ISBN 9781616497620 (paperback) | ISBN 9781616497637 (ebook)
Subjects: LCSH: Recovery movement. | Masculinity. | Meditations. | BISAC: SELF-HELP / Substance Abuse & Addictions / Alcoholism. | SELF-HELP / Substance Abuse & Addictions / Drug Dependence. | SOCIAL SCIENCE / Men's Studies.
Classification: LCC RC455 (ebook) | LCC RC455 .L243 2018 (print) | DDC 362.29—dc23
LC record available at https://lccn.loc.gov/2018020671

Editor's notes

This publication is intended to support personal growth and should not be thought of as a substitute for the advice of health care professionals. The author's advice and viewpoints are his own.

The Twelve Steps come from *Alcoholics Anonymous*, 4th ed. (New York: Alcoholics Anonymous World Services, 2001).

22 21 20 19 18   1 2 3 4 5 6

COVER AND INTERIOR DESIGN: TERRI KINNE
EDITORIAL PROJECT MANAGER: JEAN COOK
EDITORIAL DEVELOPMENT: CYNTHIA ORANGE AND VANESSA TORRADO

In This Book

Beginnings

Getting free of addictions is a long, challenging, difficult road and just the beginning of your real journey. What you learned in that struggle will serve you well as you begin to inhabit your days with the fullness of who you really are.

The journey to loving and accepting yourself is life-long. Love is simply a form of energy, present everywhere and available to be expressed through every action you take. You can invite it into your life, allow it to fill your being and light your way. I urge you to open your heart to yourself, drop judgments and notions of perfection, and feel the spaciousness and freedom within your grasp.

This is really what recovery is about, and it is only the first excursion into the power and the sweetness of discovering who you really are.

You already know that life dishes out its share of pain and disappointments to everyone. The way through these challenges involves being centered in your best self as much as possible. Cultivate the ability to reach out to others for support when needed—from those in your family and circle of friends who "get it" and who understand your unique challenges. You have to do this work yourself, but you don't have to do it alone.

The blessing sleeps next to the wound. You have suffered in many ways, and now you are ready to open a new chapter. We all have our stories, but must not be limited by them. *Why* you ended up in the throes of some destructive addictive process is less important than the *how* of remaining clean and sober, as well as getting on with creating the life you want to inhabit.

What held you back in the past is less essential than the support and inspiration available to you right now, every day. It is time to discover who you are *inside,* so you can more effectively create changes in your *outside* world. Fears will always chatter in your ear, sometimes shouting loudly how unworthy you are. You can learn to heed their warnings without letting them restrict your creative engagement with the world. Anger may try to keep you in its prison; sadness may relentlessly attempt to pull you down. But you can discover how to stay centered in the midst of any emotional roller coaster, to use the power of your mind and intention to positively shape your perception of reality.

There is nothing better than right here and right now. This does not mean that your life will not continue to unfold in marvelous ways, but rather that it is time to stop being held prisoner by your painful past or a fearful future. It is possible to get comfortable in your own skin, to find a deep peace in being who you really are. But this spaciousness does not suddenly appear; it arises from consciously paying attention to what is really going on. When you commit to getting yourself into the best possible shape—physically, mentally, emotionally, and spiritually—you open wide the gates of really learning to love and care for yourself. And it is helpful to align yourself with the simple gifts the planet offers: the embrace of mountains, rivers, beaches, and wilderness in which to soothe your deepest fears, calm your mental chatter, and bring you back to the path in which you are—and are becoming—your best and highest self.

This book is here to support you in that quest. To help you explore the different aspects of our collective masculine energy and discover the qualities you need that will bring forth the positive aspects of your inner self, the daily readings collected here introduce a different archetype each month. Archetypes are essential elements of our collective human heritage. Images, patterns, and symbols arise from our collective unconscious and permeate our dreams, fairytales, culture, and mythology. They represent universal patterns of human nature.

For example, one of the archetypes examined is the Hero. Think of a hero from a favorite story, movie, or videogame. The qualities such characters exhibit illuminate the basic essence of what it means to be heroic. Archetypes represent inner stores of energy and awareness, mirrors that reflect aspects of who you really are. They serve your development by guiding you to embody certain qualities. You can revisit these archetypes at any time, just as you return to the Twelve Steps to receive assistance in times of need or for new development.

Along the way, these daily readings help you discover these twelve essential aspects of your being that you may have ignored or never awakened. The meditations in this book were designed to lay out your journey to the principles of healthy, conscious masculinity. The path of self-discovery is also a difficult one, and there will be many moments when you will be tempted to return to old habits that do not serve you. In times of darkness, this book reminds you to summon forgiveness, kindness, and compassion, and lavish them upon your own being.

Sometimes you may feel like your copy of "The Life Manual" is missing some very important information, while other people have read the entire book and understand it. Somehow you didn't get all the correct instructions, and you feel lost. Instead of hitchhiking through heaven where no problems exist, you may feel trapped in a hell on Earth where everything seems upside down. To realize our genuine selves, we must feel the weight of our failures and our despair and intimately touch the territory of our own grieving.

As you have begun to appreciate through the process of recovery, *the only way out is through.* Recovery means you have finally said "YES" to life—to never die while you are still alive, to chart the territory of your own redemption. Ancient wisdom tells us that "a path is formed by walking on it." In the same way, every choice you make can be in service to awakening, to becoming an empowered, conscious male. Notice and become aware—and grateful—for the amount of choice you have each day. For much of human history, family and society decided one's work, life partner, religion, role in the community, and even one's values. Having the power of choice means that *you* take responsibility for your own life path without relying on scapegoats *or* saviors.

You are gradually learning to know, accept, and love yourself, even as you transform old habits and patterns that do not support your wholeness. You are beginning to appreciate the small, unique ways in which you can change the world as you live in it. You're starting to fully inhabit the space around you, without fear. You are actually learning to trust that your wounds and failures are part of the path of liberation, that they instruct you as much as your supposed successes in the world. Having intimate contact with our own human imperfections is not always pleasant, yet we often find our wings only on our descent.

Perhaps you are still settling in to the rewards of being clean and sober. Notice the inevitable ups and downs of holding fast to that commitment, because you know deep in your bones that it is good for you—and for those you love and care about. Even if you are still in the midst of struggling with addiction, I encourage you to use this book regularly to consciously nurture your inner development. Life is carrying a message from the child you were to the old man you will become. Make sure you listen to what it is whispering! Be patient with others and with your own evolution, for each stage and lesson contributes in its own way. Grieving and forgiveness are skills that life will keep asking you to summon.

Allow the ocean of who you are to gently touch and embrace the shore of who you are becoming. One conscious moment into the next, one day at a time, do your best to stay awake and aware. It is a perilous moment in our collective history. The world needs you to be whole, to offer your gifts, and to cultivate your awesomeness.

Be *your* greatest! Astonish yourself.

JANUARY

The King

The inner King summons you to examine your relationship to money, ambition, and service. As you crown yourself with a more conscious sense of manhood, generosity and abundance require your attention and awareness.

Each day of this New Year brings empowerment and possibility.

The skies of addiction are clearing, and sunshine is abundant. The worst of the storm has passed—for now. It is a bit easier to breathe, to sense the edge of possibilities waiting to unfold. Lessons have been learned, challenges overcome, some skills developed, and after a long period of struggle with addiction, there is a chance to embrace a different path. This adventure offers both sweet rewards and scary terrain—the highs and lows of everyday living. Deep within a man's consciousness, various forms of energy are available to be harnessed in service to his unique development and personal evolution.

Our journey begins with our inner king. Like the warrior, lover, and magician, the inner king is a source of inspiration, and all are archetypal reminders of basic qualities every man can make his own. In the months to follow, our tribesman, pathfinder, healer, and hero will offer the necessary internal guidance to navigate the external world. Then, our artist, trickster, wildman, and sage will bring their own dynamic forces to help inform and fashion our individual journey.

At various times, one or more of these primitive potentials will be more prominent in our life. Our task is to befriend each of these inner guides and embrace their teachings.

I can call upon many vital inner forces to assist me in discovering who I really am.

Every man yearns to be king of his own realm, to fashion a fulfilling and beautiful life. But before the king can emerge, the prince must develop his capacity to rule—not only the outer facets of his existence, but the inner challenges as well. He cannot do this alone. Different life experiences will provide their own lessons, but having teachers along the way to guide him can deepen the learning.

To manage a large kingdom, one must consider what is required to catch and fry a small fish.

There is a need for much attention to detail, a willingness to ask for help, and to use a variety of skills in the exercise of one's powers. Claiming the throne—as creator of our own life—is a daunting task that asks us to be aware of many different inner qualities, to cultivate and develop those that are lacking, and to celebrate and strengthen those we are already embodying. There is no shame in acknowledging our own ignorance. The trick is to not stay stuck within it for longer than necessary.

Reaching out to those teachers who might assist me is an important step in claiming the kingdom of my own precious life.

Many historical and fictional descriptions of kings include references to their madness. Every man has a shadow, a deep, dark forest where he has hidden all his unacceptable feelings and impulses. At some point, he must venture within to where his demons live.

The shadow king is all about control and power over others. He is primarily interested in his own self-importance rather than being of service to those who inhabit his lands. His mantra is more: more money, more power, more stuff, and more success, defined in purely external terms.

In the depths of addiction, we have been where the shadow king dwells. The Second Step, where we "Came to believe that a Power greater than ourselves could restore us to sanity," helps us realize change is possible, but we have to do our part. By observing our own destructive patterns and being vulnerable enough to ask for help, we create an empowering willingness to rule the kingdom of our own life more wisely. We can continue to align the highest part of ourselves with our thoughts, emotions, and actions, creating a sense of balance, order, and healthy limits—the opposite of what we experienced with our addiction.

I can carefully examine the unfair and exploitative patterns of my shadow king and choose differently.

The order and stability a king brings to the kingdom is grounded in his desire to serve, his willingness to rule in such a way that all may prosper. A variety of inner strengths assist him in this lofty intent. He is aware, pays attention, understands his own ambitions, and works diligently to achieve goals. Comfortable with his wealth, he appreciates the true meaning of abundance and is generous of heart and mind.

As men, we often struggle with each of these qualities and find it especially difficult to discover the balance between caring for others and attending to our own well-being. Time teaches us that the two—caring for others *and* ourselves—are intimately connected, and we are responsible for supporting both. This is a positive spiral, where service to others enhances our own vitality.

The energy of the inner king reminds us that our life gets better *one choice at a time*. We can structure our activities so that each day we move forward—even with the tiniest steps—to fashion a good life, however we define that. We might imagine placing a crown upon our head each morning as a reminder to make wise, "kingly" decisions and empowering choices as the day unfolds.

I claim a life free of addictions, a realm where responsibility replaces chaos.

There is a lot of negativity about maleness in the world. Through our conditioning, we have incorporated this into what we constantly tell ourselves about what it really means to be a man. We have been exposed to hundreds of thousands of images and impressions up to this point in our life. Many of us created a faulty foundation of great lies upon which to build our notion of manhood. We are led to believe that a "real" man is a sturdy oak that feels no pain, has no fear, and needs no one. We have been taught in countless ways to tough it out, go it alone, and bury our pain, sorrow, and fears within, entombing them in a catacomb of repressed sensations.

Such destructive notions about maleness drive us to deny our feelings; to self-medicate with substances or other addictions; to not own, acknowledge, or learn to express our deepest emotions in ways that do not harm ourselves or others. These are patterns that run deep in our culture, yet we have the power to shift them, to create a more authentic, positive version of what maleness entails in modern times.

Today, I welcome and explore a different, more empowering vision of being a man.

Every young man seeks a diploma in masculinity, for which there are no clear guidelines that determine when it is conferred. Get high, get laid, get in a fight, get a car are often the hallmarks of our rite of passage into adult maleness. How sad!

Being a real man carries so much more depth than such ridiculous choices might suggest. How do we find a path where we are true to ourselves and not to some fabricated, advertised, limited-edition notion of who we are supposed to be?

We might begin by examining the conditioning that has shaped us so far. What destructive messages did we get from family, school, friends, and the larger culture? Do we still buy into those constricting notions of manhood? We can begin to question the societal rules that tell us that men are allowed to play only a single note on their emotional keyboard: anger.

As we reflect on the conditioning that binds us, we can start to make conscious choices to seek out new role models—different from those males who have branded us with violence, shame, put-downs, and confusing messages about how to treat women or others whom we view as weak or unworthy.

Each day offers me the chance to discover what being a healthy man is all about.

Healthy manhood is a fine garment woven through time and experience. It is a comfortable fit, tailored with strong threads to endure the storms life inevitably brings. Soft and strong, flexible and resilient, its style highlights our unique characteristics, reminding us of beloved kings who were manly yet gentle, wise yet curious.

We may not be able to clearly define healthy masculinity in our own mind, yet it is apparent when we meet someone who is open, intelligent, in good shape, and committed to making the world a better place. When we encounter someone who communicates clearly and lives with integrity, we may find ourselves wanting some of that gold.

Many of the most amazing, creative, "together" men have been through the fires of challenges and temptation. Overwhelmed by their shadow side, they still managed to survive the horrors of addiction and somehow prevailed to find a good path. How did they manage that? They dropped any notions of shame, blame, and perfection and embraced a willingness to discover their authentic self. Learning to ask for and give support, they changed what they could, starting with their own perceptions and attitudes. They transformed their suffering from the inside out. They didn't judge themselves negatively or give up when things got hard. Instead, they sought support.

I can recognize and shift some of my most limiting beliefs about manhood.

Awareness creates choice, and each moment of being mindful is a hammer stroke on the chains of negative conditioning. Yet so many young men have no idea what that really means.

If we want to get out of *stuckville*, where only the most painful life circumstances are able to shake us and wake us up, we must muster the consciousness to stay awake to what is really happening right now. Shining the light of awareness in any given circumstance is not always easy. It takes practice to read between the lines, sense the music between the notes, and see what is not so obvious.

A friend who is lashing out and pushing people away is in pain and needs support. If we are triggered by something someone says, it is often because we are re-experiencing a childhood wound. When we feel cranky and irritated, the first place to look is within rather than blaming another. Each choice we encounter offers an opportunity for growth as we either take a life-affirming step forward, create an excuse to do nothing so we can maintain the status quo, or succumb to the temptation to take a step backward into an old destructive pattern.

If we practice being aware so we can better handle the little daily annoyances, we can remain more centered when a major challenge is in our face.

I can treat every unpleasant experience as a vehicle for waking up.

When we bring awareness to any difficult situation, we can choose to do things differently so that we don't react in habitual ways that fit us like a worn-out shoe. They may be familiar, but ultimately they don't help us get where we want to go.

Recovery teaches us to be mindful of what triggers our strong desire to escape, to grab our addiction of choice and run for the hills. It is not about judging these impulses or making oneself wrong for having them; it is about noticing them as they arise, even playfully naming them. "Oh, there is Ira, impulsive again" or "Here comes escaping Eddie."

It's time to just take a deep breath and do our best to stay present, allowing ourselves to feel what we desperately want to avoid. We can become aware of what our body is trying to tell us, where we are holding the tension. Such mindfulness requires that we pause *before* we act or react.

We need to take a moment to sense what is really happening inside before we change what goes on outside. When we just stop and allow whatever feelings are there to percolate through us, we taste a bit of freedom.

When I want to run is when I most need to stay present and aware.

Our ability to grow and evolve is rooted in our ability to be present, which is where our true power always lies. The past is history, the future mystery, and right now is where the action is.

We can practice being mindful throughout the day. We can pay close attention to and make conscious choices about all those ordinary activities we normally move through in the sleepy fog of routine. Waking, toileting, bathing, putting on clothes, combing our hair, eating, brushing our teeth—each and every action can be done with mindful presence. It's like going to a gym where we gradually develop a capacity to lift larger loads of awareness with less effort. We notice we are hungry, and we make a choice: junk food or something nutritious? We are aware we are getting irritated with a task, and we make a choice: take a break or grind harder? We want to chill and take a break: video game or a walk outside?

Whenever we become aware of a particular need, we have the opportunity to satisfy it in new and different ways. Without the initial awareness, there is no choice, only mindless repetition of what we have done in the past, which keeps us there and prevents us from moving forward.

Awareness creates choice and the chance to develop different patterns of being in the world.

Attention is the quality of our mind that simply focuses our awareness. We direct our mind to notice something in particular. We can point our attention inside our self, including our body sensations, thoughts, and feelings, or toward the outer world of people, places, and things.

Attention can be very concentrated—just on the tip on our finger, for example. Or it can be fairly diffuse, like when we are searching for a lost key or trying to find a trail in the woods. Attention operates in two modes: observation or immersion. For survival purposes, most of the time our attention is outward, concentrated, and observational. Is this plant edible? Does the fire we need to stay warm need more wood?

Self-growth asks that we bring our observing attention *inside*. Is that tension in our belly associated with a particular feeling? How are we right now—tired, sad, or confused? What particular thoughts keep troubling us?

Most of us have not been taught to use the marvelous faculty of attention in skillful ways. We flit from one sensation to another, often failing to notice recurrent patterns that are not conducive to our overall well-being.

Learning to play with the power of attention is fun and illuminating.

The king deeply understands that energy follows attention. When we direct our mind to a particular part of our body, for example, the blood flow increases in that area. Concentrating during an athletic activity—or even a videogame—sharpens our reflexes and enhances our participation. So it is with the flow of our lives.

When we direct our attention in productive ways, the energy we need to accomplish a particular goal emerges. Momentum builds, and a positive spiral develops wherein we see encouraging results, which then generate more energy to make continued progress.

Whether we're learning to play guitar, starting a garden, or working to remain addiction free, consciously using our attention to support creating the life we want is essential. The deliberate use of our attention begins to transform our perception of the world. We realize that what goes on inside—in terms of our thoughts, feelings, and beliefs—has enormous influence on what shows up outside. We feel less a victim and more in touch with our own internal power to alter our circumstances. Paying attention generates more possibilities and keeps us in the present, even as it informs us what might be needed as a next step.

Today, I will pay attention to whatever supports my well-being.

Learning to ride the wild horse of our mind is a skill that can benefit anyone. We think thousands of thoughts each day, and unfortunately, most of them are the same ones we thought yesterday. We tend to ruminate over the same things, day after day.

Such scattered thought patterns constantly dissipate our precious life energy into either a past that no longer exists or a future that has not yet come. When we pay attention to this internal chatter, the ongoing *thought-stream* each of us has can reveal important insights. We can begin to notice that the conversations we are having with ourselves all day long might not be very empowering. They may generate lots of anxiety, promote dissatisfaction with what we are trying to accomplish, or even convince us of things that are simply not true.

"Don't believe everything you think" is wise advice. Using the gift of our attention to just watch our thoughts floating by offers the possibility to stop and change the tune we keep playing to ourselves. When we replace a troublesome pattern with a simple declaration, such as "I choose peace right now" or "I am free of worrying in this moment," contentment and newfound energy can abound.

I will spend some time today just sitting quietly and observing the stream of my thoughts.

Ambition is the container within which our dreams are formed. It is a sacred cauldron in which we combine knowledge, skills, desires, habits, and intentions to create a magical brew of possibility. This special potion is imbued with qualities that expand far beyond the ordinary and mundane. This can be a positive driving force that enables us to overcome any obstacles. It helps us stay committed in the face of the plateau periods when nothing in our lives seems to be moving forward.

When ambition is married to our highest values, this becomes the guiding energy that keeps the lighthouse glowing brightly, even when turbulence and dangerous seas threaten to take us off course. In the chaos of addictive substance use, our ambition may have gone completely underground, lost in the haze of simply trying to find the next high, leaving us with little energy to invest in creating any future ideal.

Perhaps it is time to rekindle this essential vital force. We might begin by holding the important questions of how we define success, asking ourselves what we really want to create for ourselves in this lifetime.

I will carefully examine my own ambitions and pay attention to what they tell me about the next important steps in my life.

As any good king knows, ambition need not always be externally focused. It can also be the stimulating push we give ourselves to keep growing, evolving, and awakening to our full potential in terms of inner states of being. The positive qualities and values we bring to the world, such as kindness, understanding, compassion, joy, and peacefulness, are all worthy attributes to desire and embrace.

The purpose of ambition is *not* just for personal gain, though that may be the common image that is generated when we think about greedy Wall Street traders or the privileged "One Percent." When the endpoint of ambition is only external monetary success, it can easily leave us feeling unfulfilled and empty.

The larger view asks us to consider what constitutes a good life, and how that manifests in ways beyond more stuff and possessions. Spiritual goals, or even just the intention to be a good partner or friend, can lead us down amazing paths of discovery.

The determination and hard work involved in becoming a more conscious, loving being brings its own rewards. An inner sense of calm, peace, and satisfaction radiates outward, positively affecting all our interactions.

My ambition isn't about how to get all I can from the world; rather, my ambition can direct me how to be complete as I live in the world.

The twin pillars of ambition are enthusiasm and initiative. A king's willingness to strive for what he wants to happen is supported by both his inner passion and his outer action. His passion is infectious, and throughout the kingdom his people come forward to help him realize his dreams. As a result, he grows stronger and more confident. The most beloved kings welcome the help and creative ideas of others because they realize this involvement will make the desired outcome even better.

For many of us, living a happy, addiction-free existence was an ambitious goal when we first started down the path of recovery. Holding the clear image of our desired outcome can re-energize us over and over again and can help us keep our momentum, even when we're confronted with setbacks. Deliberate, determined, and persistent effort is what helped us get clean and sober, and it is what will carry us forth into creating the life we want.

Ambition is not about chasing someone else's dream or someone else's version of how we're supposed to be. It is about the unfolding of our most authentic self, one day at a time.

I will engage today with gusto and resourcefulness.

Finding satisfying and rewarding work can narrow the gap between what we do to survive and what we dream of accomplishing. This is about designing life and work, and our worklife with a sense of creativity. The idea of engaging in beneficial, wholesome work that honors the gifts we each have while acknowledging that bills still need to be paid may seem quite idealistic. We can view work as a calling, some form of contributing to the greater whole, beyond notions of wages and security.

Many of us never seem to find our true calling, or we remain afraid to pursue it. Our addiction may have interfered with discovering a satisfying form of employment. Often we have to explore different occupations before finding one that has the right combination of factors for our unique situation. Years spent doing work just to survive and support our habit, or being chronically unemployed, may make the whole notion of "noble" work seem rather daunting. Even dream jobs have their downside, but if we are to spend so much of our precious time and life energy working, why not look for work that comes close to something we've dreamed of doing?

I can bridge the gap between my current work and what I long to contribute.

We don't just sit and wait for our "dream job" to magically appear. Any and all jobs are valuable because working teaches us so many different lessons. We have to show up, be responsible, improve our skills, and get along with others, whether we are a janitor or a neurosurgeon. Working at a job and earning a paycheck is only a beginning step to discovering what we might have to offer the world.

With some experience and explorations in our toolbox, we can begin to ask the important questions: Is what we are doing meaningful? Does it match our talents, provide enough money for our needs, help us to grow, and make us feel good at the end of the day?

Doing what we love and loving whatever we are doing is a constant juggling act. Because life and work are so inseparably linked in our modern world, more and more people seek occupations that reflect the whole of their person. When we are at peace with how we earn a living, we have more energy to be focused, productive, and content. As with so many other vital aspects of our existence, when we have a sense of forward movement and growth, we can tolerate the inevitable little ups and downs.

Being clean and sober provides the chance to expand my work possibilities.

"Work to live, rather than live to work," proclaims a popular bumper sticker. For most of us, finding the balance between working, consuming, and living can be tricky. Determining how much we should work is often as much of a challenge as finding fulfilling labor.

Tales abound of hunter-gatherers who only required a few hours a day to satisfy their survival needs. The modern world of work demands more of our time and energy, and there are literally thousands of emotionally or physically toxic workplaces that can poison our life. We may have to forgive ourselves for staying with a deadening job for too long out of fear or inertia. If our job is draining us more than nourishing us, a change in focus or the number of hours spent may be in order.

One of the characteristics of the addictive mind-set is that we numb ourselves to distress. The personal consequences can be devastating when this happens—especially for those of us who are "workaholics," who thrive on all the praise we can get from overachieving. It is possible to find a healthy balance between work and play without a lot of internal conflict. But it takes time and conscious attention.

I choose work that is both balanced and affirming in terms of my life path.

There is a saying that money is a good servant but a poor master. Money is simply a tool that we can use wisely and skillfully to enhance our lives, or wield clumsily with poor results. Examples are everywhere of people who have accumulated enormous amounts of wealth, yet remain unfulfilled, trapped on a tedious treadmill with no idea how to escape. And it is also clear that there are many wealthy individuals who are happy, healthy, and wise.

So what accounts for the difference? Often those who feel good about their wealth are living a life in balance with their highest values. They often use their financial clout to assist others or to address critical local or larger planetary concerns. Having committed to really discovering and knowing themselves, they feel comfortable in their own skin and align their lives with what they most cherish. Yes, sacrifices were no doubt made along the way, for the road to riches is paved with many detours that can easily pull one off course from deeply held beliefs. To be in a good relationship with money, we begin with being in a great relationship with our deepest self.

Being clean and sober offers me the chance to clarify the relationship between my core values and money.

"Do what you love, and the money will follow" is insightful guidance. This often takes enormous courage, especially when both global and local economic conditions seem to be constantly teetering on the edge of a cliff. Yet the evidence is everywhere of people who followed their heart and ended up not only surviving, but thriving. This is not an invitation to be irresponsible with money, for like one of the powerful families in the popular television series *Game of Thrones*, one must "always pay their debts." Rather, it is a vision we must treasure and hold onto when we find ourselves engaged with work we know is not our true mission.

Taking the time to examine our talents and really discover what brings us joy in terms of working deepens our ability to listen and trust the inner voice that knows when we are on the right path. Then we can build a foundation that supports our highest aspirations. The cliché of the starving actor or artist is grounded in reality, but that only reinforces the importance of really going for it while still attempting to meet our obligations.

Just like my sobriety, big dreams start with paying attention to what is right in front of me.

Possessing a desired object, reaching a financial goal, or "making it big" in some fashion brings temporary joy and other good feelings, no question about it. There is a connection between fiscal fitness and feeling fantastic. Yet, in the long run, wealth is like health, in the sense that its utter absence can breed misery, but having it does not guarantee happiness.

One of the best definitions of enough is "just a little bit more." This crystallizes the dilemma for many. The natural human tendency is to want more—more comfort, power, fame, luxury—or even nonmaterial things like fitness or spiritual development. Like any addiction, chasing "more" is often a perilous dead end.

Every man must decide for himself on the endpoint that satisfies both a sense of security and overall well-being. Circumstances are always changing, so it is not so much a declaration of having finally arrived as it is an ongoing inner perspective that allows us to feel fulfilled, whatever the current status of our bank account. It is that internal gauge of success that matters more than some specific dollar amount we have accumulated.

I can be content with what I have, even as I work toward shifting my financial circumstances.

The abundance found in everyday blessings has been trampled by a world in a rush to go everywhere. When there is a natural disaster, imminent flooding, or fire danger, what do people grab as they leave their homes, possibly never to return? Do they try to take their big TVs or other expensive appliances? In an emergency evacuation, most people take old photographs, a few objects that have personal meaning, and papers and documents that might allow them to continue functioning in the radically altered world they are entering.

When we are so focused on what we don't have, we often ignore the ordinary gifts of our usual existence. It is easy to fall into a pattern of taking for granted the basics of food, shelter, clothing, good health, and enlivening personal connections.

The overflowing fullness most of us experience each day reminds us to be grateful, to rest in deep appreciation. The world offers its abundance to us, sustains us, and extends to us the opportunity to do something purposeful with our lives. The moments we have wasted in destructive addictive behaviors are behind us. Time to celebrate our many blessings.

I honor the everyday abundance in my life, which I share with others.

What we in this country call abundance, many in the world would label greed. There is some truth to the notion that the fortunes of the few are made from the misery of millions. Consumerism has become our dominant religion, and worship means going to the mall or shopping online. The religion of the marketplace promotes desire in order to continue its reign, generating new wants to replace those temporarily satisfied. This greedy state of being filled with wanting what we don't have is itself painful, yet, buried in a mountain of material goods, we seem to continually long for *more* and *different*.

The reality, of course, is that the road to acquisition inflicts enormous suffering and oppression on many. Throughout history, much violence has been done in the name of progress. We need only remind ourselves of our own addictive cravings to understand the power of consumer desire to just have more, and then attempt to fool ourselves and declare it to be abundance. There is too much waste, too much stuff, and too much apathy about it all. How do we personally distinguish between plenty and excess?

I can become more conscious about how my consumer habits affect others.

"Live simply so that others may simply live" seems a worthy ideal to embrace. While not everyone is afflicted by overpowering greed or "affluenza," this modern-day malady has reached epidemic proportions. Embracing a life of "shed and simplify" fosters living on less money, creates a lighter ecological footprint, and reduces the clutter and consumption that complicate daily life. Living simply supports being in touch with what everyone needs but no one is selling—at least not yet. It is a connection to ourselves, to others, and to the planet.

Choosing to simplify our lives is very different from depriving ourselves. Chronic suffering from hunger, thirst, poor health, or lack of shelter is not likely to promote inner development; people's physical and emotional requirements must be met first. The point is that when basic needs have been met, our continued personal growth is about *being* more, not *having* more.

It is worth considering that a greater sense of well-being is possible with "less is more" as the guiding principle. If we truly enjoy the beauty and bounty of what we consume, there will be less need for more and more. Without such appreciation, we never will have enough, no matter how much we have.

I can shed and simplify and still feel amazingly abundant.

Noblesse oblige seems in short supply. As the rich-poor gap widens, privileged people hide behind their wealth or knowledge in gated communities, closed to the world outside in their protected enclave and without empathy for those who are different or oppressed. The shadow king thrives as unprecedented corporate power mandates participation in an unsustainable consumer-madness, stuff-accumulating economy. Global warming due to human activity is perhaps the epitome of our destructive lust for more. It is easy to point the finger at the One Percent in this country for their excesses.

Yet it is humbling to remember that the majority of us in this country actually represent the One Percent in the world. We are the ones we have been waiting for. It is up to every one of us to find a path of generosity, of giving back to the planet—which amazingly continues to sustain humanity—and to other voyagers. Each day, we can find small ways to offer our resources or talents to those in need. We can begin with the temple of our own neighborhood and keep hope alive in our tiny part of the cosmos—the Twelfth Step in action is being a good king.

I can learn to be more generous with others and with the Earth and her many creatures, which sustain us all.

What is the nature of generosity? Beyond offering financial support to another being, it is an open-hearted sharing of our time, talents, and energy. How many times during our own struggles with addiction did others reach out and offer their aid? Feeling such support from others is uplifting in so many ways. It reminds us of our connection to one another and the fact that there is goodness in a world that so often seems callous to our unique suffering.

Those who consistently donate money, are emotionally available and welcoming in relationships, or volunteer in various settings comprise a force for good. Being the generous good king actually changes our neurochemistry, resulting in less depression and more happiness. It creates a life-enhancing upward spiral, a circular dance of connection in which we act our best without seeking any rewards, but receive many. As we nurture this quality in our hearts, minds, and behaviors, we become the beneficiary of tremendously favorable effects. We can gradually expand the circle of people with whom we are generous, moving from those with whom we are already comfortable or intimate to those who are not of our tribe.

I can extend a hand to anyone in need and really walk my talk.

To give is to let go. To let go is to open up. And to open up is to receive.

While giving may be second nature for many, it is often conditional. The goal is to give with love, joy, and a sense of play. When people feel the energy of receiving from others, they no longer need to take so much. As we learn to give unconditionally, we give up on a lot of things, we give in to a lot of things, and we give away a lot of things.

Our boundaries expand in healthy ways as we let others in and expose more of our true nature. Such tender vulnerability deepens our ability to discover the true language of the heart. We become more sensitive to the needs of others and begin to see clearly what is skillful in any situation. Generosity then becomes a driving force of our own personal evolution. We go beyond the amends requested by the Ninth Step, to enter the lighter, rarified air of giving completely for its own sake, devoid of any personal healing or other motive.

Today, I am generous and giving—for no reason at all.

"How can I help?" Those four words are some of the most empowering we have in any language. Being of service begins with asking this simple question. It immediately puts the other person in a more positive frame because it focuses them on both identifying what current need they may have, as well as the initial steps necessary to fulfill it. It can create a subtle but important shift and can help move someone from being a victim to being a problem solver.

This is different from the codependency so many of us who are overcoming addictions have experienced. We do not become unwilling martyrs to someone else's cause. We simply offer our assistance in a time of need and maintain our sacred right to say no, not right now, or maybe, once the other person requests something.

Being of service can mean we temporarily set aside our own needs in that moment to lessen another's distress, but we don't forsake our needs completely. The truth is that the more we offer ourselves in service, the more skilled we become at setting healthy boundaries. As we become better at relieving another's discomfort, suffering, or distress, we do the same for ourselves.

In the giving, there is always receiving.

Being of service to others is a very flexible mind-set. So many simple acts of kindness toward others are possible in any given day. We can reach out to people we know who might be lonely, help neighbors and strangers with everyday tasks, and lavish courtesies on everyone we encounter.

We can really show up and be there in many ways for our partners, our children, and our friends. It is simply a matter of focus and intent, generated by a heartfelt desire to make a positive difference. Service is about being responsive to the requests of others by honoring what *they* would like rather than what *we* think they need. This requires honest and open communication. As we tune into another emotionally, we can often be more objective and discover what they may be too overwhelmed to see. Then we can make useful suggestions, inquiring if a specific action would be helpful. The process of tuning in, carefully observing, clearly communicating, and then further clarifying is the bedrock of service, but it is incredibly important in many human interactions.

Today, I may not do something grand, but I will engage in many small acts of service, with great love.

What might we do about poverty, homelessness, hunger, inequality, violence, pollution, and ignorance? Any one of these human conditions can seem overwhelming, but these global issues usually have a foothold in our own neighborhood, and we need not travel to exotic destinations to begin to make a difference.

In any given place, there are many who are working every day to improve these unfortunate realities. And action on a one-to-one human level is also possible. As we may deeply understand from our own journey with addiction, those who most need help are often the ones most reluctant to ask for it. The chaotic nature of their lives may preclude them asking for assistance, or they may have not yet "bottomed out."

Our inner king understands that we can find a way to offer people a hand up, rather than a hand out. Many live on the edge of survival, and a broken-down car, unexpected medical bill, leaky roof, or job loss can toss them into despair. We can be part of their safety net, joining with others in our community to provide assistance, fighting those big causes one person at a time.

I will keep lighting up my little corner of the world.

FEBRUARY

The Warrior

The inner Warrior wields the sword of awareness so you might explore strength, self-discipline, and responsibility. How do you find courage, protect yourself, and deal effectively with the conflict, trauma, violence, or obstacles in your daily life?

Draw upon the energy of the Warrior to discover serenity in the midst of challenges.

To protect and to serve are the core of the warrior's credo. Society has always needed and honored this powerful energy—from Roman soldiers to ancient samurai, frontier sheriffs to modern-day military special forces. Highly solution focused, with a fierce determination to find a way through any obstacle, the warrior archetype represents the best of the human spirit. When bolstered by an inner quest to consciously expose, rather than blindly defend, one's weaknesses, a warrior's power can be highly transformative.

The exploration of warrior energy is useful in so many different facets of our lives, especially during our most challenging moments. When our sobriety is threatened, or we are confronted by a serious health or financial crisis, we can summon our inner warrior's courage, endurance, and strength. The way of the warrior asks us to not only test our physical limits, but to develop the mental clarity, emotional stability, and spiritual awareness we need in order to surrender our personal needs for a higher cause. There is a martial arts tradition that reminds us that once we achieve the rank of black belt—which takes years— we are finally "ready to learn."

I can skillfully use the powerful energy of my inner warrior to positively move forward in my life.

The shadow warrior is dark and destructive. Blinded by the concepts that "might makes right" and that violence is the ultimate solution to solving problems, the shadow warrior embraces everyone from soldiers who were "just following orders" to terrorists who kill innocents to make a political statement.

Lashing out in mindless anger and denying our addiction—and the hold it has over us—are common shadow examples we might acknowledge as our own. A warrior comes into his true power only when he has taken to heart the complexities of the Fourth Step. Through his fearless inventory, he discovers both his strengths and his weaknesses, forging a determination to nurture useful qualities and discard those that are not helpful.

Without undertaking this vulnerable inner mission to examine his faults, a warrior remains wounded, and much more dangerous. He risks becoming a fighting machine with no core values to guide him. Like a sword heated and folded hundreds of times to create a superb blade, the warrior, through many trials and tribulations, gradually begins to understand his harmful nature and what needs to be done to channel that energy in more productive ways.

I am learning about my damaging tendencies, and the steps needed to temper them.

The warrior knows when to act—and when to wait. He deeply comprehends how destructive violence (his own and that of others) can be. Through self-discipline, reliability, and taking responsibility for his actions, he forges an inner crucible; he becomes a vessel of competence. The warrior's power is complex and involves many skills. His courage and strength, understanding of conflict, and practice of inner serenity allow him to be skillful in many different situations.

The warrior utilizes the many tools at his disposal—as you do in maintaining your sobriety—techniques and capabilities honed through endless hours of patient practice and reflection.

Just as with the transition into manhood, becoming a warrior is a gradual unfolding, a steady embodying of both positive ideals and explicit expertise. Through an ongoing refinement of his capacity to discern truth, he improves his ability to make positive, empowering choices. He experiences a growing confidence in his ability to hang in there, even when his progress and development seem to be moving at a snail's pace. He appreciates that every setback is a setup for a comeback, just as it is for us, every day, dealing with our addiction.

I acknowledge the long road of awareness and practice required to develop my noble warrior spirit.

Violence is any mean word, look, sign, or act that hurts another person's body, feelings, or things. The world needs less of it, not more versions of manhood that glorify it. Violent behavior's great lie suggests that the lines between good and evil are crystal clear, rather than the messy complexities that actually exist in human relations and conflicts. Our own struggles with addictions have taught us that while black-and-white thinking may seem clearer, its rigidity actually impedes progress in understanding our own faults and those of others.

It may be easy to rationalize the harm born of revenge or retribution, or the injuries perpetrated under the influence of drugs or alcohol. But is violence ever justified, especially when defensive in nature? So much depends upon the perceptions of the person defending, the magnitude of the response, and the unknown intent of the attacker. Complicated legal and judicial systems have been established to try to sort out such degrees of behavior. The more we view violence as a *last resort* rather than a reactive, justified response, the greater our liberation from its myriad destructive tentacles.

I will carefully examine the ways in which I am violent, both subtle and obvious.

Many men today are so afraid of the warrior's force that they have become soft. In their attempt to avoid brutality, they have gone too far the other way and are unable to stand up for themselves, find their true voice, or defend what they believe in.

Pushing away anger and fear because those feelings are too scary often creates an individual who explodes in mindless, pent-up rage. He can create that which most repulses him, because he refuses to admit its existence within himself. Confronting the aggressive tendencies we *all* possess is part of growing up and becoming a balanced, conscious man. We learn to distinguish aggression from assertiveness, to find a balance between acknowledging our anger and spreading it around the living room. We observe and let go of poisonous thoughts and impulses without being chained to their mindless desire to harm.

In short, we make peace with the not-so-peaceful parts of ourselves, learning to be skillful with—rather than denying—our inherent violent tendencies. When an addiction has us firmly in its grasp, we know how easy it can be to justify cruel, irrational actions.

I vow to tame my own violent impulses without sacrificing my ability to be assertive.

Experiencing child abuse when younger, witnessing domestic violence in our household, or being victimized during blind drunken rages of parents and relatives actually alters our brain chemistry. Many victims of such family violence suffer from post-traumatic stress disorder (PTSD), often misdiagnosed as attention-deficit hyperactivity disorder (ADHD), since both result in difficulty concentrating and controlling impulses. They may feel driven by a survival need to always be on guard, and their coexisting depression and anxiety can easily lead to self-medication with a variety of substances.

For many of us, it was these initial attempts to control such pain and restore some sense of balance that first led us into addictive patterns with alcohol and drugs. We were having *normal responses to abnormal events,* but no one ever told us that! Escape—even temporary—seemed our best option. With time and various healing tools, it is possible to return the brain to a less disturbed baseline state. Everything from bullying to sexual abuse or acquaintance rape can leave invisible yet highly destructive marks on our emotional body. Out of fear or shame, we may have kept many of these traumas secret.

I will get help to heal from the wounds of violence I experienced as a child or teen.

Power has been given a bum rap in our modern world, its reputation smeared by misuse of its forceful energies.

Power *over* is very different from power *with*. The human need to cooperate is often overshadowed by our desire to be led, with damaging consequences. Those who abuse their power in various ways—from politicians and bankers, to soldiers and policemen—often operate without consequences, because they are protected by larger hierarchical social systems that celebrate the use of power for its own sake rather than in service to humanity or higher ideals.

Those who supposedly are watching out for our welfare may succumb to corruption and other dishonest practices in order to elevate their own standing. Blinded by their own greed, they see power as a force to be used for accumulating more power. We can learn from such examples how *not* to be in the world. We can seek out those who rest comfortably and securely in their power and use it to make the world a better place rather than engage in actions that oppress others.

Free from addiction, as my power grows, I will use it consistently for the highest good.

An *athame* is a psychic tool used to wield internal power. This knife-shaped implement—made from clay, wood, bone, rock, or steel—has its origins in sacred medieval practices. It was often employed to cast a protective magical circle. Its purpose is to help one ritually cut through those habits, perspectives, and beliefs that no longer serve. This is a basic transforming concept found in many diverse cultures.

An athame is a useful tool to remind us of the commitment and self-discipline needed to overcome obstacles to our growth and development. Our inner warrior develops power that uses every resource available for the highest good and furthers our personal evolution by treating every experience as a learning opportunity. We often wake up to our own self-destructive patterns through feedback we receive from the outer world, the most extreme example being the manner and circumstances under which we hit bottom with our addiction. The athame allows us to sever our attachment to unhealthy behaviors once we connect those all-important dots and recognize our harmful habits for what they are. Fashioning or finding one is a way to channel our inner power, over and over, as we make progress on the path.

I can focus my inner power to transform habits that do not serve my growth.

When we join our individual power with that of others, we create a *synergy*, a combined effort far greater than any individual component. We don't need to look far to see the amazing results that groups like Mothers Against Drunk Driving, the American civil rights and gay rights movements, or Black Lives Matter have had.

People who come together through their suffering in order to create positive change become a powerful force for good. There is joy in knowing that we can be uplifted and inspired working on whatever issue we care deeply about—related to our own addictive struggles or not—by joining forces with others.

The many streams of this human energy work together to form a mighty river, and we can celebrate our part in the movement. Being a warrior for an important social cause asks us to examine what talents and skills we have to offer and how our gifts might complement the work already being done. Feeling such group power trickles into our personal life as well, stimulating important self-reflection and growth. We see clearly the benefits of giving and receiving support, and the ways that process creates effective, important shifts in the larger world.

When I can lift myself above my own personal problems, I enjoy combining my power with that of others to manifest needed social change.

On a purely physiological level, strength refers to the maximum amount of force muscles can exert against an external load, while power is the ability to generate force as quickly as possible. We need strength to pick up a heavy baseball bat, but we use power to swing and hit the ball out of the park. The two concepts are related but quite different.

There are obvious parallels when we think about these words in terms of the inner qualities of a warrior. We generate power *in the moment* to transform a self-destructive pattern. We use power to penetrate our own defenses so that we might confront, accept, and make peace with our inner demons. Inner strength is about the *ongoing*, persistent, consistent effort required to do this work. So we need to develop both, because they so often work together. Strength endures over time, while the use of power is explosive and more temporary in nature. We might conceive of strength as a sturdy platform we construct that allows us to then move with speed and force when confronted with a situation that demands our attention and awareness.

I use both strength and power to tame my inner beasts.

The strong man at the circus is always an interesting character. He is often some version of the superhero known as the Hulk, with bulging muscles and limited facial expressions and emotional depth. Though his apparent strength is impressive, the Hulk shows us that "brute forcing" our way through any situation is often not the best strategy.

Human interactions usually require a certain amount of finesse. Aggressively pushing our ideas or making forceful demands does not usually bring the positive results we seek. Bluster, bragging, and threatening behaviors are often a front for insecurity. Many who project strength on the outside are sometimes quite scared and frail on the inside.

During the early days of our recovery, we no doubt encountered individuals who displayed an external bravado that was really quite fragile and flawed—probably because they were not willing to confront their own weakness. Those who have *true* inner strength need not constantly demonstrate it to anyone but themselves. There is a certain calm but real resolve they project without any desire for displays of machismo. They are secure in their own ability to call upon their strength when needed.

I can see through the strong external facade of others and realize that they, like me, have more work to do.

Cultivating inner strength involves walking the way of the warrior, just not the Hollywood version of a warrior. Whereas the typical champion—the hero—portrayed in the media is all-powerful and never gets significantly injured, those of us who have been through the inferno of addictions understand the enormous effort required to lift ourselves from that labyrinth of suffering. We were hurt, and we did harm to others; the admission of our powerlessness was ultimately what saved us.

We were—and remain—strong warriors who have cultivated some inner resources to fight perhaps the greatest battle of our lives. We need to honor the inner tenacity that has brought us to these first steps of liberation. It will serve us well as we move from recovery to discovery of our true place in the world. While outer strength fades with age, our inner resolve born of moving through challenges is enduring. This does not mean we can relax our vigilance or stop maintaining our inner dedication to dealing with problems and issues as they arise. We must continue to cultivate the strength we will need to move through other tests.

I will find the inner fortitude to remain drug and alcohol free.

The word *discipline* has its origins in two Latin terms, whose literal translation means to learn and comprehend what is good for one by taking it apart. Self-discipline has as its foundation the concept of teaching. It is not built upon a flimsy platform of have to, ought to, or should.

Rather, it evolves from consistently doing what we have come to know is good for us, on every level, including the physical, mental, emotional, and spiritual. It is an incredibly powerful ally on our path to discovering and manifesting our best self. Many conceive of it as some form of self-deprivation, as in eating less ice cream, spending less time on enjoyable video gaming, or even in not succumbing to the allure of a pleasurable drug.

Self-discipline is actually less about what we have to do without and is more focused on specific, empowering qualities we are enhancing. It takes self-discipline to get the most out of working out, eating nutritiously, processing our emotions, and taming our negative *mindtalk*. It is grounded in a big yes, rather than a no, allowing us to move our big visions forward and enhance our daily lives in a multitude of positive ways.

Self-discipline reminds me to keep being my best.

We learn as we go, and the path is formed by walking on it. Establishing regular reinforcing positive practices is important consciousness work. If we were to make a list of all the self-nurturing actions we engage in on a daily or weekly basis, what might we find? While many of us regularly practice some forms of self-discipline, we may not be doing this consciously or seeking to expand and refine our focus.

In all areas of life—whether eating, exercising, doing something creative, being in our living space, or engaging in our work life—we have to invest in order to be our best. Valentine's Day reminds us to love ourselves in this way. It takes time, energy, and a deep commitment to improve. Lofty goals can provide inspiration, but it is through the *perspiration* of daily discipline that we manifest them. It is the bridge, the gateway, the portal, the channel through which we gradually live into the life we deeply desire. We can begin with small steps in any important arena, and then adjust and redefine as we go. Paying regular attention to the various habits included in our self-discipline toolbox is one of the most important aspects of loving ourselves and supporting our personal evolution.

My daily choices are made easier when I stick to routines and behaviors that serve me well.

We quickly become aware of what gets in the way of our desired self-discipline practices. We can easily generate a host of excuses for why we should procrastinate or why we should quit the desired activity: it's too hard, we're feeling too tired, we have too many other competing interests—there are so many possible impediments to doing what we know is good for us.

When we observe such defeating impulses arising, we need only remind ourselves of our original commitment and take the first steps to get us in motion and out of our excuses. Often just honoring that prime impulse toward our practice enables the follow-through to happen. It is just a matter of overcoming that initial resistance, which everyone experiences to varying degrees. And if we do slip, there's no point in beating ourselves up for the misstep; we can just get back on the horse. Because self-discipline is not a response to some external "should," it is a part of our inner strength—an internal locus of control through which we hold true to what energizes us. While not always a smooth path, it is one with rich rewards.

Obstacles to doing what is good for me are to be expected, and I can move through them.

To be reliable means to show up and to be trustworthy. Bumper sticker wisdom reminds us: you must be present to win. For anything of any import to occur in any situation, we must first be in attendance, available with our time, energy, and talents. How many times did we get nothing—and contribute nothing—to group counseling sessions when we first started in recovery, because we were somewhere else in our hearts and in our heads?

So showing up is the first requirement, but then we must also be willing to honor our word and actually *follow through*. When we do this, we gradually learn the critical importance of doing what we said we would do, even if we encounter difficulties. This opens the door to other important lessons, including the value of asking for help while we are doing our best to stay true to our intent.

And being trustworthy also includes holding close anything confidential someone else shares with us—in or out of a Twelve Step program setting. When we put the concept of reliability into practice, we nurture many positive attributes: being present, asking for support, keeping our word, and following through with our actions.

Being reliable teaches me in many different ways.

Reliability is not about constantly pushing ourselves harder; it is remembering the good feelings we have when we accomplish what we said we would do. And that means we really pay attention when we agree to do something—for ourselves, or for another. Reliability constantly instructs us in setting healthy boundaries.

Many of us found ourselves people-pleasing during recovery, saying yes to many things that we would eventually ignore or have to drop because we were overwhelmed. We lied to ourselves, and that lack of living with integrity was damaging. Inherent in being trustworthy is that we honor our own limits so we actually have time and energy to follow through on the covenants we make.

So many in the modern world do not live by their word, and we all suffer because of that. As with many other attributes of being a warrior, embodying reliability is not necessarily an easy path, and we will find many obstacles along the way. Yet such impediments are actually helpful. We can greet them with open arms because they help us build resolve and see where we need to pay most attention.

I honor all the challenges to being reliable, for they are my teachers.

We have all known people in our lives who supported us when we were most in need of their assistance. We knew we could count on them—not in some codependent way, where they just continued to let us stay stuck in damaging addictive patterns, but by lending us a hand up to help us out of the mire of self-destructive behaviors.

Often, we did not acknowledge them for their important aid or for their actions that made a difference in our lives, because they were so reliable. Not only are such people ongoing good role models, but they can also inspire us to embody this important quality ourselves. This quality of being a reliable helper is not limited to teachers, health care professionals, or family. We are lifted up by the many individuals in the world who work with integrity and consistently do their job well. Their reliability is what enables the world to function, from the person who grew the food we ate this morning, to the mechanic who worked on our car, to the individual who made our clothes, to the person interviewing us for a job we really want.

I honor those whose reliability assists me in everyday tasks, as well as those who lifted me from the abyss.

Responsibility is simply defined as the ability to respond to what is actually happening. In order to accomplish this, we must acknowledge what has occurred, see it clearly by unpacking its various components, and then bear the consequences of the choice we made or the actions we undertook. We stop trying to minimize, deny, bargain, or otherwise escape the adverse effects of our thoughts, words, or deeds. We fully proclaim that we are sculpting our own reality, moment by moment.

We are coming to understand the law of cause and effect, which states that everything we think or do produces ripples that manifest in our lives. From science to metaphysics, from religious teachings to common proverbs, the notion that "we reap what we sow" is universal. Often it takes time and reflection to see the connection between what we are putting out and the feedback we get from the larger world.

Responsibility means we are willing to do that detective work, to tease apart the links in the chain of causality, in order to adjust our course and become more skillful in the future.

I can practice taking responsibility for everyday small things, to build my capacity to do so when more difficult predicaments arise.

The warrior counsels us to expect nothing, but be ready for anything. To expect the best, yet prepare for the worst. We are constantly reminded that we are not in charge of everything, that so much is beyond our command. To believe otherwise is simply folly. As much as we tried to manage our addiction, in the end we were defeated by such attempts. Only when we surrendered to the reality that we were not in control were we able to really make progress on the path to sobriety.

We create our own reality. This does *not* mean that we orchestrated or invited all the bad things that may have happened to us, but rather that we *are* accountable for how we react to them. We don't have influence over the creation of every negative situation we encounter, but we can alter its course by the responsible choices we make. Whenever we are emotionally triggered by a remark or something that happens, we can pause and reflect before responding in a habitual—and perhaps unskillful—manner. When our actions have caused harm to another—inadvertently or through direct malice—we can take stock of what we have done, face it full on, and then find a way to make amends.

Taking responsibility means I stay conscious of how I am reacting to difficult situations.

Responsibility is to be taken, not assigned. We are often eager to point out the faults of others, especially when they have not accepted the degree of culpability we think they should. Placing a burden of shame or blame on another—or tossing it upon our own shoulders—is not what responsibility is really about. It is not a constant barrage of incrimination, making others wrong because of their mistakes or putting them down for making less-than-skillful choices. Nor is it about drowning them in a sea of regrets—a fate we also must avoid ourselves.

The accountability that taking responsibility requests is born of a deep desire to grow, to look first within ourselves before pointing a finger at another. To ask, over and over, what is—or was—my part in creating the current dilemma, and what do I need to do about that? This places us squarely in solution mode rather than remaining stuck in a painful past or an imagined, fearful future. Responsibility keeps us present, willing, open, and in discovery mode. It sorts through what is really mine and what is theirs, a liberating perspective that empowers everyone.

When I assume responsibility, I free myself from being a victim.

Courage evolves from the roots of internal power and strength, self-discipline, reliability, and responsibility. We nurture it by consciously reinforcing these inner potentials. Everyone has moments of fortitude and moments of weakness. We need only reflect on our journey from addiction to sobriety to realize the many mountains we have climbed and valleys we have traversed. Remaining in denial about our fears means we never learn to consciously shift to a courageous perspective where we can realize the abundance of gifts that can come from such resourceful actions.

Bravery begins by accepting that we are afraid, that our fear has something to teach us, and that pushing it away only serves to strengthen it. It's not that some of us have courage and some of us do not. Courage is a universal quality that each of us can access, a beneficial force available anytime and anywhere, under challenging circumstances large and small. Courage becomes self-reinforcing over time, as we realize we are capable of pushing through our fearfulness. Fear always brings with it the energy to ignite our pluck, our spunk, our moxie. We can reach for the light whenever the darkness of fear threatens to overwhelm us.

I can find the courage to remain on a good path, just for today.

Courage asks us to act, even in the face of uncertainty. It is momentum that generates forward energy to deal with whatever trouble we are facing. We've already learned through the practice of the Twelve Steps that the first strides are often the most difficult, requiring a unified breakthrough. We align thoughts, feelings, and actions to move in a positive direction.

Rather than being paralyzed or limited by the grip of fear, courage helps us extend beyond—and through—the apparently insurmountable walls our apprehension creates. Every mountain of fear comes with a burst of sunlit heroism hidden behind it. We discover that bravery by naming the fear as specifically as possible and then illuminating a larger perspective from which more possibilities can emerge. Encountering a rattlesnake, being threatened by a violent individual, facing a serious injury or illness, or coping with the potential loss of a loved one—these situations are not that different. In each, clarifying and identifying the fear helps us summon the determined energy to find a way through it. We refuse to be held prisoner by our fear or be victimized by its power. Fear may visit us again and again, but so will the brightness of courage.

I invigorate my capacity for courage every time I face an obstacle and move through it.

Taking the time to honor courageous deeds is a long-held tradition. Most countries around the world have some celebration to honor their veterans and heroes—those who sacrificed for the benefit of others. But we all know that heroic acts are not limited to police, fire, and military personnel.

We need a medal of valor for every person who has come through the battle of addiction and stood ready to help others do the same. So many give their time and energy, volunteering to assist those just starting on the long journey of recovery. Their selfless, timely support and skillful interventions often go unheralded.

We see evidence everywhere of those who have overcome obstacles, transcended their limitations, and often triumphed against horrendous odds by claiming the dominion of their own daring determination. We have our own memories of courageous actions we ourselves summoned in frightful times.

The Sioux phrase *hoka hey* is uttered in times of duress and roughly translates as "hold fast, there is more." This reminds us that the trials and tribulations generated by fear will always arise, as will the courage, found in many individuals, to meet them.

I honor and celebrate all those courageous beings who are now in recovery and helping others to achieve sobriety.

Conflicts are a natural and normal aspect of any relationship. So why do we try so hard to avoid them, push them under the rug or into a closet, hoping they will magically disappear? Conflict avoidance is so common because few of us have been trained or have experienced any positive modeling for handling conflict. We didn't learn how to safely navigate interpersonal dilemmas. Most often, we are afraid of the strong emotional undercurrents present in significant quarrels. We may also be scared of what we might say or do in the heat of the moment that will hurt the other. So we build barriers that sometimes break with destructive emotional mood storms or ooze out in passive-aggressive ways.

The ability to discuss anything and everything that arises between two individuals is facilitated by clear communication. The focus is on determining and sharing what each person is feeling and needing rather than assigning blame or pointing fingers. To successfully resolve a conflict—or even get to the point where we respectfully disagree with each other—we need a toolbox of essential skills. The abilities to actively listen, share openly, and make requests instead of demands are paramount.

Managing interpersonal conflict well involves utilizing the learnable skills of conscious communication.

The war within is the most difficult one most of us will ever fight. The incessant clamor of "shoulds" and the turbulence of competing desires can fill our heads with chaos and confusion. In our addictive attempts to self-medicate and quiet the inner voices of discord and pain, we often took less-than-skillful actions. Rather than resolving deep emotional conflicts, we added more disorder to the battles unfolding inside us.

The true warrior is aware of the violence he perpetrates against himself. This includes negative thoughts, put-downs, and self-destructive habits. Unless we begin to regularly observe our inner workings, we can remain blind to the damage that occurs within our own mind— the rampage caused by our internal dialogue. The inner critic must not take command, nor must we surrender to the forces of despair and hopelessness. Simply observing the negative chatter is an important first step that already reduces its power over us. Then we can begin to create a ceasefire, lower the volume on the negativity, and shift to more empowering conversations with ourselves.

Today, I will be tender with myself and take a break from any conflicts raging within me.

An old Celtic proverb reminds us to never give a sword to a man who can't dance! Being in touch with our destructive power must always be balanced by a deep appreciation of the sweetness of life itself. It is a useful practice to make a list of the people with whom we habitually experience conflict and the situations that often create it.

How might we dance with our disagreements, relax into our struggles, twirl and whirl our way through arguments? The point of dancing is not to get to the end of the song, but to move gracefully somewhere through space and time, connected to another. The same is true with conflicts. The idea is not to finally get to the end of them, but rather to disarm the discord and find the path to satisfying resolution. We realize we may never be free of all conflicts, yet they need not hold us hostage or escalate. For some, conflict is a way to feel alive. How many times during our recovery did we add fuel to the fire, lash out at someone who was trying to help us, spawn a squabble to push others away?

Careful observation can clarify my patterns around how and with whom I often experience discord.

A strong and noble tradition once existed among ancient warrior priests or monks, men who dedicated their lives not only to learning the ways of warfare, but also to forging their spiritual weapons in order to dispel ignorance and promote peace. These spiritual warriors were consistently instructed to defend rather than attack, heal rather than hurt, preserve rather than destroy. Their whole community understood deeply that without cultivating inner peace, there is little chance of finding it in the exterior realms. They also created meditative techniques by carefully observing the natural and animal worlds, appreciating and practicing the transition from stillness to action, tranquility to powerful storm.

By both imitating and embodying qualities of the forces and creatures around them, spiritual warriors discovered a deep, harmonious way of being in the world. Regular meditative studies—including both sitting and movement activities—deepened their capacity to find a stable, serene core, even in moments of great physical and emotional duress. The true warrior does not act from anger or fear, but from a more centered place of interior calm. It takes time, focus, and commitment to create such a wellspring of inner quietude.

I can start each day in deep serenity, prepared to be a peaceful warrior.

Can we truly imagine acting wisely to defend or protect from a place of deep serenity? Having such a reserve of inner calm helps us remain confident in the face of extreme fear and challenges. The samurai of ancient Japan would awaken in the morning refreshed by thoughts of their own death. This was not a bizarre, morbid outlook, but rather a sincere practice designed to place front and center the realization that—at any moment—they might surrender their life in service to a higher cause. By starting the day with such awareness, they remained mindful of how precious life is, and they could rest peacefully in their resolve that whatever challenges were encountered, they would do their best. Keeping thoughts of death close by allowed them to move in their world with clear intention and commitment.

Such a centered way of being in life takes years to develop and is not found simply by reading self-help books or going to a weekend therapy seminar. The daily practice required to achieve serenity is not for the faint of heart, yet it is eminently achievable by anyone dedicated to the path. Take the extra leap that this year provides to cultivate such inner calm.

Every day brings me a chance to deepen my sense of inner peace, which is so important to maintaining my sobriety.

MARCH

The Lover

The inner Lover seduces you with sensuality and sensitivity. When creating and leaving relationships, emotions such as anger, fear, and sadness become familiar, accessible territory—no longer relegated to the shadows. Sexuality delights, as love and intimacy become living, breathing aspects of your conscious manhood.

The Lover's influence teaches us to listen from the heart.

The archetype of the lover is dedicated to the exploration of intimacy—on both a personal and a relationship level. The ancient wisdom "Know thyself" and "To thine own self be true" resonates deeply within the heart of the lover. How can we expect to find profound connection with other beings when we remain a stranger to our own deepest feelings, dreams, desires, and gifts?

The path of intimacy begins when we take the first steps of exploring within ourselves to discover who we really are, what we love, and how we might manifest and share our inner light. But learning to nurture and appreciate our whole selves can be a long, difficult journey, since most of us have had many experiences that drove us to hate parts of our essence. Some of that self-loathing found expression in our addictions, but our sobriety is testimony to our intention to continually expand the depth and breadth of how we actively express love for ourselves. Each day we can begin to be softer with ourselves, rather than being harsh and judgmental, when we look within. We can appreciate the beauty of who we really are, focusing on the positive while not ignoring our flaws.

Loving myself begins with accepting myself—even those aspects I don't like.

The First of the Twelve Steps asks us to admit we are "powerless over [our addictions]—that our lives had become unmanageable." This Step is actually a "lover's cure" for what ails us. *Loving ourselves*—in some ways our most important life's work—is grounded in accepting our own imperfections. When we do this, we can drop any pretense that we have it all together. We see clearly our own shadows, yet we somehow find the resolve to keep moving forward.

Every human being has a dark side, a part of themselves they would prefer to reject or remake. And coming to terms with that reality is one of the most important tasks of the lover. The beauty of imperfection is more than a comforting phrase. It is deepest truth. When we can be vulnerable enough to disclose our shortcomings—to ourselves and to others—we are on the road to accepting the fullness of who we really are, warts and all. Without such acceptance, there is no possibility for healing change, and we remain stuck—hiding and ashamed. When we face and accept our imperfections, we can stop carrying those wounds into every other intimate relationship, so we don't repeat the same destructive patterns.

Even when I am at my worst, I can find some aspect within me to love.

To be a lover is to understand the deep currents of our own passions. It is to have a sweet familiarity with the ever-changing seascape of the ocean of our own emotions. As we engage and understand the flows of our inner life, we open ourselves to fully experiencing the depth of our feelings. When this happens, feelings become familiar companions—rather than scary enemies—reflecting back to us how we perceive the world, which greatly enriches our existence.

The energy of the lover is always available, allowing us to be joyfully touched by the beauty in the world, saddened by its suffering, afraid for those we cherish, and angry about injustice. Learning to skillfully express our feelings alters our lives in immeasurable ways.

From that clear foundation, we become capable of exploring sexuality and the deeper hidden jewels of intimate love. Our boundaries clarify, and we see the exquisite loveliness of our *interdependence* with others. With time, we realize how love can infuse every aspect of our daily lives, how by loving we transform ourselves and the world. We open more and more, and become sensitive beings reaching out and touching others in profound and meaningful ways.

The more I connect to myself, the greater my capacity becomes for loving others.

Feelings represent the interior experience of our limbic system—the part of our brain that deals with emotions and memories. It is a sort of inner navigational compass. Direct immediate sensations and feelings are a natural consequence of being alive, painting our world with the basic four tones of mad, sad, glad, and afraid (to which some researchers would add surprise and disgust).

Emotions are a more complex state, involving a complicated stew of thoughts, feelings, and body sensations. Guilt, grief, shame, and desire are examples of this multifaceted complexity. Emotions have been described as energy in motion. Fear is the energy to do our best in a new situation, guilt is the energy for personal change, unworthiness keeps us on track, hurt feelings remind us how much we care, anger is the energy for creating boundaries and change, and discouragement reveals our courage. Moods surface when a dominant emotion persists. We can conceive of our moods as simply fluctuations in the quality of our internal weather, where one of the basic feelings predominates. Moods are ever changing, so we can be grateful for high moods and graceful in low moods.

Today, I can observe and experience my feelings, emotions, and moods in new ways.

All feelings are okay, but not all behaviors are. This is the basic guiding principle for our emotional lives. "Emotional fluency" is the ability to be in touch with whatever we are feeling inside and able to communicate those sensations to ourselves—and others—in ways that are life enhancing rather than destructive.

We develop this capacity for emotional fluency gradually, starting in childhood, as we learn to identify and name certain bodily sensations. We then expand the vocabulary we use to express the continuum of each core feeling. Using "I" statements, followed by a feeling word, helps us refine our ability to take responsibility and make these internal sensations our own. I feel scared when I see you drinking so much. I feel upset and angry with myself when I mess up.

Mood storms teach us about the ever-changing tempestuous nature of our emotional life. We all go through times when our emotions seem to have *us* in their grasp, more than we are having *them*. Through all these developmental phases, we learn to experience, recognize, name, and then express our internal experience to others. Addictions commonly interrupt this growth and tend to leave us with less mature skills in identifying and revealing our inner states. Sobriety allows us reclaim what we have been missing.

Whatever I am feeling is valid; how I choose to express it needs healthy boundaries.

In recovery, we learn to accept the deep truth that we were taught about expressing emotions by people who were often totally confused themselves. What was (inappropriately) modeled for many of us was a combination of denying or minimizing our feelings, which disempowered us rather than increased our ability to navigate the wave of emotions that rise and fall in the course of a day.

Now we're learning not to fear, avoid, or squash our feelings, but to embrace them because they offer us a greater depth of aliveness and often serve to get us out of our heads and into our bodies. We have each developed a backpack of habits related to how we interact with our "feeling self"—but many of those ingrained behaviors are not helpful or appropriate and can cause great unhappiness.

In order to make progress in life *and* in recovery, we must lighten this load by developing new techniques and skills for caring for our most challenging states: anger, fear, and sadness. We can imagine each of these as expressions of a wounded child who requires our concern, compassion, and contact. Addiction helped us shove these feelings into a closet by medicating away whatever unpleasant sensations were arising. Now it is time to call upon the lover within to allow our feelings to emerge, with tenderness and acceptance.

I resolve to reverse some of the faulty teachings I received about my emotional life.

Anger is often an unwelcome guest that shows up in the living room of our consciousness. Is anger good or bad? The reality is that it is neither—it just *is*.

But how do we handle the energy generated by this strong emotion? The behavior that erupts under anger's influence is what leads society to label it as good or bad. But the core feeling itself simply exists, without any moral judgments. Anger lives in our bodies, generated by a complex brew of hormones and neurotransmitters that result in the physiological cascade of fight, flight, or freeze.

Anger exists along a continuum. We can start out being mildly peeved or bugged, then go through the sensations of irritation and being ticked off, and before we know it end up fuming, explosive, and raging. As our individual, unique "anger meter" rises, it is a very useful practice to notice exactly where in our bodies we first get feedback that anger is about to storm through the door. Rather than being blindsided by its going from zero to sixty in the blink of an eye, we can learn to sense its beginning signals *before* it fully develops and we do or say something we might later regret. It then is possible to choose a coping strategy and prevent its escalation.

Today, I will notice in my body where the first edge of anger begins to simmer.

We see evidence everywhere of men who have no clue about how to skillfully deal with the fire in their belly that is stoked by anger. While some may equate its powerful force with the sensation of being alive, its energy is most often blind. When embroiled in its flames, we often think, say, or do things we later regret. The male emotional funnel is a useful image for understanding the conditioning that most men receive around their emotional expression.

The majority of us have been taught that anger is the *only* allowable male emotion. We're led to believe that fear and sadness have no place and must be controlled and eliminated in order to be a real man. Even though we experience a wide range of complex emotional states—like all humans—men have been taught to channel them all into the one acceptable emotional expression of anger. We transform a whole host of feeling states into one predictable, but ultimately destructive, state of expressing what is going on inside. Our addictions only reinforced this destructive conditioning by masking our fears and grief, hiding these important feelings—and burying them alive.

Every time I am irritated or angry, I will look beneath my anger to see if fear or sadness is what is really there.

We often become angry for one of four reasons:

1. We have an *unmet expectation,* such as when we nicely ask our children to do something and they do not respond.
2. We have an *undelivered message,* which often occurs when we have something important to say and the other person is not listening or does not want to hear it.
3. We experience a *blocked intention;* for example, our car breaking down when we are ready to go camping for the weekend.
4. We sense *a violation of personal boundaries,* as with a neighbor's trash spilling into our yard.

The reality is that no one else makes us angry. Such feelings are generated in *our* body, and they are *our* responsibility. It does not matter if we are "right," and they are "wrong." Whatever the initiating trigger, we need a toolbox that helps us get the energy out. We can draw, write, sculpt, exercise, play, dance, or talk our anger out. But whatever method we choose, we need to release our anger in *harmless* ways that won't hurt others *or* ourselves. Learning and using the technique of a temporary time-out whenever we notice angry emotions and voices are rising is another skillful practice.

I will expand my available coping strategies for expressing my anger in healthy ways.

Anything can happen at any time. This is the mantra fear foists upon the human psyche. While we move through life most of the time avoiding this precarious truth, we know deep down that at any moment our lives could be turned topsy-turvy through injury, illness, death, or natural disaster—affecting ourselves or loved ones. This knowledge lies deep within the dark room of our negative thoughts and can easily generate anxiety—or full-blown fears—that can limit and control us.

But fear is also a useful survival mechanism that has enabled humans to survive, both individually and as a species. In terms of physical threat, fear allows us to react quickly, without even thinking about what we're doing. There is no time to contemplate the tree that is falling on us, or our hand that is on the hot pan, or the fist heading for our face. We react first, both physiologically and with our whole being, to get out of harm's way.

Although fear can be an ally that serves to protect us in times of actual danger, it most often lurks in the background, sapping our vitality and holding us back from taking risks that might help us to grow.

I acknowledge the prison of fear and regularly ask what I might be doing differently if I were not so scared of failing.

The well-known saying "There is nothing to fear but fear itself" seems somewhat simplistic, as does the advice to always "choose love instead of fear." How do we actually embody these bits of wisdom?

We begin by learning the art of centering by focusing on our breath whenever fear or anxiety starts to grab us. Centering allows us to blend and flow with the current situation rather than block and resist it. Instead of reacting habitually, we pause and begin with our breath. We slowly breathe in through our nose and then hold that breath for a count of four. Next, we breathe that breath out through pursed lips, relaxing our facial muscles, for a count of eight. We repeat this process until we calm down.

With each breath, we can intentionally allow our abdominal breathing to get slower, quieter, and more regular, which communicates to our entire nervous system that we are safe. Breathing in, *we are present to whatever is.* Breathing out, *we calm ourselves.* Our breath is the bridge from where we are to where we'd like to be. We ride the waves of our breath to a calmer, safer place, where we can more easily problem-solve and take positive action.

Whenever any strong emotions threaten to overwhelm me, I can practice the art of centering.

Coping with fear does *not* mean ignoring it or pushing it away. However, some of us became very good at doing just that. We used substances to keep the walls in place, trying to turn down the volume of our deep-seated anxieties. Each time we call a fear by its name and welcome it as a friend that warns us of danger, we make progress on the path.

Fear comes dressed in a multitude of cloaks. The *loss of self* is a frequent concern with any significant injury, illness, or emotional crisis. Fear might also be present when we experience distress about being dominated, overcome, or overwhelmed in a close relationship. The ultimate expression of this disguise of fear is seen in our worry about death—the loss of our very existence. Another common mantle of fear is woven from the *I-am-not-good-enough* cloth. Feeling rejected, abandoned, condemned, or alone reinforces our deep-set notions that we may be defective, inadequate, or unworthy of being loved or wanted.

When we are wrapped in *I-won't-get-my-needs-met* attire, fear convinces us that we will be deprived unless we stay in control: an impossible bind in an essentially uncontrollable world.

When I name a fear as specifically as possible, it loses some of its power over me.

Sadness is anyone. Sadness is anytime. Sadness is everywhere. It lurks behind the scenes in the happiest of moments, sneaks up around the corner to surprise us, wraps around us like a heavy garment we cannot shake off. Sadness delivers low energy, emotional pain, and grief—it is a uniquely personal expression of a universal experience.

Human sadness and emotional hurt are like lightning that does not choose its targets, but strikes with no regard for position, success, or moral stature. For men especially, it is not an emotion to which we easily surrender. We will commonly try to stay busy, because stillness often lets the hidden sadness in, brings it to the forefront of our awareness.

Depression is a general, pervasive sadness. Some of us may have a brain biochemistry that predisposes us to extended periods of melancholy, a feature we share with other family members. Trying to medicate away our sadness is often what introduced us to the minefield of substance use. We can learn healthier coping strategies, such as talking with a friend, journaling, or getting out into nature, whenever this emotion threatens to drown us.

I can be curious about what makes me sad, rather than pushing the experience away.

Given how much suffering there is in the world and in any given individual's life, it is astounding that we are all not having a good cry at least once a week. Such regular cleansing is good for body, mind, and spirit. Many men have overcome the negative conditioning that prevents them from shedding healing tears.

When sadness is particularly prolonged, intense, and focused on a specific loss such as the death of a loved one, divorce, or loss of a job or significant functional ability through injury or illness, it transforms into the more complex brew of grief. Initially, grief always disorients and overwhelms. It represents an arduous transition from loss in some form to reintegration. One never "gets over" difficult experiences, but we can somehow fit them into the fabric of the big picture of our life.

Grief cycles and past losses may unexpectedly arise when least expected. A new sorrow may trigger memories of older ones. Grieving is more a marathon than a sprint. The more we feel our sadness and allow our grief, the more spontaneity and aliveness we will have.

Grieving well is a skill I can learn over time, and letting myself cry is good medicine.

Suicide can happen when a person who is experiencing deep sadness wants desperately for it to end and sees no other way out. They may not really want to die; they just want the pain to stop. Coexisting disorders, such as anxiety, PTSD, and substance abuse, only intensify the desire to permanently escape their suffering. One of the most dangerous scenarios is when a person who is on antidepressant medications suddenly decides to stop taking them because of unpleasant side effects, money concerns, or the belief that the meds are not needed anymore. The abrupt changes in brain chemistry that occur with such sudden withdrawal can trigger highly intense suicidal thoughts and urges. It is a tragedy that we lose so many people this way.

We can each be part of the solution of suicide prevention by learning the common signs of depression, such as changes in eating or sleeping, persistent low mood and low energy, and losing interest in formerly pleasurable activities. The most dangerous signals—when someone openly talks about hurting themselves, starts giving away their stuff, and withdraws more and more—require immediate action. Helping friends, especially those still embroiled in destructive substance use behaviors, involves getting them needed evaluation and counseling, even if they are initially resistant to such interventions.

I will educate myself about depression and suicide, and reach out to friends in need.

We get so many mixed-up messages about sex. We might hear that sex is dirty or be told to save it for the one you love! So many of us have been fed a great lie or a crazy perspective that we have not yet purged from our belief systems. Our inner lover is often confused, and the shadow side may emerge in unhealthy attempts to find sexual release and intimacy. The truth is that sexual exploration is part of being a vital male, though we do not have to act on every desire.

As long as there is honesty, safety, kindness, respect for self and the other person, and mutual consent, there is no harm in enjoying the delight of sharing our body with another consenting adult. Any messages we received to the contrary were usually fear-based lies, told in an attempt to somehow control the enormous energy of the life force that pulses so beautifully within us.

Religious and societal views differ widely on the subject, yet we get to decide whether and how we act on our curiosity, what kinds of touch are fulfilling, and the forms our sexual expression may take. This is not a license to force ourselves onto another or assume that because *we* feel sexual desire that the other person does too. Rape and pedophilia—which are more about "power over" than sexuality—are unacceptable, violent expressions, because by definition, mutual conscious consent is missing. These behaviors indicate we need some help and healing.

I honor the beauty and passion of who I am as a sexual being.

Some of us have sex with women, some with men, some with women and men. Homophobia is a fear-based dislike of homosexual people, which can manifest in bias and violence. Mutual respect and tolerance are just as easy to embrace. Homelessness, alcohol and other drug abuse, suicide, and being bullied are all consequences of societal prejudice, bigotry, and discrimination. A lot of people are able to come out during their teenage years, a time of accelerated learning about sexual identity. Or, since coming to terms with sexual feelings can take a long time, later in life may feel a safer time for allowing others to acknowledge one's being lesbian, gay, bisexual, transgender, queer (or questioning), intersex, or asexual (LGBTQIA). The process happens in different ways for different people.

Coming out does not mean telling everybody about our sexual orientation; it's better to first choose carefully those who are more likely to react positively and be supportive. The larger sphere of loving and accepting ourselves has to include our sexual orientation. We get to decide as an adult how to inhabit our own body and in what ways we express our sexuality. When people trust enough to openly share what separates and connects them, the world is a richer and safer place to be.

I can be supportive of all my friends—gay, straight, intersex, transgender, bisexual, or asexual.

Sexual addiction can be a very painful form of losing control. In our modern society where so many commercial messages are delivered through sexually subtle—as well as more explicit—advertising, and where endless stimulation is readily available through *sexting* or a click onto a porn site, we can easily mistake this preoccupation with sex as the "new normal."

The "everybody is doing it" mentality can push us into destructive patterns of random hookups and porn dependency. Porn can become a habit that bombards us with images, invading our minds throughout the day—even while lovemaking, which risks taking us away from being *present* with our partner.

Deciding where we stand on pornography is to step into the morass of the collective archetypal male shadow—the history of male domination, repression, and oppression of those deemed "lesser than." Why have we turned to it, and what might we be doing instead of it? Do we regularly use porn as an escape when feeling lonely or unmotivated, a secret that separates us from our partner? Given its downsides, does porn really agree with our well-being? Based on our own deeply held values, we have to determine what is okay for us.

I will observe my efforts to control certain sexual activities, which might indicate their addictive power over me.

While many of us go through periods of "recreational" sex, we usually discover that sexual expression is most satisfying when combined with a deep emotional connection with another person.

Being true to ourselves is as important here as it is in other realms of our life, but we must attempt to come to terms with our sexual desires and preferences consciously, rather than through blind conditioning. Men, in general, are taught that they must always be ready for sex—anytime, anyplace—and that sex is always natural and spontaneous, that we have no specific conditions under which it feels better, and that no education is needed. Many of us have been indoctrinated with the idea that sex is a performance and the grand finale is always orgasm—which denies the whole spectrum of pleasures available before that final release.

It is doubtful that older men have given us much more than locker room talk, as opposed to real bits of helpful advice. It takes patience and practice to be able to look our partner in the eyes, learn about the difference between orgasm and ejaculation, ask our partner directly what acts might be pleasurable, understand our basic anatomy and physiology as well as our partner's, and build true physical and emotional intimacy. Recovery allows us to explore this as we were never able to before.

I can still obtain the healthy sexual and emotional education I was denied when younger.

Heaven and hell underneath one roof—such is one poetic description of intimate partnerships. Close emotional relationships are a great laboratory for healing, awakening, and understanding our whole selves, serving as both crucible and sanctuary. Some experts in the field of psychology think that we are attracted to partners who embody the best and/or the worst of our parents or members of our family of origin. They say that when we do this, we re-create situations, conflicts, and wounds from our childhood at a point in our development when we are more empowered to heal them. For example, if our mother was an alcoholic, we may find ourselves in a relationship with someone who also has trouble with alcohol. This can cause many of the same issues we experienced when younger to resurface.

In a coupled relationship, the marvelous possibility exists that we can help each other move through these past emotional injuries to arrive at a place of aliveness and wholeness. By unconsciously attracting the correct partner to help us do this, we are then able to consciously heal.

I acknowledge that one reason I am partnered with someone is so we both can heal childhood wounds.

Successfully being in an intimate partnership with another human requires a dynamic toolbox of communication skills. Whenever we are emotionally triggered by something our loved one has said or done, the first step is to actually notice that we have become upset, so that we can pause *before* reacting. We can take a moment to center ourselves and communicate to the other person that we have been triggered. Before engaging in a conversation with our partner, we need to first inquire *within* what our upset might be about, especially as it relates to earlier wounding.

By self-calming in the moment, we optimize the chances of not falling down the rabbit hole of unskillful responses. This is challenging, difficult work, but ultimately it is what will free us from conditioned and habitual responses with each other—reactions that only keep us stuck and in conflict. Clarifying, listening, making requests rather than demands, taking a time-out, or expressing affection even in the midst of turmoil are all ways that keep us moving forward. The pull of our past patterns of using substances to escape when triggered may be strong, but we now know better and can call on our support systems when situations with a partner are particularly demanding.

Conflict and getting triggered are normal in any close relationship, and I need to respond skillfully.

Breaking up is hard to do. As the Paul Simon song goes, there may be fifty ways to leave a lover, but some approaches are definitely more skillful and sensitive than others. There is bound to be a complex brew of emotional upset, with fear, anger, sadness, and inadequacy competing for dominance at any given moment. This will be true on both sides, but more intense for the person who is being left or rejected by the other.

Taking time alone to process all these feelings is very important, and journaling can be very helpful. While healthy distractions, new activities, and old friends can support our healing from the breakup, medicating the situation with a new relationship is generally not a good idea. We need *time* to appreciate what worked and to pay attention to what didn't work well in a relationship before re-engaging intimately with another. Jumping right into another *affaire d'amour* or courtship after a breakup usually keeps us blind to the lessons of the previous one. While it may feel like a healing balm for what ails us, ultimately rushing into a new romance on the heels of the former one leads to the same old, same old. In recovery, we learn that there are no real failures, only lessons from experiments in relating that did not produce the results we wanted.

When a close relationship is dissolving, I can find many forms of healthy support and avoid slipping back into destructive patterns.

The quality of our lives is highly dependent on our capacity to communicate clearly. The lover knows that the ability to listen deeply in relationship is one of the essential skills required to be a master of mindfulness. Active listening creates spaciousness with another being; rather than trying to make a situation be different from what it is, or attempting to "fix" anything, we instead allow it to just *be*. It creates possibilities for deeper connection.

We cannot always be certain that we have really heard what another person wants to share, since it comes through the filters of our own beliefs and perspectives. And when what we are hearing is negative, we may be triggered with guilt, shame, sadness, or anger. Profound and attentive listening helps us sort out our feelings by focusing our attention on the *intent* behind the message, by focusing on *the other person* rather than on *ourselves*.

We all know people who are "listening impaired." In recovery, we learn there are no stupid questions, but there are plenty of useless answers from people who enjoy spouting their advice without really lending an ear to our real situation. We encounter many such individuals in meetings and counseling sessions who do not edit themselves and who prefer to talk rather than inquire. They remind us to continue to hone our own listening abilities.

Listening well is a skill I can practice all day long.

The lover knows how to listen to the still, quiet truth within him. He is familiar with the chorus of different perspectives within his consciousness. While one voice may say "go" and another "stop," he can discern where his authentic values lie and peer beneath apparent inner conflict to discern the guidance he requires.

Listening to our hearts—hearing the unspoken truths, sensing the power of silence, and feeling the sentiments floating beneath the words—comes only through practice. When we regularly take time to quiet all the voices around us that offer suggestions and tell us what to do, we create the space for deeper understanding to be revealed. We begin to nurture the wise, intuitive aspect of our being that knows that answers will emerge to our deepest questions only when we can really hear—and fully live—the replies. We learn to trust both our hearts and our guts, grounded in lessons learned. Our addiction prevented us from accessing and hearing our own true voice. Sobriety allows us to have confidence in ourselves, to finally listen to the intelligent wisdom that has always been there.

Whenever I listen deeply within, I intently attend to the insights of my own counsel.

Intimate partnerships are tremendously enhanced as we learn to listen with the third ear, just as we see with the third eye. Listen with a connected heart. Listen with what the Eskimos call *seuketat,* the ear of the animal that is attuned to nature and other members of our tribe. Listen as if there is a thief in the house. Listen with the intensity normally reserved for speaking. Listen as if to hear the songs of the birds that populate the secret places of the forest.

If hearing is the act of receiving sound, then listening is the art of decoding messages. When we engage its magic, we become more present and available to another person. We let go of thinking about how to respond, offering our own thoughts on the matter, or focusing on what comes next in the conversation. We are fully present, listening with our whole being, not just our ears. This can provide a healing experience for both of us when we have no agenda to push, no point to make, no intention other than really deeply comprehending whatever they might be sharing—good news or the suffering of their struggles. We do not judge, we do not withdraw, we simply open to just be with them.

Practicing active listening is both rewarding and enlightening.

A lover possesses many qualities, but one of the most underrated—yet critically important—is his sensitivity. This word might conjure images of an effeminate, somewhat spineless or weak person, or someone easily offended or hurt. But the lover understands the deeper meaning of the word, which exalts one's ability to be in touch, in tune, and responsive.

Balancing our assertive "yang" with some receptive "yin" brings a greater awareness to many diverse situations. We enhance our ability to understand what other people are feeling and needing, to offer kindness whenever and wherever we see suffering. The self-absorption and narcissism of addictions often blunts this natural human capacity. How many times were we completely insensitive, indifferent, or inconsiderate to those around us, even those we loved? As we live into our sobriety, day by day, we may find that many new sensibilities are enhanced.

We can invite the power of sensitivity into our lives at any time by fine-tuning our senses to receive and perceive that which is normally lost in the busyness and hustle of daily life. To be sensitive, we must slow down, appreciate, and be curious, open, and vulnerable.

My sensitivity training begins with a delicate, tender receptivity to whatever is occurring.

Ultimately, our body is the temple within which we find ourselves. All that we are, and everything we learn, emerges from our physical body. It is the starting point for all our explorations—including those with other people. In this moment, where are we on the continuum from dis-ease to discomfort, from good health to well-being and optimal flow? Being receptive to the feedback our body constantly offers us is a discipline worth developing. We have many chances to really pay attention to the signals our body is giving us that are connected to nutrition, exercise, and the ways we manage stress.

Our addictive self may have encouraged us in various ways to ignore the wisdom of the body. We can now reclaim it, nurture it, comfort and respect it for the sacred container it is. We might even try pampering it with massages, hot baths, and healthy skin products. Enhancing our sensitivity to the body's messages is strengthened by any body-mind-spirit integrative practice, such as yoga, martial arts, or even sports. In these and other disciplines, we focus on listening to the body and aligning it with its truth.

I may like or hate my body, but it is mine for the duration. I can learn to listen to the subtle truths it has to tell me.

Besides an enhanced tenderheartedness and openness to others, as well as to his own body, a lover brings the same delicate perception to the wonders of the natural world. He is inspired by the beauty that vibrates everywhere: in the sunrise sparkling in a jungle, snow falling in the vastness of the desert, moonlight dappling down deep into the forest, sunset over the endless horizon of the ocean.

Life is a truly amazing tapestry, and humans have managed to survive in nearly every extreme condition the planet offers. During our most difficult times with our addictions, some of us found some comfort in the spacious stillness that being outside offered. Maybe it was just going to a park or a vacant lot or sitting by a fire, but something pulled us to experience the healing powers of our environment. And now that we are clean and sober, we are free to explore the magic inherent in wild places, the deep silence and quiet moments offered to us as we continue our healing journey. Nature can move us to write poetry or compose a song, touching our inner core with its surprises and inspiring us to protect it.

I open myself to the healing gifts nature lavishes so freely upon me.

Love is an action verb. It is nurturing, caring, giving. Love is full of different flavors. It is boisterous, quiet, wildly demonstrative, and softly tender. Love has many different languages of expression.

Some people feel most loved when they receive presents, others by physical touch—including holding hands, embracing, cuddling, and kissing, even when not progressing to lovemaking. Still others prefer compliments and verbal appreciation, including love notes or texts. Some experience feelings of love most through time spent together, receiving the other's undivided attention. Performing acts of service for our beloved can also be meaningful—cooking a meal, repairing something, or organizing a surprise party.

While all of these expressions are important for everyone, when done in a positive, kind spirit, usually one or two are most satisfying. What does our own unique love language look like? In our own family of origin, we may have never experienced certain love patterns, and they may seem alien to us at first. During our struggles with addiction, we were often unable to let in the love of others. Now we can open up and become aware of just what forms are most appealing to us.

I strive today to express my love for those close to me in ways they most appreciate.

Self-love can seem a confusing maze in which many of us feel lost and hopeless. We hold on tightly to memories of the love we did not receive in the past, using them as a shield to protect us from being vulnerable and hurt again. Our hearts stay closed, although the yearning for deep connection may remain.

Self-love asks us to be mindful and hold our own well-being and happiness in positive regard. This is not a narcissistic, selfish perspective, an always aim-to-feel-good state. Rather, it is an honoring of our very being. It is a dynamic appreciation for both our strengths and weaknesses, grounded in the gradual acceptance of who we are as a whole being—with all our unique physical, mental, emotional, and spiritual flavors and flaws. Addictive behaviors helped us run from our faults rather than learn to accept and then, perhaps, transform them. Knowing what we feel, think, and want leads to a deeper understanding of self-care and healthy boundaries. It is a lifelong journey that we nourish by small actions and wise choices each and every day.

Today, I will focus on improving one personal quality that will help me love myself more.

Expanding the circle of those we love is often challenging. People can be gnarly, prejudiced, insensitive, mean, and greedy. They may regularly and unskillfully spread their anger and stress around the office, public places, or intimate living rooms. Those who are very difficult, who trigger and challenge us the most, can often be our greatest teachers. They instruct us in patience and compassion and lead us to examine our own limiting beliefs.

But what should we do when someone's negative, blaming, shaming, angry energy is directed at us? As emphasized in the popular science fiction television and movie series *Star Trek*, "Shields up and open a channel!" In other words, we can first protect ourselves, and then try to understand what the other person's need really is. When someone is emotionally dumping their garbage, we need to give them space, both emotionally and physically, so it doesn't have to land on us. We can practice expanding our love and acceptance of others by reminding ourselves—especially when they are at their worst—of the simple phrase "This, too, is within me." Identifying with them can temporarily suspend our harsh judgments, which opens up the possibility of change and reminds us that our own journey to wholeness has been fraught with its own predicaments.

May all beings be free and find happiness.

APRIL

The Magician

The inner Magician invokes a spell of insight, intuition, and flow. He knows the secrets of confidence, as well as the alchemy required for your growth—and can reveal them to you. His visioning allows you to manifest intentions and commit to life-affirming habits, even as you dance with uncertainty.

The magician in each of us is no fool, seduced by easy parlor tricks, but is an agent of awakening. This aspect of our being knows that developing sacred space is an intimate and creative process, and the rituals involved slow us down, remove us from our habitual ways of seeing the world, and remind us to expand our possibilities. Such rituals can feel transformative. Even magical!

Most of us are familiar with ceremony and ritual: we have witnessed graduations, marriages, funerals, and religious activities in some form. Even a simple birthday party has the essentials of ritual: a predetermined form (who comes and where it is held), function (desired outcome of a happy child lavished with love), and sense of structure (playing games, opening presents, blowing out candles, and then eating birthday cake).

Our inner magician understands the power of such ritual undertakings when they are performed with positive, clear intent to improve our life. We might imagine a daily practice that inspires gratitude, a monthly ritual that honors our sobriety, or a seasonal ceremony where we envision and open ourselves to the continued blessings in our life. Words spoken, formal dress, and symbolic actions might combine to create an empowering ceremony—with unknowable, unanticipated, unpredictable results.

My inner magician holds many gifts that I can begin to access at any time through inventive ritual and ceremony.

The world is full of magic. Serendipity, synchronicity, and random revelations appear on a regular basis. Some might call these wondrous moments of connection fate or karma, coincidence, or messages from our Higher Power. Whatever we call them, altered states of awareness and energy fields beyond our ordinary perceptions do exist, and they manifest each day to those who are willing to look.

During our perilous times with substances, many of us were somehow rescued from horrific situations by benign forces of unknown origin. One way we tap into the Great Mystery that surrounds us is by paying attention to the subtle signs that are offered: the chance remark of a passerby that delivers an insight we need, a book screaming out at us from a bookstore shelf, finding a lost object whose return leads to unexpected adventures. The magician reminds us of the Third Step, when we make "a decision to turn our will and our lives over to the care of God"—or to whatever we understand the Higher Power beyond self that influences the course and patterns of our lives to be.

Magic and mystery are everywhere, calling me to experience wonders in ordinary moments.

Magicians don't save us, but they do show us how to save ourselves. Their tools are not ancient texts or mysterious tomes, secret spells, or ritual objects of divination that foretell our future. Rather, they marshal the forces of visioning, intentions, and habits. Magicians understand the inner workings of commitment and confidence as they wield the mighty sorcery of intuition and insight. Because they are grounded in compassion and empathy, they become skilled at knowing what magic—what transformation of consciousness—they need to work in any given situation.

Without getting caught up with the trappings of ego and how special they are, magicians humbly use their abilities to discern beyond ordinary reality the underlying truths of our universe and find practical ways to assist others on their journey. They are filled with deep understanding for the plight of others, in large part because of their own transformational journey. Their suffering, mistakes, and missteps now become the light that guides others. As many of us have experienced in treatment or Twelve Step meetings, those who have been through the fire are often most skilled at illuminating the way, providing insightful strategies.

Part of my own magic is learning to save myself, to find a clear path of personal transformation.

Traditionally, a vision quest was a rite of passage for young males on the threshold of adulthood. Found throughout the world in many diverse indigenous cultures, this initiation was designed to instill in the youth responsibility for his life within a tribal community.

The essential elements of a vision quest include elder-led ceremonies and isolation in a natural environment—often a known sacred site—where a boy undergoes physically challenging tests, including fasting and sleeplessness. The intent is to obtain information and guidance about his life purpose, specific role in his community, and what unique talents he can offer to the larger tribal group. By tuning into nature over the course of many days, with its inherent magic and mystery, these insights and perceptions may appear in the form of dreams, natural signs, or waking visions. The rituals involved help him to purify and prepare for—as well as to integrate—whatever insights are harvested through the experience.

Such positive, life-affirming traditions continue to this day in many cultures. By following such examples of establishing our *purpose*, we can create meaningful encounters to guide ourselves.

I see the value in creating the sacred space to better discover my purpose.

As we consistently act to move our lives in the direction we want, we can remember to call upon the booster power of visualization. Many in recovery call this process *acting as if.* When we repeatedly visualize a specific desired outcome over forty days, we create new neural pathways—our brains actually rewire connections, so the new perspective or positive thinking habit becomes stabilized. The key is to make our visualization practice clear, vivid, and real. We want to see the desired outcome in our minds, as if we have already achieved it, and in as much detail as possible.

Smells, sights, sounds, actions, and positive feelings can all be added to the mental picture we create. The imagination inherent in visualization is more powerful than willpower, and it helps us get back to persistently broadcasting our original intention. Our power doesn't create the desired or needed change; we just open the gates of our mind with desire, intention, and attention to what needs doing. We keep acting *as if* we already have what we want, for the highest good of all concerned. We reinforce our emerging purpose and life design as we continue to practice the art of actively imagining our results, throughout each step of forward progress.

I can use the potency of repeated visualization to help manifest whatever is most needed on the next step in my journey.

Besides using the energy of visualization for manifesting specific goals, we can employ it to regulate internal experiences of our body, and thus reduce physical discomfort, mental confusion, and emotional upset. We can learn to temper physical pain by imagining that we are fluffing up white clouds at the edge of our pain—not fighting it or pushing it away, but simply softening its edge.

Whenever our mind threatens to overwhelm us with its runaway negative thought train, we can summon assistance by conjuring images of purifying calm—perhaps a soothing waterfall or deserted ocean shore. When we are emotionally upset, held in the constricting grip of fear, the bottomless abyss of sorrow, or the damaging blindness of anger, we can visualize breathing in calm, healing blue light and exhaling whatever dark turbulence is consuming us. Such actions enable us to transform our situation in the moment, which is the real magic of altering perceptions and consciousness. All of these examples represent very useful tools we can use whenever old habits or impulses might want to take us down the destructive path of visiting an old addiction.

I can use the splendor of my imaging imagination to transform unpleasant current realities.

Habits contribute in a big way to human evolution and to our individual developmental journey. To deal with ever-changing conditions and create some stability, our body develops and relies on habits, which our brain thinks of as being energy efficient and for our greater good. Habits keep us safe by offering the illusion of some control; they allow some respite for the part of our brain that plans and organizes, making multitasking possible.

Habits, because they are automatic, are sometimes difficult to see—they are so embedded in our lives. Habits can also be a self-created prison of sorts: we take refuge in old habits of mind and body. While certain habits feel comfortable, they may not serve us well. This truth was quite evident in the destructive patterns we created while addicted. At times they are like an old shoe that fits well but may not be in our best interest to wear as we explore new territory. We stay locked in habitual patterns because they are familiar and reinforce our sense of self, not necessarily because they work to make us feel happy or improve our lives. Practice makes permanent, not perfect! Transforming such unskillful patterns is true magic!

I can easily generate a list of habits that no longer serve me, discovering perhaps they never really have.

One familiar definition of *insanity* is doing the same thing over and over again, expecting different results. We are always getting results from our thoughts and actions, just maybe not the ones we want, in part because we are stuck in habits that do not promote our well-being or do not support the edge of our growth.

Brains are designed to store, and they don't particularly care what gets stored. Just think about all the old ads and jingles from childhood that are still stuck in our heads! We form new habits by combining awareness with the energy of motivation to develop the skill we need and capacity for the specific tools we can use.

Awareness creates choice, and this is especially true when we really examine our stuck places. Like the water fish swim within or the air birds fly within, the regular routines and habits of mind, body, and spirit are often invisible to us—they are part of the fabric of our daily existence, an unconscious garment we don every day. The first step is to become aware, through self-observation, of those habits that need changing, whether they relate to bodily self-care or predictable emotional reactions to common triggers.

I can observe and become aware of my most destructive patterns.

A natural progression occurs when a new habit is formed. First we are "*unconsciously* incompetent"; we barely realize something is not correct. Then we become "*consciously* incompetent," where, through feedback, flaws become obvious.

Think about learning a new musical instrument, language, cooking technique, or sport. Gradually we become consciously competent, where we get it right, but *only* when we pay lots of attention. Eventually, we achieve being unconsciously competent, where the habit is ingrained and embodied, and the action happens automatically. The cues and rewards for the brain to activate the new loop and habit become firmly established.

Some research suggests that it takes forty days for consciousness to solidify a new brain pathway. Neurons get wired together in their new firing pattern, and the full energy of commitment builds. Embodied spontaneous action arises after at least five thousand repetitions. Changing a habit is always based on reaching toward the new rather than rejecting the old. Automatic routines and behaviors remain flexible throughout our life—we are not powerless before them! We know from our own experience that the Twelve Step principles comprise a really ginormous, successful awareness mechanism for shifting habits. Many men before us have successfully embraced this path.

I am always using outer situations to change inner states and perceptions.

We are biological beings who manifest intentions. Imagine that we wake up in the morning with a desire to eat a specific food. This is just a thought formed in our mind. Then, with some focused attention and actions, available supplies, and some minimal skills, we are eating our creation fifteen minutes later. This is how the whole game of life operates, though not quite so fast and efficiently.

Through combining the motivation of desire with informational knowledge and practical skills, we have the capacity to generate in the physical world what began simply as thought energy. This is true magic, and it is always available to every one of us. However, there are some techniques and rules of the game that make us more effective players, just as in the video gaming universe. Once we understand the basic structure of how using intentions to manifest reality works, we still need to practice, except we learn to do this in the real world rather than losing ourselves inside a gaming console. We each have a fairly predictable future, based on our past. Unless we shift something, we will continue to get what we have always gotten rather than what we intend or desire.

I am realizing the magnificent and magical power of creating clear intentions.

The first step in forming an intention or establishing a new habit is developing *awareness*. We must become conscious, as clearly and specifically as possible, of what we want to manifest. This may require that we carefully examine what is and what is not working well for us in our lives.

It may take some time to get really clear about the one thing we want to prioritize shifting or transforming. Journaling and contemplative time by ourselves can help uncover what aspects, habits, and patterns in our lives need alteration. Next, we must believe that the desired change is actually possible. The best intentions are grounded in reality, though still expanding our perceived limitations. Awareness helps us see if we are focusing on external items such as financial attainment or developing skills and nurturing ambitions unrealistically quickly, which may be rooted in a desire to disprove or overcome negative ideas of who we are.

Stating "I am willing" with awareness and intent opens tremendous possibilities, freeing internal obstacles and blockages, so that our mind can operate in many creative ways and our lives can transform. Beliefs reflect our emotional core. Beliefs are the cornerstones upon which we build the change we want to make. We become what we think.

I know it is true: what the mind can conceive and believe, it can achieve.

Awareness and the belief we can change are the first steps. Then we have to face the next component of manifesting our intention: *commitment*. We have to *commit*. A commitment is a promise. When we wholeheartedly promise to do what is needed in terms of being-having-doing-interconnecting, we express the big "yes." We state our willingness to risk, to be vulnerable and open to possible failure—all of which fuel our desire to really *go for it*.

Commitment also means we marshal the preparations needed for action and enlist the support of others by making our intention public. Commitment is followed by a sense of *just do it*. Constant effort with clear intent produces change. What gets stimulated gets enhanced. What gets rewarded gets done. Clear intent and positive action feed off each other in an uplifting spiral.

The ancient wisdom that tells us "the path is formed by walking on it" acknowledges that when we do something every day to move our change forward, we gather momentum. Our cumulative small actions eventually create the larger change we seek. Committed action continues, despite any rationales or excuses. We need warrior discipline to follow through, and some days will be harder than others, as we know well from our struggles with changing our patterns of substance use.

Commitment and action create the center of the wheel of forward progress.

When we have traversed the steps of **ABCD** (**a**wareness, **b**elief, **c**ommitment, and **d**oing), we arrive at a new destination: **E** and **F**, where we must **e**valuate and **f**ocus.

Things going wrong is part of the unfolding process. Resistance is expected and normal. Though we want to embrace transformation, a small part of us that doesn't want to change begins to resist, freak out, and may feel threatened. Ever watch a baby learning to walk? They fail more than succeed, but they get lots of positive encouragement and keep adjusting their movements until they get the flow right. So think "baby steps" as we move from breakdown, to breakthrough, and then breakout.

Evaluation feedback—the kind we give ourselves and invite from others—is simply an invitation to pay attention to what we most need to observe and adjust. It moves us toward the final accelerator, in which we come back, again and again, to *focus* on our original intention and recycle through the various steps involved.

Focus is ongoing engagement with a desired outcome until the outcome manifests and becomes reality. This process is about *skillpower* rather than willpower. Like an airplane that keeps correcting its course as it goes, we must refocus on what needs doing to make forward progress. Things may not be developing exactly as we wished, so we need to stay open to daily fine-tuning.

Everything dances on the point of intention.

People often make lots of resolutions for New Year's but then fail to materialize any of them because they usually choose too many and commit to none. The big "yes parade" soon turns into a sputtering, dribbling march of "no's" and "maybes." The flow of forward momentum dissolves, leaving us more discouraged than determined.

When this happens, it's time to reexamine what inner gates might still need opening, asking ourselves what *inside us* is getting in the way of a complete commitment? What internal obstacles are still keeping us chained? Is our fear of success, fear of failure, anxiety about not being perfect, or negative *mindtalk* keeping us stuck? When we face our fears, we can actively imagine the inner gates opening wider, effortlessly casting aside self-imposed limitations. As we allow the "yes" of an open gate, the "no" we have been generating will dissolve on its own. All our negative energy must be released and channeled into the unwavering commitment to manifest what we desire.

Positive affirmations can be useful in this process of inner release, gradually altering core belief systems; they are strongest when they are specific, expressed in the present tense, and have strong emotions connected to them.

I am capable of keeping my commitment to sobriety.

Pledges, covenants, agreements, and the vows we make to ourselves to stay on a good path of recovery and well-being always encounter resistance. We might wake up in the morning uninspired and lethargic about getting done what we said we would. *Carpe mañana*—I'll do it tomorrow—becomes our theme song, with the someday isle (meaning "I'll") as our background default setting.

Resistance with a capital "R" is a subtle inner mechanism that urges us to back away from life's difficulties and demands, often revealing itself as negative *mindtalk* and self-defeating behaviors. The big R uses avoidance and procrastination to intensify problems, tasks, and routines, even as it undermines enthusiasm and energy. Unless addressed, its subversive, pervasive, and persuasive nature destroys our commitment to fine and healthy intentions. When we hold back yet yearn to go forward simultaneously, we do not act as boldly and firmly as we could. Confusion, self-doubt, fear, apathy, and restlessness arise. We must acknowledge their presence, call them by name, accept them rather than fight with them, and just keep on keeping on anyway. We might imagine each of them, whenever they arise, as bags of rubbish that obstruct our trail; garbage that simply needs to be picked up and cast away.

My commitment to sobriety teaches me about how to actually keep my promises.

Struggling to keep a commitment we have made is simply feedback that we also want something else. Articulating our competing desires is often the key to moving through resistance and struggle. Yes, we want to stay in our warm bed, but we have a commitment to exercise daily. That candy bar is appealing, but we have committed to eating less junk food. Just one beer can't hurt, yet we have pledged ourselves to abstinence.

What can we do in the moment of struggle in order to choose wisely and honor a promise we made to ourselves? We can turn down the volume of the voices that encourage us to stray and turn up the bodily sensations of the good feelings we have when we do what we said we would. We can feel the lightness, expansiveness, and burst of energy that arise whenever we respect our own promises and thereby nurture our underlying, treasured values.

What we resist persists! This is especially true of whatever wants to sabotage our commitment, including the chorus of self-doubts beginning to hum its tune. We must face these obstacles, rather than keep them hidden, in order to diminish their power over us.

I let go of struggle easily and keep focusing on my original commitment.

As we move toward the higher reaches of our energy and intentions, the lower, less helpful habits just fall away. This developmental process builds confidence over time. We begin to trust our own word, to have faith in our ability to follow through and accomplish whatever we set out to do—in the inner *or* outer worlds. Our inner magician operates best when confident in his ability to transform reality. Over time, the magician's ongoing commitment to transcendent change makes him more and more resilient when difficulties arise.

Following the magician's example, our self-assurance will blossom with our growing appreciation of our own abilities and qualities. Arrogance—and its cousins of superiority, self-importance, and conceit—plays no role in this unfolding; it is counterproductive and an impediment we must root out at every opportunity. While our self-esteem is dependent on the respect of others, self-confidence is a quality we can continually nurture within ourselves when we diligently "Photoshop" and create our own mental image of ourselves. From grooming to our choice of clothes, from speaking slowly with authority to standing tall, our habitual mannerisms can support our sense of certainty. Building confidence takes courage, curiosity, and constancy.

Whenever I take a moment to appreciate myself, the inner light of confidence grows stronger.

Confidence is consistently choosing *self-reliance* rather than *self-indulgence*. It is grounded in self-competence and self-control, and fostered by the deep realization that we are valued by our significant others—those important people in our life who build us up rather than put us down. Strength-based perceptions and skills help us evaluate and respond effectively to challenges and difficult situations, to make judgments with responsibility and integrity.

Such maturity develops gradually as we become more skilled at interpersonal communication and problem solving. Confidence flourishes in a supportive atmosphere of instructive positive reinforcement. Many of us only began to experience this when we entered treatment or started to participate in Twelve Step meetings. Before that, we may have been mired in endless loops of self-doubt and low self-esteem, unsure of ourselves in every realm: work, family, relationships, and purpose. The sense of feeling good about ourselves was buried in the haze of just trying to cope with emotional pain and disappointment, by-products of deep childhood wounds. Confidence is not some mysterious quality given out to a lucky few. It is an inner light that is available to us all and can be illuminated by small victories and great quests.

I am becoming a capable person.

The inner magician knows that getting comfortable with uncertainty is a very useful skill. We are, in fact, dancing an eternal tango with the unfamiliar. Those many moments on our life journey when the universe does not seem to be aligned with our vision can be painful and obstructive. And it can be overwhelming when we're faced with a big life decision. Thoughts of a new job, the next step in a relationship, moving to a new place, a big health decision, or the leap of committing to be a father can paralyze us. These large choices can unearth lots of fear and unfinished business—and sometimes push us back into our addictive patterns.

There are very specific steps that can help us to get unstuck. The first is to honor and accept uncertainty as our teacher. Uncertainty accompanies our most dogged attempts to figure things out. Not knowing what to do happens so often in life, we'd think everyone would get good and more relaxed about inhabiting our uncertain lives. A really common barrier to life's flow is that most of us repeatedly respond to uncertainty with fear and withdrawal rather than curiosity and openness.

I will start to notice how I normally react to uncertainty in my life.

It's often suggested that "When you get lemons, just make lemonade." While this adage may be true, usually no one teaches us how to do that. Making the best of things is not about pouring positive nonsense over a situation and hoping things will improve. Wisdom manifests *not* when the brain is humming along, but when it is puzzled or gets stuck!

The initial step in removing an obstacle is to change the belief that there is an obstacle. Remember that challenge and opportunity are *positive* words, as opposed to "problems." When we embrace uncertainty as our mentor or guide every time we experience it, we begin to shift our mind-set and view our state of confusion as helpful and interesting. We magically transform something unpleasant into an adventure in possibility. Most of us hold tightly to the idea that we can think our way out of every dilemma. To move from *stuckville* to *clarity-town*, we have to be willing to hang out with our confusion for as long as it takes. Only from a more grounded and centered place can new possibilities emerge.

When faced with any troubling dilemma, I can learn to relax and go with its flow, trusting my best choice will eventually become obvious.

What is really meant by the truism "When there are only two apparent choices, always pick the third"? What color is an apple? Red or green would be the most common response. Yet we might also answer white, referring to its interior, or brown, in terms of inner seeds or decay.

Black-or-white, either-or polarity-based thinking is common and has clear survival value; it can also lead us down the path of addictions. Refusing to flush out the nuances and in-betweens of any emotional situation can push us to seeing escape as the only option. We risk the danger of seeking relief through substances because of the tension and stress inherent when we are confused. The drive to "figure it out" often invites a fear-based process of going over the situation repeatedly in the hopes that something helpful might emerge from this incessant mental thrashing around. Instead, we might try to remember the magic inherent in just shifting our perspective. Contemplative quiet time can open us up to seeing more clearly. It can take us out of ourselves, helping us embrace an eagle-eyed view through the timeless wisdom of "sleeping on it."

I can just observe, without judgment, where "should," "try," and "but" are limiting me and my options.

Insight can simply be a **BFO**—a **b**linding **f**lash of the **ob**vious. We may suddenly understand that our father was beaten by his father and was in chronic pain, explaining—but not excusing—his constant irritability and abusiveness with us. We see clearly that we picked a partner with substance use problems so we could work out some of what we had experienced with a parent, who also has problems with drug use.

Something that may be a new realization for us may have been painfully obvious to many others who are close to us. What is important is that we utilize this recently discovered, clear perception to enlighten our path. Insight is always about enlarging our perspective, offering a sense of spaciousness beyond the previous prison of our limited understanding. Information that has been gathered, clarified, compacted, and crystallized over time finally bubbles to the surface of our awareness.

What appears magical is really the result of the experience, knowledge, and awareness we have gradually built up. Insight is just a seed, and to grow into a valuable tree, it must be continually nurtured through our positive actions. Insight without action quickly loses its potency.

I value the insights that come to me, and use these precious gifts to make my life better.

We can try playing with the notion that insights are really *upsights*, since they so effectively *up our game*—serve to propel the trajectory of our life forward and enable us to reach for the highest and best parts of ourselves. Once we connect the all-important dots and find that missing puzzle piece, we alter our awareness forever about that particular aspect of our journey.

Of course, while the upsight may seemingly occur in an instant, we are often blind to all the preparatory development behind it appearing. We're learning that integrating insight fully into our thoughts and behaviors is something that unfolds over time.

We need to translate insight's kernel of wisdom into practical actions. That compressed, potent, sentinel "aha" moment of realization when we grasp something important is only the beginning of the shift. Such breakthroughs can produce a sudden and overwhelming unfolding of freedom from long-held limitations, making what seemed impossible, possible. Unless such insights are translated into meaningful changes, every aha is just a prelude to a "so what?" Insights expand our palette of choices, allowing us to react in more empowered, skillful ways—even though a situation or person about which we've had the insight remains the same.

I can easily translate insights into positive, practical changes in my life.

When an *upsight*, or series of them, is especially clear and powerful, we may experience a complete paradigm shift. When this happens, the universe offers us a veritable internal earthquake rather than just a gentle nudge in the right direction. A paradigm shift is defined as an important change that occurs when the usual way of thinking about or doing something is replaced by a completely new and different way. The initial use of the term in science and business environments has now expanded into the realm of personal growth.

Maybe we get in touch with a talent we never appreciated before, and that new reality alters virtually everything—from how we make a living to the quality of our relationships. Rather than an incremental advance or slow, steady progress, we leap! Sometimes, such dramatic changes are preceded by a significant wake-up call. This could be someone close to us dying or getting severely injured, resulting in a significant change in our worldview and behaviors. Or we might develop a serious illness and suddenly realize how important spending time with family and loved ones really is. While sometimes such jolts are painful, the changes they engender often produce some of the best moments and outcomes in our lives.

I pay special attention to the insights offered by wake-up calls and paradigm shifts.

Most people have many instances of intuitive functioning. It might be a conversation overheard in a restaurant that seems directly uttered for our ears, or knowing who is calling before we pick up the phone. Perhaps an impulse tells us to bring something we might have forgotten, or a friend shows up at the perfect, oddest times even though previous attempts to call or keep an appointment with that person were in vain.

While the dominant culture tends to minimize these "coincidences," intuition is, in fact, a very valuable tool that can be strengthened and cultivated. Some of us, no doubt, used its guidance to find the right combination of support that really helped us get free of our addiction. When pruning trees, we try to increase spaciousness for more air and light to enter; the light can then penetrate deeper and more profoundly into the dark places as the vitality rises. Our receptive intuitive faculties need similar affirmation and openness. Intuition is a felt sense rather than an externally sourced guide. We gradually learn to tune in more, listen more deeply, and then trust our intuition enough to act on what it is telling us.

I honor my intuition as an important source of messages that are useful in my life.

From infancy, our natural curiosity enables us to learn an enormous amount of information in a short period of time, because our brains are designed to grow in response to the stimuli they receive. As a species, most of us simply don't know yet how to teach or turn on our intuitive faculties.

Intuition is not an appliance we plug in when we need to use it. It functions more like a telephone network into which we are always connected. This whole process is clearly facilitated when we cultivate a calm, inner, wakeful, and receptive state, where we keep our mind free of unnecessary static while maintaining high alertness. Our normal everyday web of emotions, desires, and trains of thought covers up and obscures intuitive truths by absorbing our entire attention and keeping our consciousness at a superficial level.

To penetrate our intuition and go deeper, we can become proficient in various techniques for quieting the mind—including prayer, meditation, yoga, and journaling. Each of these practices enhances our ability to be fully present to whatever is happening, which allows us to detect subtle information from within.

As I build intuitive capacity through practice, I understand what I need more of and what I need less of in my life.

Intuition enhances the knowledge we have gained and the expertise we have developed. Described by Buckminster Fuller—a highly innovative and creative architect, author, and visionary—as "cosmic fishing," this natural faculty of mind has great survival value. We might imagine our intuition as a divining rod that helps locate underground streams, so we know where to dig. Or we might visualize it as a simple lifting of the veil, a flash of lightning, or dipping our finger to touch the cosmic ocean of information.

Intuition allows us to tune into the voices of unseen inner guides or whispers heard in the middle of the night, despite the normal bubbling of thoughts in the jumble of our mind. Just like we are learning to be more fluent with our feelings in recovery, intuition asks us to recognize and decipher our body's vivid messages—verbal, visual, or kinesthetic (body-felt awareness). Then we will appreciate that those everyday hunches, which seem to descend like an offering from outside, are really a direct line to our connection with all that is. We flash on what normally might be missed in the daily hustle and bustle of our lives to gain insight on what could be.

I welcome the magic of intuitive knowledge in things both large and small.

The magic of the *flow state* is something most of us have experienced. It is composed of those moments when everything seems aligned in our favor, and what is normally difficult acquires an aura of effortlessness. This can be something as simple as moving easily through a stuck place in a video game, or coasting along on a snowboard, where we are indeed one with the activity.

We may have felt such flow-state moments when high—they are part of the allure of addictive substances. In recovery, we discover that those special moments are possible (and ultimately more rewarding) *without* chemical assistance. *Flow* has been described as an effortless, optimal, deep concentration and a well-ordered consciousness where all thoughts, feelings, and senses are harmoniously directed toward the same goal. Flow engenders a creative feeling of being transported to a new reality, pushed to higher levels of performance and to a different state of consciousness where attention is effortlessly focused, shutting off all physical or mental processes but the relevant ones.

Our inner magician knows that a key characteristic of flow is that we are dynamically relaxed, in a place where thought, action, and transformation occur simultaneously and spontaneously. Reaching a state of flow as a result of true harmony within the self feels wonderful.

Because I know what flow feels like, I can expand its possibilities in my life without relying on substances.

We spend a great deal of time and energy observing the world around us, and this capacity has certainly helped our species survive. This type of observation is like watching ourselves in a movie versus being immersed and feeling like we're actually living in the movie or getting so involved with it that everything else disappears. When our attention is immersed, we often use terms like "lost in thought" or "in the flow."

Humans really enjoy states where the sense of flowing and immersion is paramount. While we tend to think of such experiences as ones in which we are physically very active, they do occur in more passive situations as well, such as sitting on a beach and being fully engulfed in watching a sunset, enjoying the antics of animals, or listening to a concert. What we are able to perceive is dependent on what state we are in. When we are rushing about and multitasking, what arises to our awareness is very different from what happens when we sit quietly gazing at a flower.

I will notice today when I am fully immersed in an activity and how good that feels.

Is it possible to cultivate more moments of flow in our lives? What are the conditions that maximize the possibility for such wondrous states to arise? While the cultivation of positive habits can help us transform as people, routine can also be a killer of spirit. We crave novelty and stimulation because they also play an important role in personal growth; at the same time, our cravings may have been part of what got us in trouble with substances.

Throughout our day, we can play a Sherlock Holmes–like role, noticing when we are more in flow and when whatever we are doing generates boredom or restlessness. Flow is not a state we can maintain throughout the course of our everyday life; rather, it is an opening into what is possible, an ephemeral state to be experienced and released, meant to be lost and found again. Such peak performance memories tend to be characterized by their effortlessness. Many times, dynamic relaxed attention—dropping effort and struggle—creates the portal into flow, and such centered, calm presence is what achieves full benefit and best results.

Our inner magician offers us many tools for creating a good life, from setting intentions and changing habits, to understanding commitment and confidence, to using insight and intuition to guide us to higher states of being.

I honor the gifts of flow whenever they arise.

MAY

The Tribesman

The inner Tribesman offers you the support of community and the gifts of resilience. Alongside him, you discover the sweetness of solitude and the force of friendship, both of which help you move beyond the wounds and shame that might have taken root in your childhood.

With pain from your upbringing transformed, the Tribesman helps you embrace fatherhood and community as a conscious path of awakening.

Originally an ancient northern hemisphere spring festival, May Day—also known as Beltane—later also became a celebration of the struggles for workers' rights. We enter this world held within the embrace of many diverse ethnic, cultural, and social traditions and practices. Each of us is born a member of a tribe, but in our modern world, we often lose sight of our tribal identity.

Our inner tribesman knows we must forge healthy, caring connections to be successful. The broad circle of giving and receiving is one of the most powerful tools humans have. We are social animals ill-equipped to survive on our own. Our parents are often the first to introduce us to this, although their version of belonging to a tribe may be distorted and not match our own reality.

Emerging science shows us that we are biologically hardwired to relate to a tribe. Our brains are designed to interact with a community of individuals who form a web of mutual exchange and kinship. Cooperation is a key element in human survival. We can take a moment to appreciate that our sobriety would not be possible without countless moments of support and assistance from others. Finding our own tribe—people with whom we resonate easily and who lift us up toward being our greatest—is one of the most important aspects of loving ourselves.

I will examine the characteristics of the tribe in which I really feel at home.

As we grow and age, we find ourselves drawn to others with whom we have common values and interests. In effect, we begin to create our own tribe—those individuals with whom we share a sense of natural affinity, kinship, and connection. And within that community, we experience both the joys and challenges of relating closely. We willingly shoulder a mantle of responsibility for our actions as we continually strive to keep good relations and open and honest communication.

Being part of a larger whole helps us place our unique problems into a broader perspective. To flourish, we learn to practice the Ninth Step: we make "direct amends . . . wherever possible, except when to do so would injure them or others." Our inner tribesman knows this is the essence of walking our talk, of truly finding our place in the great circle of relations.

Hiding, escaping, minimizing, or refusing to deal with the inevitable conflicts that arise among our tribe only keeps us trapped in destructive patterns. To admit we were wrong about something—and to attempt to make it right—takes courage and vulnerability, and has its own deep rewards.

I am learning about the give-and-take that is part of every healthy relationship.

To be a good tribesman, we must actively be involved with and contribute to our community. We help foster resilience, express loyalty, and share both burdens and joys. We develop deep friendships, which are important building blocks within any tribe, that offer us both counsel and comfort during trying times.

Most men live their lives in constricting boxes others have fashioned for them. Discovering a truly supportive tribe helps us safely experience the fierce power of breaking out of ourselves. We can move beyond our comfort zone of isolation and loneliness rather than remain locked up within ourselves—an often painful, but secure, prison. We know that previous patterns of isolation often contributed to our staying stuck in our addiction.

Sobriety requires not only our own commitment, but also the ongoing support of others. We may need to redefine our tribe and choose wisely those with whom we spend time. The presence of other positive, caring travelers on the road to recovery uplifts and nourishes our own journey to wholeness. The world needs us to be ourselves, to participate in a creative, courageous community, and to awaken from the illusion of separateness.

I will take the ageless wisdom that "no man is an island" to heart.

It often seems that parents are always wrong, doing too much or too little, but never just enough. While it is true that they are often in error, they are usually doing the best they can, given their own upbringing and challenges.

Every child receives both gifts and wounds from their parents. As we grow and evolve, our job is to learn to appreciate the gifts, even as we do what we can to heal the emotional injuries. As we learn in recovery, we cannot change the past, but we can alter our relationship to it. We do this by being willing to explore the darkness of some of the difficult things we experienced and by slowly connecting the dots to see how those early episodes still influence us.

Everyone harbors a shadow, where they tuck away things they would prefer not to see. It takes both courage and support to look at parts of our self that were rejected by our parents, society, and even us. Our shadow is a natural part of the self, a reservoir of human darkness, but also the wellspring of creative expression. We must first acknowledge and access it before we can accept it—thus bringing us closer to wholeness.

Shining the light of awareness upon the shadow of my family wounds helps diminish the pain.

Ideally, from generation to generation, we pass on a bit less confusion and greater clarity about how to function and be happy in the world. Raising children and trying to be "good enough" parents is hard, tiring work. It demands a level of conscious awareness that many people lack. Rather than labeling our parents' behaviors—past or present—as dysfunctional, it often helps to try a dose of empathy. When we do this, it is possible to conceive of our parents as caring people stuck in difficult situations. That is not to deny emotional or physical injury that some parents inflicted upon their children.

For children raised with the unholy triad of violence, substance abuse, and mental illness in their family of origin, the magnitude of the wounds can be enormous. The multigenerational transmission of faulty learned behaviors may have contributed to our own tangle with addictions, as we did our best to cope with the emotional injuries: all those times when we felt misunderstood, endured "you're too . . ." put-downs or "you're not enough" shaming, suffered those little wounds that happen in families, and survived the big traumas—abuse and abandonment—that occur as well. We begin to understand—not excuse—that some of the ways they wounded us, they themselves also experienced.

I am freeing myself from childhood wounds by becoming more aware of where they still influence my behaviors.

Some of us are screwed up, and some of us are screwed up and can explain it! "Paralysis of analysis" serves no one, and we don't get to the light by the endless examination of the dark. Childhood wounds don't just dissolve over time. They require awareness and healing, a gradual making peace with our parents or our memories of them, or those significant others who raised us.

We must make peace with the patterns of behavior we learned from our family. How are we to treat people? How do we deal with conflict? How should we navigate our often-overwhelming emotional waters? To what rituals do we turn for comfort (that might be harmful)? Most of us received conflicting, confusing, and constricting conditioning from those who raised us. This doesn't give us a license to wallow in chaos, however, or use it as a reason to relapse or as an ongoing excuse for not creating the life we want. Nor does it make it acceptable to deny the real pain or cover it with some positive new age goo.

It *does* mean we have to develop some of the communication and relationship skills we missed along the way. As the Twelve Step saying goes, "We learn to keep what is good, and discard the rest."

I see more clearly the negative ways in which I am like those who raised me. Awareness is the first step of transformation. I will use those insights to build positive relationships.

While parental, family, and tribal affiliations can be up-lifting and inspiring, they can also generate enormous suffering. The essence of shame is not only that we believe we are bad to the core, but also that we hold it is our fault. The toxic mix of guilt, negative perceptions of one's defects, and scornful self-deprecation is difficult to transform. Instead of drinking from an inner wellspring of positive feelings of worth in times of duress, we submerge ourselves in a poisoned well of negativity. We may resign ourselves to a "why bother," self-defeating attitude and find that the only relief from such profound feelings of unworthiness comes from addictive escapes.

The way through this tangled psychic mess is to gradually purify our inner source—to slowly, with small acts, begin to love and accept ourselves. We silence the inner critic and give voice to an expanding chorus of affirming voices from the healthy tribe we are creating.

Whenever we notice the old negative songs playing in our head, we immediately shift the tune to something more empowering. This inner transformation requires awareness and attention, as well as the presence of kind people who see clearly our value and talents, even as they accept our current shortcomings. There is the tribe into which we are born, and there is the tribe we create or choose.

I have the power to gradually release the shame that binds me.

It is a sad and alarming statistic that before reaching age eighteen, one out of six males is victimized by some form of sexual abuse, including fondling and inappropriate suggestive remarks, up to actual penetration. Rather than the stereotypical pedophile stranger in a van committing these harmful acts, data shows that—similar to other forms of violence—sexual abusers are most often someone we know and trust.

Healing from such assaults to our core being is often a long process. Fear of retribution or ongoing trauma empowers secrets to become full of shame, an emotion that erodes a healthy sense of self and increases a person's chances of developing substance abuse, eating disorders, and other addictive behaviors.

When we bury the negative emotions rooted in our past, we bury them alive. Important parts of our true beings are often buried with the shame. Too often we allow the negative emotions that emerge from the abuse to become a destructive force that wreaks havoc on our own expressions of intimacy and sexuality.

With help, I can release any shame I feel from being sexually abused.

In childhood, many of us repeatedly experienced what is known as the *double bind*. This emotionally distressing dilemma offered us two or more demanding, conflicting messages. We were often left feeling "damned if we do, and damned if we don't," with nowhere to run and no tools to resolve our feelings of shame and unworthiness.

To cope, many of us "went underground" to survive. We sacrificed our true being to belong, which often meant connecting with the wrong group of friends, many of whom contributed to our addictive lifestyle. This probably made sense at the time, but it hurt us in the long run. As part of that process, we constructed our own prison, whose bars both protected us *and* enslaved us. In the darkest, deepest part of that inner chamber lies the shadow, the parts of ourselves we don't want to face.

The shadow lies under the psychological "clothing" of the person we present to the world, the human we think we want to be. The shadow is composed of those parts of ourselves we fail to see or know, the refused and unacceptable characteristics that were repressed so we might behave in a manner consistent with particular family and cultural expectations. Truly, we are as sick as we are secret. All the defects—real and imagined—that we try to hide never see the light of healthy healing, until we are willing to be vulnerable and reveal rather than conceal.

Doing healing shadow work involves releasing secrets I have hidden for too long.

We may someday take our place as a father in our tribal community. Hopefully, we enter the magical realm of fatherhood by conscious choice, rather than through unintended consequence.

Fatherhood is less about biology than about showing up, since we may parent the children of another man because of our love for their mother, or we may partner with another man and adopt. However we get there, the journey of healthy fatherhood begins with the awareness that parenthood is a life-changing process. We don't have to have all the answers, but we need to be a willing pupil. We will have to learn a whole new set of communication skills as our offspring pass from infant to teenager and beyond.

In addition to the rewards and challenges inherent in each developmental stage, fatherhood will call forth illuminating qualities from deep within us that we did not imagine we possessed. Making our children a priority by being fully present with them and gifting them our time is a great bounty beyond what we might provide materially for their betterment. Our presence is the best present! We honor them as *our* teachers because they test our kindness and patience in innumerable, unimaginable ways. They'll make us laugh as never before, reminding us of the playfulness we may have lost along the way.

Remaining clean and sober is the best gift I can give my children.

If and when we do become fathers, we will realize that, despite doing the very best we can, we are passing both gifts and wounds onto our children—just as our parents passed gifts and wounds on to us. We may react with dismay when our offspring use a similar nasty tone of voice or develop some of the same negative habits we exhibited in the past. Becoming a father always sheds new light on the struggles our own father experienced. Though we may be very different from our parents, the process of raising children is a common bond we have with all our ancestors. In our attempts to correct the mistakes our parents made, we may choose a completely different style of parenting from that of our father, but we still walk in his shoes some of the time. This opens the door for us to have compassion for the times he was not the father we wanted, hoped, and needed him to be.

Perhaps, for instance, when we were in the throes of our addictions, our father had to withdraw to protect himself, even though we longed for his support. We do not condone his most serious errors, but we hold them in a larger field of understanding. This new perspective can help put us on a path of healing our relationship with him.

Raising my own children offers new possibilities for healing with my father.

The challenges of maintaining a close relationship with our children after divorce can be overwhelming. Research shows that children suffer most with divorce when a father drops out of the picture, parents remain in significant conflict, or the family experiences a significant decline in socioeconomic status. Divorce is one of the most traumatic events in a child's life and one of the most traumatic experiences we can have as a father. Divorce is a common reason men fall off their path of sobriety.

For the sake of our children, we must summon the resources—both financial and emotional—to remain actively involved in their care and upbringing. Somehow, despite the wounds we have sustained, we must find a way to treat our former partner with respect to ensure the best outcome for our children. We must not bad-mouth, threaten, or blame those we have divorced, and we must do what we can to minimize conflict. Money, custody, and visitation issues can be a battleground. Thankfully, most states now recognize the importance of both parental roles. Of course, to maintain our parental rights, we have to accept the responsibilities of parenting, including our responsibility to remain clean and sober. We can always strive to be better at fathering, one day at a time.

If I am a divorced father, I commit to remaining actively supportive of and engaged with my children.

We will be successful fathers whenever we are affectionate, attentive to our children's needs, actively engaged, accepting, and available emotionally. Should we not be fathers ourselves, these qualities are worth remembering in other interactions we have with boys and young men, many of whom suffer from a deep "father hunger." Such boys often exhibit an aggressive style of relating. This may include a hypermasculine interest in muscles, guns, and trucks. Other immature behaviors can be derogatory attitudes toward women, individuals who are LGBTQIA or of a different ethnic or racial origin, or other prejudicial behavior born of fear and ignorance.

Boys and young men often lack the skills for expressing appreciation, making apologies, or resolving conflict. Their emotional fluency tends to be minimal. They are at much greater risk for developing addictive patterns of coping with inner emotional distress.

It is important to remember that "under-fathered" youth need the assistance of every older caring man who is willing to show some positive modeling. We may encounter these boys and young men through our work, sports, or faith community, and no matter our time limitations, we can at least show them that a better path of masculinity exists.

I can be a contributing member of my tribe by reaching out to help young men who have received the worst, rather than the best, from their own fathers.

Being a tribesman isn't, of course, only about connecting with others in our tribe. We need to be at ease within to build healthy "outer" relations. Feeling comfortable in our own being requires that we learn to enjoy solitude. As the often-used saying goes, being alone is not the same as being lonely.

At this point in our recovery, we have hopefully begun to see the value of accessing that place of deep peace, tranquility, and comfort within us, which then naturally supports the process of opening our heart to our self, to others, and to the world. When we sit still and allow insights to arise from observing how much internal movement there is in our mind, we become more intimate with our self. When we appreciate what is, we expand what is possible. When we stay fully engaged in the here and now, we deepen our experience of appreciating and savoring life. For most of us in recovery, the only space that ever felt comfortable and safe was found in being high, an illusion that reinforced the power our addiction had over us.

Where is the place now where we can take refuge, refresh our spirit, and regain our strength? What people, places, and practices always welcome us back, like the shade of a tree where we might rest and feel content?

In discovering how nurturing quiet time alone can be, I take another step in loving myself.

Everyone needs a sanctuary, yet few take time to create one. Many people have favorite spots in the natural external world they enjoy visiting, places where they renew themselves, such as a garden, beach, or forest path. For others it might be a city sculpture garden, a cozy library nook, or a tranquil café. Even a pen, a journal, and a quiet place might suffice for some.

We just need to turn off everything else! We can also use our creative imagination to build and enjoy an inner haven that is extremely calming and empowering. The setting and overall structures may be anywhere, with any special features or chambers we might want to conceive. Perhaps there is a waterfall where we can allow whatever quality we need at the moment to penetrate every cell of our being. Maybe there is a healing grotto, a wisdom altar, or a gazebo where our Higher Power or other guides offer advice on dilemmas.

When we take the time to slow down and go within, we discover that we are both architect and interior designer of our sanctuary. *We* determine how grand and elaborate, or simple and cozy, our place of calm and peace needs to be. Our sanctuary—inner, outer, or a combination of both—is our own personalized, private enclave of possibility.

I see the enormous potential in establishing a sanctuary— inside and outside—for myself.

Stillness is not so much the absence of noise and activity, but rather the presence of transparency, an invisible openness to the immediate world about us. Heaviness falls away from us, and a richer, deeper life appears. Time alone, in which we can be curious and question everything, is the only true way to get to know oneself.

When we take a spell away from the daily race, quiet the turbulence of our normal pace, and slow down to the speed of life, we stimulate a different part of us, which opens us to new ideas and puts us more in touch with what we really love. The sense of spaciousness to just *be*, in a world so consumed by *doing*, is good for us on every level and reinforces our commitment to remain clean and sober.

We may have to actually schedule such time for ourselves—make an appointment with solitude—to create the space and place to go deeper within. At first, we will encounter both battles and peace there, just as in the outer plane of existence. Through awareness, we eventually will surrender struggle, creating greater harmony between our inner and outer worlds.

I welcome stillness and the peace it can bring. Today, I will do less and be more.

We experience many transitions in the course of our journey. Deep ties are often formed and alliances initiated through the commonality of shared hardships. In Zambia, the friendship that develops among those who have endured a rite of passage together is known as *wulunda*. During their time of ritual seclusion, participants sleep together in clusters around fires and partake in special ceremonies, creating unique bonds that last even into old age.

Those in recovery, college buddies, veterans, or others who have shared experiences or had similar life challenges may develop long-term relationships like those of the Zambia tribesmen. Sometimes, members of these tribes offer comfort by just sitting in silence together. At other times, their simple words can be touchstones that bring them out of confusion. Like a rock cairn, they provide a strong foundation. They help each other recall the path and return to it.

Best friends know the song of our heart, and they can sing it back to us when we forget. Since they have probably seen us at our best and worst, they are a reminder that, despite imperfections, we are accepted in our tribe rather than abandoned. Lifelong deep friendships are immeasurable treasures, and there is much truth to the adage that "We can't find new old friends."

I can strengthen contact with dear friends with whom I share a special bond.

To have good friends, we first need to practice being a good friend. We can make the effort to remember birthdays—even if Facebook doesn't remind us—and uniquely special events. Our close friends can act as our support system when we need it, but by putting energy into returning the favor, we create a balanced circle of giving *and* receiving.

Small gestures that show we're thinking about the people who love us go a long way. We might take a few moments to regularly express our thanks and appreciation, especially when others have extended themselves. Friendship is much more than just a dumping ground for our pain. If the only time we have contact with a friend is when we are in need, our mutual bonds will not grow.

Good friends know how to listen intently, paying attention to what we say and to what we *don't* say. Close friends embody safe space, are nonjudgmental, and do not discount our feelings or invalidate our experiences. They have a healthy respect for our boundaries, and they honor confidentiality. These are individuals who remember our beauty and wholeness, even when we feel horrible and broken.

I will put energy into cultivating and keeping good friends.

We may have learned the immense value of a weekly support group during the process of our recovery. It is now possible to create one that includes our close friends. Rather than limiting our time together to engaging in outdoor activities, discussing sports or politics, or playing video games, we can establish a regular sacred space of deep sharing about the joys and challenges of being a man. Our most intimate dreams and passions, as well as the landscape of our struggles and stuck places, can find voice within the space of our friendships.

Every man wants to be appreciated for who he is and to contribute in some way to the greater whole. Establishing regular contact with others with whom we feel kinship engenders a certain inexplicable bonding, a resonance that seems natural and easy. This breaks us out of the isolation that engulfs so many men. Standing shoulder-to-shoulder regularly with other men strengthens our listening skills, increases our ability to be present and open, and helps us work through some of our issues—qualities that also tremendously enhance intimacy with our partner. An old tribal proverb remembers that shared joy is double joy, and shared sorrow is half sorrow.

Joining a regular men's support group is enlivening, offering many benefits.

Ever notice how, deep in the woods, the morning sun first hits the tops of the trees, then works its way down the trunk? How the life-giving moisture ascends from the network of roots? So, too, we are nourished our whole life by early experiences and connections, rootedness, and an early sense of self, family, and cultural identity.

The open arms of community may have softened some of the blows we experienced in our family of origin. We may have found temporary comfort and relief from the home craziness with the support of an encouraging neighbor, relative, coach, teacher, or spiritual figure. For many men, "support" feels like someone is getting on their back, telling them what to do. Their reaction is often "Just leave me alone!"

When we allow someone to help us, we're helping ourselves in the process. True support is asking for assistance in the form we need, not blindly taking what others think is good for us. This give-and-take of working on and improving ourselves by helping others in our tribe is a very satisfying spiral that takes us beyond desires for approval and status.

I engage positively with the many communities of which I am a part. Each offers opportunities to give and receive encouragement and comfort.

We have to do it ourselves, but we need not do it alone. In fact, we usually can't do it alone, despite what countless movies and adventure tales might suggest. We need the support of our tribe.

When entering a sweat lodge of the Lakota tradition, one utters *mitakuye oyasin*, words that honor the connection to not only one's ancestors, but to the whole human family and beyond, to all the animal, plant, and mineral kingdoms, as well as the forces of nature—the wind, rain, lightning, and thunder. This expression encompasses a consciousness of the fundamental truth that everything is interrelated, and nothing exists in isolation.

We dance in a fine web of each other's creation. We are patterns in a tribal or community tapestry that constantly enriches rather than confines. Survival has dictated for millennia that humans are hardwired to relate to not only the natural world, with all its forces and inhabitants, but also to their elemental extended clan. The ability to connect, maintain good boundaries, and communicate clearly comprises a host of capabilities, without which satisfying relationships become much more challenging. Every interaction with those with whom we share some form of community provides our practice ground.

I honor the special connections that exist everywhere, all around me.

Community is formed when we expand our sense of belonging. As a culture, we have gradually moved from plaza to front porch, to backyard, to living room, to our own rooms and spaces where we relate to each other through screens. Having online connections is not the same as having in-person interactions!

Participating in community can enhance our sense of competence and provide opportunities to do something meaningful for other people, giving us a chance to feel the simple power of being heard and accepted—as many of us finally discovered in treatment. Many in the world have come to believe that anger, resentment, jealousy, rancor, and hatred are simply by-products of disconnection. Truth and love will trump ignorance, hatred, and isolation.

In community we are assisted to grow up, grow out, and grow in. Forging an empathetic community that nurtures and sustains us is a lifelong, essential human need. Yet we can keep circling back to the essential question "Where do we find connection?" That is what leads us to joining forces with others in our tribe of like mind, heart, and spirit. This is the essence of conscious fellowship.

Wherever I feel connected, with a deep sense of belonging, is where my true communities live.

Resiliency is the ability to bounce back from adversity, to cope positively when one is affected by negative influences and events. The essence of resilience involves the ongoing presence of at least one older, caring, loving adult in our world. As a member of a tribe, we have at least one person who "gets it" and is in our corner. Sometimes this person functions as a fair witness. They know and verbally acknowledge that what we are going through is not right, not fair, and not our fault. They see through the veil of secrecy thrown up by the family—or the tribe—that we have been wronged and that what is being blamed on us is really the crazy, shameful behavior of others.

Such individuals not only see our preventable suffering—from violent, abusive, alcoholic family members and from those who betrayed or abandoned us—they also take steps to alleviate our suffering. Most of us are capable of walking around or dealing with trouble if there is some place to walk to and someone to walk with. Treatment programs help us to fashion those critical links that comprise our own safety net—helping us find "who we're gonna call" when times are tough.

I honor all those who have in some way been a fair witness to my suffering.

To move from risk to resilience requires our wholehearted participation. We cannot depend entirely on the kindness and goodness of others to save us. We know from our own process of recovery that being resilient means that when things are really tough, we will find someone offering a hand up—but it is still us who has to stand up and carry on.

Characteristics of resilient people include the ability to fortify their psyche by realizing that bad times are usually a temporary state of affairs—and that these periods offer opportunities for growth. Resilient people practice positive *mindtalk*, seeing themselves as competent and capable human beings. They tend to seek out and surround themselves with others who are also resilient, discovering that the uplifting presence of those who know how to just be with adversity inspires them to do the same. Rather than toughing it out, always seeking to be harder, stronger, more armored, they are flexible and go with the flow; like a tree in a powerful storm, they have strong roots but flexible branches. They have learned how to fill their own cup with positive self-care when life seems too much.

I am slowly building a resiliency toolbox, which will serve me well in times of life's trials and tests.

We can think of resiliency in youth as three complimentary circles of fortification that become our foundational sources of encouragement and support. The *circle of the individual* includes traits such as a sense of humor, the ability to have fun, and a sense of healthy detachment from the adverse conditions with which the child is confronted. This means establishing and maintaining healthy boundaries and not taking all the mess of their family on their little shoulders.

The *family circle* includes "good enough" parents who, at least half the time, provide a caring and supportive environment. They also hold high, positive expectations and provide opportunities for participation.

The *community circle* includes schools with a caring and supportive staff, strong extracurricular programs, and much youth involvement. Some of us were blessed with these resiliency-building opportunities; some were not, as we fell through the proverbial cracks into the despair of early substance use.

Who do we know who might benefit from *our* involvement in their life? Someone for whom we can be the fair witness, offer a more empowering perspective, and serve as a reminder that many, including us, have been through the same fires and not only survived, but thrived.

I will reach out and become part of someone's support system.

Loyalty is a double-edged sword. In the modern world, it has lost some of its noble luster and become mired in the shadows of keeping secrets and fostering injustice. We may think those who followed orders to kill in concentration camps, or those in corporate boardrooms who turned a blind eye to their company's polluting or inhumane practices, were just being loyal. While these individuals were perhaps loyal to their organization—maybe motivated by fear of reprisal—they were certainly not being faithful to themselves.

It's easy to point the finger at others, yet we know all too well the shadows of this quality, for we let our addiction become our best friend, showing loyalty to it rather than remaining true to our higher self. We gave up our ideals and principles for a quick fix, a temporary lift, and the fulfillment of an impulsive desire.

Now our recovery is teaching us to be trustworthy, to honor our own being physically, mentally, emotionally, and spiritually. Such allegiance to our core will only strengthen over time as we continue to remove whatever obstacles interfere with our own self-love.

I can remain loyal and true to my highest values.

When my external daily life is in line with and reflects my most deeply held internal values, then I am loyal to myself. When I "walk my talk," I free myself from hypocrisy and strengthen my resolve to be my best in any situation. This is not the stale prison of perfection, nor is it the rigid confines of a universe of "should" imposed by others. It is an inner flowering, a pruning away of all our considerations in order to allow the light of authenticity to shine forth from within.

Loyalty, in this sense, is a surrendering to the brilliant lighthouse beacon of our principles. We don't have to figure everything out; we just need to listen to our own true voice articulating what we know to be most important. The old saying "Blood is thicker than water" reminds us that we all have loyalties of differing strengths, scopes, and legitimacy—each one potentially resulting in different levels of sacrifice.

Do we protect a child or parent who has done wrong? Do we shield a co-worker from his or her substance-induced mistakes? The ethics of loyalty can be tricky, but if we always first consult our own moral compass, then the way can become clear.

My ultimate loyalty is to my own truth.

Rather than getting lost in lofty philosophical discussions, we can look around us for examples of loyalty. What does it really mean to be trustworthy, steady, and reliable in our daily lives? What cause, country, group, or person inspires us to be devoted—far beyond casual interest—with wholehearted commitment? Who is really deserving of our loyalty, worthy of our ongoing willingness to be in their corner, to be tight and remain bonded with them, no matter what is happening?

Dogs embody what it means to be loyal. With their attentive presence, willingness to serve, and protective spirit, they often place themselves in danger for our benefit. They remind us to accept less than perfection and to make allowances for human weakness.

The fierce commitment and respect inherent in loyalty can infuse our daily actions with an unshakable determination to keep revisiting the Ninth Step, to continue making amends, because we can finally be loyal to our highest values and self. With loyalty comes trust. Trust develops over time and is continually reinforced by honesty. Those we have harmed may take some time before they trust us again. Some never will. Either way, we continue to be true to ourselves.

I will look all around me to learn from the profound gifts of everyday loyalty.

Competition is a fundamental human impulse. It is entwined with the natural laws of evolutionary pressure. It can drive innovation, motivate us to achieve greater success, and prompt us to explore new frontiers. Games and tournaments have long been a part of human history, designed, in part, to encourage the training and development of useful survival skills.

There is a dark side to competition. Many of us had negative early experiences with competition, feeling excluded, less than, or being pushed to win at any cost. Through rituals of celebration or loss, many of us were taught very early that alcohol or drugs are an essential part of relishing a win or surrendering to defeat.

There is also a light side to competition. Playing to win enhances coordination and concentration in an individual, and develops teamwork, cooperation, and creativity in a group. The inevitable times when we lose remind us to keep our heads up, because we did our best.

Losing is not failure, and loss carries its own lessons of supporting each other when victory is lost and of persisting in the face of obstacles. Winning isn't everything, and it's not the only thing. While it is an important goal, the bottom line is more about enjoying the competition and developing respect and other positive attitudes toward others.

Competition, like any human impulse, has positive and negative attributes.

The Buddha taught about four sublime states of mind that, while focused on the well-being of others, have the clear effect of generating happiness for the person practicing them. These four "immeasurables" include compassion, lovingkindness, sympathetic joy, and equanimity.

Sympathetic joy—also termed empathetic or appreciative joy—is the wholesome attitude of rejoicing in the success, happiness, virtues, or qualities of another. There will always be those who are better than us at something, who have more possessions, and who achieve greater heights of triumph and prosperity. Wanting what someone else has, and resenting them for it, is the invasive, smoldering sensation known as envy. It is fueled by our own sense of lacking something. Jealousy is a fear-based concern—we feel threatened, thinking that someone will take what we already have.

Envy and jealousy can infiltrate and poison our consciousness, destroying both friendships *and* community. The antidote is to bring to mind genuine, positive feelings of happiness for the other. Rather than experiencing envy or jealousy over the good fortune of another, we can quickly transform those emotions into more positive feelings, creating a greater sense of spaciousness in our own life.

I can generate sympathetic joy rather than remain mired in envy or jealousy.

The individual human heart is the foundation of all our social engagements, generating both power and purpose. Meeting others in vulnerable, honest *heartspace* revitalizes us all.

Being a healthy tribesman involves working through our childhood wounds and shame. It is finding an empowering balance between solitude and time for friendships. We ask—over and over—not just what we might get from the different communities in which we are involved, but also what we can *give*. Fostering resiliency in others becomes part of our contributions.

We can learn to gather the best fruits from the trees of competition and loyalty, while casting aside the rotten elements of those qualities. With practice, even the twin poisonous weeds of envy and jealousy can be rooted out, replaced by the beautiful flowers of sympathetic joy. Our role as a tribesman helps us grow and evolve, allowing us to offer even more gifts to the community at large.

As tribesmen, we revisit the Ninth Step and try to make amends for the wrongs of our past, while minimizing the missteps of the present. We willingly take responsibility for the person we are—and are becoming—within our tribe.

I honor all those who participate with me in creating a healthy, caring tribal community.

JUNE

The Pathfinder

The inner Pathfinder requests that you clarify your true purpose and distinguish your *wants* from essential *needs*. Embrace your destiny; listen to the call of your deep desires! Pilgrimage and adventure promise the revelation of your highest values and deepen your sense of spirituality.

It is said that all paths lead *home* and that we always carry our true home with us in our heart. The inner pathfinder knows that each of us needs both a center and an edge. Center is home, in every sense of the word. It is all our relations, everything we deeply love, all that nourishes and supports us. Home is also that little happy peaceful place inside, our inner sanctuary.

We each travel the world in search of what we need, and ultimately find our lives much enriched when we return to our roots. We try to carry with us on our journey only that which is both useful and beautiful, and our passage is often turbulent, confused, and uncomfortable—made great only in the retelling of the adventures.

Our *edge*, then, is the territory of growth, risk, change, and evolution, where deep desires drive us to a path of growth-infused uncertainty. Somehow, each day we manage to navigate the stormy seas between home and edge—between the life we now have and the one we would like. This is the territory of the pathfinder, where we embark on both inner and outer quests in order to discover what we most need to know.

Strengthening my center allows me to explore my edge.

Some of us became lost in the labyrinth of substances, thinking they might provide the answers to our dilemmas. We often found despair and disappointment instead. The Eighth Step—"Made a list of all persons we had harmed, and became willing to make amends to them all"—became a road map for taking responsibility for those times when we were truly missing in action.

The inner pathfinder often summons us more with questions than answers, reminding us of the false summits and mirages that inevitably appear on any journey. Denial and escape are replaced by the more useful compass found in *really* listening to our heart. Experiencing a better, more authentic, more fulfilling life comes from asking ourselves some important questions about needs, desires, purpose, and happiness. And, with right timing, an adventure or pilgrimage can add its own truth to the garden of living a good life.

We are always—every one of us—coming together and falling apart at the same time. Searching and seeking always lead to victories and defeats, illumination, and further confusion. One day at a time, with each conscious step a liberating moment, we make progress.

I am learning that an apparently easy path can become a long and suffering way, and a roadblock to an opening into liberation.

Like flowers in springtime, the lessons culled from different life experiences arise slowly, with their own unique form and beauty. No one knows in advance what each day might bring. We do understand that we either wake up with fear and anxiety, inundated by a mountain of shoulds and have-to-dos, or with a more peaceful center full of gratitude.

What is the feeling tone of our average day? Are we mostly stressed, pressed, and overwhelmed? Are we enthusiastic, enjoying, and energized? Or are we somewhere in between? It is possible to remain relaxed and content, even in the face of uncertainty and fear.

If our struggles with addiction have taught us anything, it is that there really is nowhere to run and nowhere to hide. We cannot escape our demons by traveling far. We carry them with us. What we do with desire, and how we channel its energy into fulfillment of our purpose, will determine whether we starve or feed the scary monsters within us.

Pathfinder offers us the possibility that we can develop new and interesting ways to get our needs met, that we can forge a more empowering perspective in any situation.

As I explore my needs and desires today, my path can be both tranquil and exciting.

Needs represent the basic requirements for sustaining life found in the physical, emotional, mental, and spiritual aspects of our being. They involve physiological necessities like air, food, water, sleep, and some protection from the elements, including clothing and shelter, access to health care, and medicines.

Humans also have emotional needs for safety, identity, connection, participation, and cooperation, as well as mental needs for creative expression, ways to satisfy their curiosity, and opportunities to learn new skills. We also have what some consider spiritual needs—connecting with the Great Mystery to make some sense of the meaning and purpose of our life, so we can continue to evolve and develop an expanding sense of freedom.

The psychologist Abraham Maslow visualized needs as a pyramid with physiological and safety needs at the base, followed by the need for belonging and love, then esteem. Mental and creative needs were built on top of those. The top need to be fulfilled in the pyramid is *self-actualization*, the need to be our true self. From a motivational viewpoint, we start at the base, and as each level is satisfied, we attempt to get the next higher level of needs met.

I see clearly what basic needs I still have trouble satisfying.

It is helpful to distinguish needs from wants. Simple wants often show up in the realm of having, such as possessing a different car, upgrading to a better cell phone, or experiencing a beach vacation. Wants are so woven into the fabric of our daily life that they often become invisible to us.

Our wants constantly evolve over time, just as we do. Preferences are the priorities in the jungle of wants. They speak to basic rhythms, satisfying habits, the kind of place and personal environment where we enjoy living. Preferences can be rooted in our body. For example, we might be a morning person, or we feel better when we eat a certain diet. They can also be grounded in personality. We might be extroverted and prefer big parties, or introverted and prefer to spend time alone or with a few close friends. Or they can show up in activities we enjoy, such as biking, watching sci-fi movies, or listening to live jazz. Preferences also influence our choices in relationships—we might enjoy spending a lot of social time with one person; we might be attracted to a certain body type or personality. Whatever our preferences—from simple wishes to intense wants—the train of *more* is always running.

I will pay more attention to what is a want and what is a need.

Because they are so linked with our survival, needs are deeply meaningful and universally valued by all people, regardless of age, gender, race, ethnicity, or culture. But we often misuse the concept of need in daily language and employ it to sugarcoat demands ("I *need* you to . . .") or to justify cravings ("I *need* more money so I can buy . . ."). We also confuse wants and preferences with basic, real needs.

Under the illusion of "need," we can easily give in to consumer madness, with an endless thirst for sense pleasures, the fever of longing for more and different. Although capable of providing pleasurable and satisfying moments, the double-edged sword of *craving* is that it can lead to out-of-control accumulation, greed, and chronic dissatisfaction.

As we know all too well through personal experience, addiction in many diverse disguises has its origins in such patterns of craving *more*. Like money itself, wanting can be a good and helpful servant, but a poor and dangerous master.

How much is enough is not always an easy question to answer. As we learn in recovery, ultimately it just feels better to hang out in continuous gratitude rather than be in a state of constant wanting.

I can create a healthier relationship to both my needs and wants, and how I communicate them to others.

When most people use the term *desire,* they usually view it as something fleeting, impulsive, or limitless. Or they use it in a sexual context, often in the framework of a drive that needs to be controlled or repressed.

Consider for a moment a different perspective, the notion of *deep desire*: a lasting, loftier challenge, the elegant juice of life that thirsts and quenches, a heady realm whose powerful energy can assist us in learning about delayed gratification, impulse control, future orientation, and hard work. Deep desire invites us to dare greatly, to be vulnerable. It can inspire us to believe that things will continually get better and that it is possible to manifest something we really want.

What are the deepest aspirations we hold for our life? Some may have been present in childhood fantasies, the realm of what we always wanted to be or to explore. Wanting to be a doctor, live by the sea, or play jazz might be examples. The specific form is yet to be created, but the impulse is alive and full of energy. This is very different energy from our wants, preferences, and needs.

My addiction made fulfillment of my deepest desires difficult, but now I can explore them.

Deep desires are really about exploring our edge. They are the quests that keep tugging at us, demanding our attention until we recognize their importance in our life. Their ultimate purpose is to guide us to experiences that help us to grow. They are a repository of seeds, which when planted allow us to evolve, for it is through manifesting such inner visions that we really learn about life.

Passion is one form of desire; it is energetically engaged enthusiasm, with wild moments of abandon. Our personal passions are always ready to welcome us back. The inner necessity of deep desire channels that passionate energy into specific pursuits.

Deep desires are like orchards. The more attentive focus we put into them, the more fruit they will bear. While such a driving force ignites needed changes and growth, it is often a pain in the ass because it can create much suffering as it leads us down paths that challenge us on every level. Sometimes we wish we could just let go of our need to pursue our deep desires and step back from our commitment to change. But our deep desires will always surface throughout our life in some form, until we heed their call.

I welcome the changes that come from following my deep desires, and I will have a healthy respect for the demands they make upon me.

Everyone struggles with conflicting needs, desires, and wants, and balancing them all is part of the challenge of living well. We need independence, yet we seek connection. We enjoy luxury, yet we also want to maintain simplicity and fitness. We like the satisfying feeling of accomplishment, and we also enjoy chilling out and doing nothing in particular. Perhaps we want to achieve certain benchmarks in terms of having money and *things*, but we also feel the drive to contribute, to make a positive difference in the world.

Balancing work and family, paying the bills and doing what we love, embracing the new while rooted in the old, can tug us in different directions, dispersing our focus. It takes a centered person to be able to navigate the different responsibilities and choices that pull on our limited time and energy. While in the throes of our addiction, we often just gave up trying to juggle all these different demands. Our focus was stolen, our passions locked in the basement, as our most creative urges took a back seat to the drive for another hit, another fix, another drink—another descent into temporary relief from our pain.

Sobriety gives me the gift of attending to needs, wants, and deep desires in healthier ways.

Purpose can be defined as the reason for which something is done or created, or for which something exists. It often implies determination, objectives, intent, and the focus of one's efforts and actions.

To seek our purpose is to ask, "What does it all mean?" These five powerful words embody the ultimate quest to understand our *raison d'être*—our reason for existing—to deeply *grok* that which has meaning and significance for us throughout our life. The critical, meaty, consequential actions we tackle each day are buoyed by the realization that they can contribute to living our purpose. The healthy interaction between routine activities and higher mission is where the rubber meets the road.

We infuse each moment with purpose when we wholeheartedly instill it with our presence and attention and place it in a larger field of intentional movement. Even eating can become a meaningful activity that ensures our body is fit to do its purpose—as are all the other small bits of daily self-care. Remaining addiction free is a conscious choice we make to provide us with the energy we need for doing good in the world. Even the smallest acts of kindness to others can become the vehicle for expressing our deeper values.

I align all the little actions I take each day with a greater, more expansive sense of purpose.

Once our basic survival needs are met, we humans have the opportunity to regularly engage in nine sacred arenas: **family, friends, fitness, fun,** our current **field of endeavor** (work), the **fortress of our home,** the **frontier of our personal growth, finances,** and being a **force for good** (being of service).

Each day offers us limited time and energy, and we must choose activities that nurture these diverse aspects of our life while somehow striving to align them all with our higher purpose. The richness of this tapestry is evident when we examine any one of its life-affirming threads. Every one of these realms can bring about satisfaction and a deep sense of fulfillment.

We want it all! We want to be a good friend and excellent partner, feel healthy and in great shape, find meaningful work that makes a difference, and have a well-appointed castle to retreat to at the end of a long day. It is easy to see how our recovery makes it easier to experience success in each of these realms.

In recovery, we discover that we can rest in gratitude for what *is*, right now, even as we continue to make things better.

Being clean and sober helps me find purpose and meaning in each of the sacred nine realms of my daily life.

A key aspect of any exploration into purpose involves the concept of right livelihood—finding work that offers us something we believe needs doing, beyond pay benefits, vacations, and security. Right livelihood narrows the gap between what we dream and what we do, and deeply honors the gifts we have to offer the world, while acknowledging what is required for survival. This notion intimately weaves together work, money, and creative expression. A basic principle is "We must not work hard to get what we don't want!"

How do we define success for ourselves? Much flows from that deceptively simple query. Meaningful work marries passions with skills, allowing us to measure success in any currency we choose: money, people helped, habitats saved, the degree to which we are experiencing peace, health, and love—whatever our own personal criteria may be. Most people direct their precious time and life energy into accumulating money and the stuff it buys, trying to create a sense of security and diverting themselves. But does it make sense to give up five days doing what is not fulfilling, so we can enjoy the other two?

Even if we can't live it right now, we can at least envision work that is more satisfying, the first step to making it so!

Freedom from substances offers more opportunities for meaningful work, aligned with purpose.

Our destiny awaits us on the road we have taken to avoid it. This principle of "uncommon sense," revered by the pathfinder, reminds us that the wounds from our past cannot remain buried if we are to make forward progress. Working the Twelve Steps regularly reinforces for us the need to keep finishing unfinished business. We profoundly realize—perhaps for the first time—that the choices we make today influence the quality of our lives tomorrow. This seems such an obvious truth, yet our addiction kept us blind to it.

There is a strong belief in many cultures that the effects of our actions determine our destiny, in this life or the next, and that this "karma" affects the fortune of our friends and family as well. The parallel Western idea is "As you sow, so shall you reap." The essence is that whatever thoughts and actions we extend out into the world will very definitely return to us in kind. In this sense, destiny is not some predetermined future, but rather a malleable unfolding, an ongoing karmic accounting, in which we are not passive victim, but rather active creator.

By doing my inner work, I will resolve my main issues and gradually live the life I hope to manifest.

Who are we? Are we loved? Who can we count on? What are we here for? These queries make up the fabric of the tapestry of our destiny. As pathfinders, the accumulation of all we have thought and done in this life produces the path we walk upon. What we do and how we behave along this trail involves free will, choice, and transformation.

Each and every day, the accumulation of right actions alters the path as we walk upon it, creating the future we desire—or not. Bearing the burdens of today's hardships sows the seeds for the blessings of the future. Destiny is determined, not predetermined. If we look at where we are today, in relation to the past suffering we experienced from our own addiction, we can grasp how alterable our future is.

Continuing to become more conscious of our destructive patterns, and working diligently to shift them, ensures that we will alter the course of the flow of our life in a more favorable direction. All is not lost, and never has been. With support, we continue our journey to wholeness, weaving the threads of our own destiny.

The choices I make each and every moment can contribute to the unfolding of my higher purpose and delightful destiny.

Although the concepts are used interchangeably in many cases, *fate* and *destiny* can be differentiated. Fate is the development of events beyond a person's control, often regarded as determined by a supernatural, or higher, power.

In many traditions, there were three goddesses, sometimes depicted as sisters, who wove a tapestry on a loom that determined the fate of mortals. The key principle of such tales is that people will always act, or things will turn out, in a particular way. Fate is the power that predetermines and orders the course of events, decreeing and defining these occurrences as things "meant to be."

Destiny is more uplifting than fate, suggesting a positive outcome, as determined not only by chance and good fortune but also by the actions and intent of the person. The inner pathfinder reminds us that while we cannot control all the events that happen to us, we can influence our reactions to them. We can evolve to the point where we outgrow our habitual reactivity and drop more and more of the conditioning that does not serve us well. While becoming addicted may have been our fate, our *destiny* is changed by the efforts we put into remaining sober.

What happens in my life is neither predictable nor inevitable.

Our individual journey as pathfinders can be brimming with negatives such as beating ourselves up and constantly feeling like we're "not enough," or we can choose to experience the path as a pleasant walk of mind-body awareness.

An old adage states, "If we don't know where we are going, we will end up someplace else." We operate in a culture where the mantra is "More is better," and *more* then becomes what fuels our sense of importance and status. Living our core values can bring us back to *enough*. Living smart implies listening, reflecting, and then acting, rather than reacting out of social conditioning.

Having clear values builds confidence in our instincts to do the right thing in the moment when we don't have time to sort through particulars. When we regularly act in accordance with our own inner guideposts, we grow in insight and understanding and strengthen the muscles of self-respect and self-awareness. Consistently making choices based on values helps us learn about our strengths and notice our weaknesses. Embracing what is most helpful to our evolution enhances our inner power. Again and again, we affirm our essential authentic self through our choices, even as we reject old cultural conditioning and societal programming.

I embrace my most cherished values.

Words have power. Words create a landscape for us to enhance with our actions and intent. Honesty, kindness, loyalty, responsibility, contentment, generosity, creativity, and love are the concepts that hold within them the potential for guiding our daily actions. Consistently holding these notions—and others like them—at the forefront of our awareness creates the foundation of our prime, keystone values.

These elemental belief systems often developed in relationship to our core issues. If we had a largely absent and nasty father, for example, we may make it a priority not to repeat those behaviors with our own children. If we grew up in poverty, we may have a deeply held value of sharing whatever we have with others. If we witnessed parents working at jobs they hated, we may hold expressing our imaginative creativity as most important.

What top values do we strive to live by or admire in others? We can pick five and post them on our refrigerator. We might ask ourselves each day if we are living a life that is in harmony with the principles we hold as most important. These can positively influence the many choices we make each day and the path we carve for ourselves across our lives.

My daily actions are where my values actually manifest in reality.

If our life is a book, and our current situation a chapter, what might be their titles? It can be fun to come up with some entertaining and insightful answers. Our inner pathfinder asks us to frequently reflect on where we are on our journey. Taking an eagle-eyed view can help us truly understand the larger perspective and appreciate the progress we have made.

Is my life better than it was a year ago? Has my progress in recovery opened up new horizons, allowing me to navigate the low valleys more easily? Creating time once a month to contemplate the simple question "How am I doing?" and then journaling our insights can be very helpful. This practice is similar to regularly consulting a map when on a long expedition. Such check-ins help us examine if we are indeed living what we say is most important to us. We notice where we stray from our desired path and how we inevitably manage to get back on track again. Just as an airplane is constantly course-correcting as it flies from one place to another, our journaling allows us to adjust our direction.

Regular writing about my life helps clarify and reinforce my core values.

The urge for adventure seems instinctive to the human species. Our natural impulses of curiosity, creativity, problem solving, and exploration have helped us colonize our planet. We have found ways to survive and thrive, even in places with the most extreme, hostile conditions. Technological advances continue to offer us the equipment and resources to survive harsh circumstances in relative safety. Deep sea and outer space investigations continue to capture our imagination, and every day, what once was science fiction becomes our current reality.

Whether it is a weekend camping trip, longer vacation travel, or a full-fledged expedition, the unknowns and uncertainty inherent in adventure pull us out of ourselves, expand who we are, and allow us to marshal inner resources we did not know existed. Now that we are in recovery, we have the opportunity to discover such possibilities. No longer consumed with just satisfying our addiction, we can choose to explore new frontiers. Saving money to travel for a few months, or getting it together to visit a destination we have always dreamed of seeing, can now become reality. Name the place, create the space, and enjoy the novelty we will face!

Every day, I am grateful for the new adventures sobriety allows me to undertake.

On the inner plane, the call to explore our edge involves risk, facing our fears, and a willingness to embrace uncertainty. The essence of an adventure—inner *or* outer—is encountering the unknown and unpredictable, which can be both scary *and* exciting. For many men, venturing into the vast terrain of their feelings can be such a long, illuminating voyage. For others, really listening to their heart for the first time, dropping the noisy expectations of others so they might hear their own truth, can be a rewarding odyssey. Learning to perceive more clearly the feedback our body is offering us in terms of stress and anxiety can also be a novel frontier filled with helpful insights.

Being in treatment has helped us begin these perilous but rewarding journeys within. We finally grasp that creating lasting changes in the outer circumstances of our lives begins within. We have, no doubt, come to realize how much unexplored territory there is within our own being. Perhaps we have even become inspired by the imperative "know thyself," which holds enormous relevance for us in our daily lives.

I am in awe of how much there still is to discover about myself.

Primitive activities are good for us: a walk in moonlight, sitting around a fire, wandering in the woods, beach-combing, or exploring a jungle path can fill some deep yearning. We are part of, and in, the universe, and the universe is in us. Our very atoms came from the stars, and we share them with other voyagers and creatures. Lying down, embraced by the Earth, we gaze at a starry sky and realize both our incredible significance as a sentient being *and* our miniscule place in the vast universe of things. We are humbled and inspired.

Now that we are clean and sober, we can truly feel at home in both ourselves and the planet. Adventuring offers us time away from our routines and normal ways of thinking and being. To not make it a regular part of our life is to deny ourselves some basic connection for which we will always yearn. When we engage with the planet directly, leaving behind our usual creature comforts, we experience some of the wanderlust our ancestors had. We feel the joy of new discoveries and better appreciate the comforts of home.

Adventuring in nature, I honor the sweet precariousness of my own survival.

Notwithstanding the inherent spirituality of practicing the Twelve Steps, spirituality has become an alien concept for many of us. Having rejected the religious credos and dogma of our families, some of us fail to define for ourselves a new code of ethics—those rules provided by an external source or Higher Power—or a basic sense of morality, defined as an individual's own principles of right and wrong. And many also cease to establish a meaningful connection to what might be termed the Great Mystery, that which is beyond one's individual ego, "small-self" consciousness.

Every major religion promotes the principles of kindness, forgiveness, and generosity—all transformational ideals. Active spiritual practice can take many forms, including rituals to honor the changing seasons, phases of the moon, sunrise and sunset, periodic fasting, tithing, and other forms of service. Each of us must determine for ourselves what is most fulfilling and what rings true in terms of our own worldview and belief systems. We may even come to appreciate the religion of our parents, reaffirming and redefining its teachings to make them our own, and find renewed faith by participating in their religious community events.

I can use my everyday experiences as a well from which to strengthen and deepen my spirituality.

Spirituality is a personal journey, while religion is an organizational road map. Sometimes they cross and overlap, and while they can support each other, often one can be a barrier to the other. One can be spiritual without embracing a variety of rules and codes determined by a group of people with shared beliefs about the nature of a divine being.

While religion can be full of ritual and meaning, it can also be narrow, exclusive, bigoted, and full of prejudice, a cloak one can wear or discard depending on what circumstances dictate. The great societal lie in religion is the oft-expressed *certainty* that heaven and hell are other than here on Earth, that in order to experience a shared community of compassion, with meaningful ritual, we *must* embrace a religious belief in a god—often a god who monitors our every thought and action, and who will punish or reward us for the things we do.

We need not blindly accept what traditions, books, or even teachers say we should. We can believe only what resonates in the deep chambers of our heart and the investigation of our own life. Even the Twelve Steps acknowledge this by using the term Higher Power and the phrase "God, *as we understood [God].*"

I can keep clarifying my beliefs and distinguishing between spirituality and religion.

So does it really matter whether our spirituality looks like a little old black-and-white TV, or something that isn't even on our radar screen in terms of what we consider important at this point in our lives? What if humanity's spirituality is really what helped us to survive, based on the values it generated? The skills and wizardry of science leaping forward has created for many a techno prison: a daily life filled with materialism, expediency, narrow self-centeredness, and frenzied endless spinning of having to work, produce, then consume.

Lessons learned from traditional cultures with their embedded values are often left behind. As a result, our connections to a sense of seasons, the rhythms of labor needed for survival, daily rituals, stages of life, and other essentials of living have become precarious. Many young people have never witnessed a birth or a death, two of the most fundamental spiritual experiences. The disconnect many of us feel will not be resolved by getting more Facebook friends, Twitter followers, or Instagram pals. Recovery gives us the chance to *really* discover what is meaningful and true for us, in terms of concerns much larger than our small ego and its issues.

Spirituality matters, and its exploration can provide critical insights for my personal evolution.

When we infuse a sense of spirituality into an adventure, we create a pilgrimage.

Such journeys invite us to suspend modern-day thinking and drop into a more primitive, "body-based" way of being in the world. Being rooted in our senses, our intuitions, and all those subtle feelings that helped our hunter-gatherer ancestors survive creates an aliveness in which our thinking mind is embedded in the natural world.

While a pilgrimage may have elements of mechanized travel, ultimately it involves some walking or traveling, with the assistance of our four-legged animal brothers. We slow down to the pace of life's natural rhythms. We walk under the open sky, with only our wits and what we can carry on our back for sustenance. Sometimes we journey with others who seek similar benefits. At other times, the solitary quest is what calls us.

The concept of pilgrimage is ancient—a time when we can become an open mirror of emptiness, taking in whatever is there. The joys of adventure and the excitement of wandering around combine with clear spiritual intent to forge a powerful exploration of quiet mind and open heart.

I honor the sacred tradition of pilgrimage and will listen when my own deep restlessness compels me to journey.

From Stonehenge to Easter Island, Machu Picchu to Mount Kailash, Lourdes to Mecca, humans have always been drawn to special, enchanted places on the planet. People regularly visit innumerable sacred sites scattered around the world. Many books describe the profound experiences generated by such encounters. Some involve religious rituals, others just an immersion into the divine expression of Earth's magnificent beauty. Whenever we are able to journey to such locales, our beings are filled with awe, and the pilgrimage opens us up to receive the unique blessings of the site. Sometimes these spiritual quests involve physical hardship—part of the sacrifices necessary to obtain the transformational results.

But the pathfinder doesn't have to travel to the far corners of the Earth to reap the benefits of pilgrimage. The temporary highs of our addiction, which often took their toll on our health, allow us to appreciate even more, in our sobriety, the beauty of enduring difficulties for spiritual benefit. We make a conscious choice—rather than the unconscious fallout from substances—to surrender ourselves to the passage, to learn larger lessons from moving through the physical challenges. We are capable of much more than we had imagined. Our inner world enlarges through exploring the outer in a sacred manner.

I will consider a pilgrimage to someplace I have always felt drawn to.

Imagine and accept that we are animal creatures, rooted in the planet's embrace. Only then can we discover our elemental places of power. We realize we need not go to the other side of the world to experience a pilgrimage. We might establish a sacred grove in a nearby woods, adorning it with only natural objects we find in the vicinity. We can make this altar as simple or as complex as we wish—on a beach, jungle, forest, plain, or even in a city park. We can mingle our prayers with the prayers of the wind, the sunshine, and the rain.

We can create our own path and our own sacred place where we can be silent and just observe, letting our senses bathe in how good it is to be alive, free of our addiction. Our pilgrimage may be as simple as packing a lunch, driving somewhere, and then walking to our uniquely exceptional spot—extraordinary in how it touches us. This can be a place where we can be a part of the ever-changing patterns of animals, minerals, and plants; where dialogue with a world of intelligent, powerful presences is possible. The topographic marvels of *landscape, seascape,* and *skyscape* allow the fullness of our humanity to be expressed.

I need not travel far to regularly experience the marvels of the sacred, natural world.

Most people have some idea of what makes them happy. Happiness bursts forth when we want exactly what we have, right here, right now, this very moment. Although it is often equated with having more, sustainable happiness is always rooted in wanting what we already have. It most often involves being present and appreciative.

This type of happiness is very different from the craving trap, wherein the desired, future "there" seems so much better than "here." When our there has become a here, we will simply obtain another sought-after there, which will look better than here. Our own journey with addiction has taught us the destructive futility of constant craving. The prevalent societal big lie is that whatever emptiness we feel inside can be filled by the accumulation of material things, unlimited wealth, power, recognition, and sensual pleasure. While all of these important elements are part of everyone's life, they certainly don't guarantee that we will be happier. We must dig deeper inside ourselves to find the true sources of our joy.

I will observe my moments of happiness and notice how they usually involve being present and grateful.

Everything is great as it is—and there is always room for improvement. Just as there is no one "right" way to live, people define happiness for themselves in different ways. The truth is that we are all seeking to find happiness and to avoid suffering, and this common human striving connects and bonds us all.

It is useful to remind ourselves that we each go through periods of feeling lost, and then found, as we endeavor to find joy. Our own struggles with addictions can be perceived as misguided attempts to relieve pain and find good feelings. All our mistakes and missteps are just variations on this basic human theme. What we may finally realize, with time, is that pleasure is not synonymous with happiness, but rather a temporary gratification of a desire.

Is it even possible to stabilize happiness, when everything else is constantly changing? Perhaps we just learn to appreciate and enjoy it when it presents itself and let go of seeking and struggling to achieve it. We can have a good time with all the variations along the happiness continuum, from contentment and delight to elation and ecstasy, each experience emanating a deeply felt, complete sense that all is well.

I hold the keys to my own happiness. Where have I hidden them?

Some believe we cannot seek happiness directly, that we can only prepare the soil and cultivate the seeds from which it might arise. Others conceive happiness as our birthright, believing it is always available, requiring only that we shift our consciousness and maintain gratitude for the many blessings at the forefront of our awareness. Still others are convinced that lasting happiness only comes when we live with lovingkindness, compassion, and being of service to others. In such open-hearted giving, there is always joyful receiving.

What everyone seems to acknowledge is that happiness is an inside job, less dependent on external circumstances than on our own perspectives, the lenses through which we view and inhabit the world. Just as one candle lights another and in that moment of contact seems to grow brighter, so joy multiplies as it spreads, growing and blazing from its own energy.

Our inner pathfinder reminds us to be grateful for everything: our needs, wants, deep desires, purpose, and values. To enjoy the adventures, the dance of destiny, the pilgrimages we make—inner and outer—in pursuit of meaningful spiritual connections. An attitude of gratitude nurtures joy in every circumstance, promoting appreciation for any situation.

Happiness cannot be grasped, only held with an open, grateful hand.

JULY

The Healer

The inner Healer reminds you that you are worthy of
forgiveness, appreciation, compassion, empathy, and
lovingkindness—qualities important to give to others
but also to yourself. Self-care, fitness, and harmony
within will carry you through challenging times of
being stuck.

Our inner healer asks us to embrace a path of well-being, wherein we declare to the universe, and all those around us, that we intend to thrive, whatever circumstances we encounter.

Healing can be defined as any change for the better. It is focused on whatever produces forward motion in any of the four windows through which we experience the world: physical, mental, emotional, or spiritual. In recovery—and whenever we are working intensely to improve current conditions—we encounter positive and often unexpected effects in all of these realms. We move toward the light, bringing more awareness and mindfulness to wherever our current dilemma might be.

Physical changes—more exercise, better nutrition, getting a checkup we have been avoiding—bring emotional benefits. Getting more skillful with our relationship with anger brings us a quieter mind. And deepening our spiritual practices brings profound emotional benefits. The healing needed to get free of our addictions involves—and continues to ask us to make—many internal changes as well as external supports in each of these four arenas. We welcome all forms of medicine to assist us with real well-being: laughter, music, arts, and love.

I honor all the progress I have made in healing, even as I realize there is still more to repair.

The inner healer reminds us of the Eleventh Step: "Sought through prayer and meditation to improve our conscious contact with God *as we understood [God]*, praying only for knowledge of [God's] will for us and the power to carry that out." The surrender, acceptance, and positive intent inherent in this Step are all essential components of any healing regimen.

We cannot continue our healing path without regular doses of each of the Twelve Steps. Working and reworking them helps keep our focus on moving forward. We each found apparent comfort in the cocoon of our habitual suffering—sometimes the changes required to take the next healing step seem too difficult. This is why deepening our spiritual practices can be so important. We simply cannot continue to respond to new situations with yesterday's old solutions if we want to experience positive results.

Asking for assistance from realms greater than our small self—whether we name it God, Higher Power, Life Force, or something else—summons and connects us to larger healing possibilities. We may never know if such aid is externally sourced or generated from the depths of our own being, but we welcome it, whatever its origins.

Healing occurs from the inside, with help from the outside.

In recovery, it is important to repeat this mantra, reminding ourselves often, "The blessing sleeps next to the wound." This principle of uncommon sense reminds us that whenever we are summoned to engage in active healing, there are gifts to be discovered along the way. The dis-ease of addiction shakes us up, calls forth as yet undeveloped inner resources, and offers us lessons in terms of asking for and accepting support. Part of the hidden beneficence lies in teaching us about the difference between what is, and what *is not,* important.

No matter what illness, wounds, and trauma we have experienced, we are capable of finding and empowering our true self, developing peace of mind, our capacity for unconditional love, the courage to be oneself, and the belief that we have choices to create our own version of the good life. This type of healing expands our capacity to deal with the misfortunes and difficulties that every individual life contains. Its energy renews and transforms us, increasing our confidence that we are more prepared for the next dilemma. The old adage "If it does not kill us, it will make us stronger" is true, but only when we stay aware and harvest the teachings concealed within the challenge.

As grateful as I am for my continued sobriety, I also appreciate all the healing lessons that brought me here.

While pain is inevitable, suffering is optional. On our journey to healthy independence, painful and challenging events happen, and we respond in the best way we can to survive. If we journal about a past difficult time, we will discover the gifts that were uncovered by moving through such a challenge. In the beauty of our own discomfort we then find the source of our power, and our divine discontent alerts us to undeveloped gifts.

Sometimes it takes an illness to put us on a path of self-realization; our body has to get sick in order for our life to heal. Some of the most exciting opportunities of our life come cleverly disguised as seemingly unsolvable difficulties. Suffering arises whenever we are in resistance to what is happening. The more we try to push away, minimize, or deny our pain—on any plane of existence: physical, mental, emotional, or spiritual—the greater our suffering. Not only because what we resist persists, but also because we waste enormous amounts of energy trying to defend against what is already affecting us. We guard the wound rather than letting it heal into its gift. But we can choose to do pain differently—to accept and move through it and sidestep the associated suffering.

I can learn to distinguish between pain and my resistance to it.

Like everyone else, we have experienced our share of not getting what we want or of dealing with what we don't want. Right here, right now, what is the primary cause of our own suffering? We need look no further than whatever we are experiencing that we want to push away—from physical pain to feelings of sadness or fear, negative mental chatter, or a sense of disconnection from our Higher Power. We generate suffering when we avoid addressing whatever is causing significant discomfort or dis-ease.

We know that our constant attempts to escape—through drugs or alcohol—only brought us more misery in the end. Whatever we were running from did not magically disappear; our suffering diminished only when we finally were able to confront and address the wounding. "If we can name it, then we can tame it." We first must call whatever we don't want by its name, as clearly as possible: this pain in my knee, these feelings of unworthiness, our obsessive thoughts about how someone has done us wrong. Then we can create a shift by putting our healing energy into new solutions.

Suffering can be reduced at any moment by naming what is and focusing on what might make it better.

Sacrifice, struggle, and suffering have been elevated to high ideals, the transformational compost of saints and martyrs. Yet do we really need more of these in our lives in order to heal? Perhaps we can take a holiday from these three champions of misery and instead embrace generosity, harmony, and bliss.

What if, just for today, we lived our life determined to be kind and giving, going with the flow, and experiencing joy, even in the midst of discomfort or unpleasant sensations? We must always honor what we did to survive our earlier challenges. At the same time, we can create different coping strategies. Recovery expands our capacity to choose healthier ways of moving through difficulties. We are no longer chained to the destructive patterns of our addiction.

Whenever we start to experience what we don't want today, and those same, nagging, threesome patterns begin to appear, we can replace them with a deep breath of awareness and positive images of the situation already transformed. When we do this, we put our energy into solutions. In the moment, we may not be able to disarm or discard all the pain, but the attendant suffering can be reduced.

Part of my healing is letting go of old patterns of suffering and struggles.

Wake-up calls, desperate to get our attention, may start as polite requests, gentle shoulder taps, whispers in the night, and they escalate to rude shoves or strong-arm tactics only when we continue to ignore them. Our inner healer will speak as softly as possible, and as loudly as it needs to. Some changes must be initiated this way to overcome the stubborn inertia of habit, fear, and laziness.

Like a shipwrecked sailor, the part of us that wants healing will use every resource at hand. The word for *development* in the Pali language is *vaddhana,* which translates roughly as "making messness." Good things, problems, suffering, and chaos all have their place in our unfolding. While in the midst of this, all we may experience is the sense of *stuckness,* of nothing moving forward, mired in old patterns and destructive habits.

Hitting bottom has its own wisdom. It may be the point where we finally realize we cannot climb out without help—that we are not destined to remain trapped, and healing is possible one step at a time, day after day.

I will pay attention to wake-up calls, both large and small, that nudge me along my path of healing.

Everyone who overcomes difficulties must seek to create meaning from their experience. Why did this happen to us? Why did we survive when others did not? We seek meaning by creating narratives about our life. We establish a story about what happened, which helps us shape the events and fit them into our life. This is all part of surviving. But even though it was just one more event in our life—although a very difficult one—because we do not grieve well or know how to heal through surrender and forgiveness, the danger is that we allow the story to become the characteristic that completely defines who we are.

We may even engage in "wound worship," using the past as a giant excuse for why we are not stepping up in the present. This form of being stuck can be very subtle, and highly invasive. It eats at the roots of our desire to evolve, destroys our capacity for being satisfied and experiencing joy, and shifts our consciousness into a depressive, fearful, "why bother," mind-set.

Getting free of the stories we constantly tell ourselves about our painful past is an essential component of getting unstuck.

The past is history, the future mystery, and each moment a chance to get free.

Being stuck means we're not listening to what life is actually telling us, stubbornly demanding that life comply with our preconceived version of how it should be, what it is supposed to be delivering in this moment. Getting unstuck—part of any healing process—involves a willingness to explore, to risk, to go beyond our habitual in-the-box ways of being and doing. Most important, it helps us realize that the dream of a life without obstacles is an illusion.

Our real life is *right now*—that includes all the unfinished business and daily challenges to our well-being. The idea of recovery is not so much to fix all our dilemmas or to finally arrive at some perfect summit, but to become more fully alive, aware, and adaptable.

Our life will never be without quandaries. We can try to consider difficulties signposts that lead us to necessary change. We can enjoy our life deeply, just as it is, with all its wild imperfections. Part of healing always involves the willingness to live with uncertainty, to hold fast patiently until the next step becomes obvious.

Recognizing I am stuck helps me to unwind it faster, knowing I will get stuck again in a different form.

There is no shortage of people in the world who have been hurt—by someone they love, by a friend, or by a stranger. People often undergo many ordeals across their life journey: accidents, illness, depression, divorce, imprisonment, even torture (emotional and physical).

Considering trauma as a topic might bring to mind a wounding experience from childhood, adolescence, or recent times. We can re-experience for a moment the sensations that were painful and overwhelming. In that recalling, we may feel as if we were stranded in an inner wilderness, yet we must realize that we are not alone in facing such challenges.

The purpose of replaying any traumatic memory is to bring awareness of what can be done in the *present* in order to release the pain of what occurred in the past. It is not about mining the memory for more recollections. The endless repetition of examining the story and experience does not bring relief. Whatever sensation or emotion rises to the surface, healing is being asked for.

Forgiveness can be a healing balm that releases us from the prison of traumatic memories. It opens the door to a new story, releasing us from victimhood.

I commit to healing past trauma that impedes my present path.

Many of us experienced early childhood traumas and also witnessed horrible circumstances while grappling with addiction. Post-traumatic stress disorder (PTSD) can be shifted for the better, but first we must recognize it.

Symptoms of PTSD include recurring intrusive recollection of the traumatic event, persistent avoidance of stimuli (sights, sounds, feelings, and so on) associated with the trauma that remind us of what happened. These are *normal* reactions to *abnormal* events. Yet they can be confusing, shameful, and remain a destructive secret for too long.

To better understand PTSD, it may help to think of allergies. With an allergy, our body may respond to the presence of a foreign protein like cat hair by trying to wall off and dilute the offending substance. The protective immune response may include an outpouring of secretions—runny nose, irritated watery eyes, or airways filling with mucus. Over time, our body's protective response is what creates the unpleasant symptoms we associate with the allergen. Similarly, without appropriate treatment for PTSD, what begins as a helpful physical response, designed to put our systems on alert in times of danger, continues to be stimulated by circumstances that trigger fragments of memories wreaking havoc on our sleep, our moods, and sometimes our entire lives.

Seeking appropriate help for any PTSD symptoms I am experiencing is an important component of my recovery.

Often the wisdom of our inner healer illuminates the need for forgiveness. An aspect of forgiveness is letting go of our judgments and need to be right about what happened. When we view the world through the lenses of "forgiveness glasses," we often experience the profound realization that we can't control another. No one can make other people in life behave kindly, fairly, and honestly at all times. It takes too much energy to judge, analyze, or attempt to change others into what pleases us just so we can keep them from hurting us.

Forgiveness is often perceived as a sign of weakness or submission, a pardoning of an offense. But forgiveness does *not* mean forgetting or approving hurtful events from the past. It means not making someone else endlessly responsible for our present well-being by constantly fueling and feeding our resentments and thoughts of revenge. We might think that keeping a grudge helps toughen us up by offering a good defense so we don't put ourselves in the original situation that hurt us. But living in a state of resentment often ends up hurting us more.

It is hard to give up grievances toward people we believe have wronged us. If we can't blame our misery and touchiness on them, then we have to take full responsibility for ourselves. That can be a scary prospect!

Forgiveness helps me stay sober. Recovery reminds me of the many people I need to forgive and from whom I need to ask forgiveness.

So how do we actually begin to forgive someone who frustrated, hurt, controlled, or abandoned us, or who did not recognize, respect, or respond to us? Untangling ourselves from the hates, reactions, judgments, and grievance stories we tell ourselves involves softening our sense of "the other" as enemy.

We don't have to like the offending person or spend time with them socially, but our willingness to see them as beings who are also wounded presents the gift of being able to put ourselves in their place, of feeling the weight of their burden and guilt. To do this we first must grieve, which allows us to feel everything related to the incident. Since grief cycles, we must acknowledge its call whenever it arises, and each time it does arise, keep placing the whole experience in a larger perspective.

Like grief, forgiveness is a process. Similar to rinsing dirty laundry in clean water, we need to keep renewing the purifying waters. The essence of forgiveness is accepting that what happened, happened, and what is, is. We drop the blame by gradually releasing the negative emotions and thoughts we have been holding. This includes all conditions, expectations, and demands—of ourselves or of the other.

When thoughts of the offender arise and I feel more peaceful than stressed, I know forgiveness is taking hold.

Self-forgiveness carries its own healing energy. Mistakes help us grow. They are vehicles for learning what we most need to understand. That does not mean that we don't experience regrets for our wrong actions or that the inner work of forgiveness can be ignored.

To forgive ourselves, we can make a regular practice of gazing at ourselves in the mirror with eyes of forgiveness and love. Try it—sometimes it's not so easy. It helps to remind ourselves that we are always doing the best we can under the circumstances in which we find ourselves. Forgiveness is always in order! It is part of letting go of whatever the experience was, which allows us to move on and emerge hopefully a bit wiser.

Forgiveness can only occur if we allow ourselves to feel all the emotions bundled together in whatever happened: the sadness, fear, anger, and even joy. And that requires some time and attention. Pushing it away makes forgiving that much harder to achieve. We can create some quiet, extended time in a lovely place and then allow these diverse feelings to flow so we can let them go. We can keep going deeper to new levels of forgiving ourselves—for not being perfect, for being human, and for not always walking our talk.

I embrace the power and teachings of self-forgiveness.

Just expressing that we are feeling "sorry" does not communicate acceptance of responsibility. When asking forgiveness from another, it is helpful to understand the anatomy of an apology. The essence of apology involves the five R's: **r**eal, **r**ecognition, **r**eveal, **r**emorse, and **r**eparation.

An apology is **real** when it is wholehearted and sincere; it cannot be faked. We **recognize** the wrongdoing and acknowledge the offense. Then we can **reveal** some of our perspective, giving an explanation, knowing that there is often more dignity in just admitting there was no excuse rather than attempting to offer a fraudulent or shallow reason. We show an honest expression of **remorse.** Finally, we state our willingness for **reparation,** because as we've learned in recovery, making amends compensates in a real or symbolic way for our transgressions.

An effective apology is an essential tool that requires honesty, generosity, humility, and courage. Sincere apologies not only help people calm down and move toward forgiveness, they are a critical part of our recovery process of making amends. We do this for the benefit of the other, with no expectations of being forgiven or absolved. However, when the apology meets the offended person's needs, forgiveness often comes spontaneously for everyone concerned, as the gift of release from the burden of carrying it all.

I am learning to apologize effectively.

To surrender does not mean we *give up*. Rather, we *give into*, with full, wholehearted acceptance of what is, coupled with the determination of Phoenix rising. We can and will survive, revive, and thrive. Rebirth can be the defining characteristic of embracing our inner healer.

When we surrender, we embrace ourselves with love, surround ourselves with healing light, and feel the tender compassion we allow to flow within us. As we do this, we release all expectations and demands of how life *should* be different in this very moment.

When we first entered treatment, it may have seemed like a defeat or resignation. Gradually we realized it was really a new beginning. When we surrender to physical pain or to our fears or sadness, we give in, in order to rise above. The very act of submitting is itself transformative. We embrace uncertainty as our teacher. We drop preconceived notions, and we trust deeply what life provides. We quiet the disparate inner voices and in the moment of release feel relaxation and relief.

The triad of acceptance, release, and trust become surrender's trident, the three-pronged spear of the healer we've been given to pierce the veil of the illusion that life has forgotten us. And we discover how the universe can respond positively, with surprising kindness.

I practice surrender in small things, preparing myself for doing so with greater challenges.

Surrender is full attention with appreciation, nonjudgment, and an opening to what is right in front of us. There is no need to be anywhere but here and now. It is simply amazing how tenaciously we cling to what we beg to be released from. To surrender is to affirm one's own destiny. It is dropping—at least temporarily—the continuous effort to tell life how it "should" be.

To surrender means to settle back into the natural awareness of whatever is present. To let it go really means to just let it be—the thoughts, the emotions, even the pain. This may never have been explicitly explained to us, even when we were dealing with so much wrenching chaos as we started on our path of recovery.

The secret to dealing with pain is to embrace it fully with a sense of spaciousness and expansiveness. We shift the narrow awareness around something painful to a larger perspective. Everything comes and goes by itself and we don't have to do anything to make it come, make it go, or let it go. We just let it be. Pain is still there, but our relationship to it is now quite different.

Spacious surrender allows for greater possibilities to move forward.

Like a waterfall, the soft yield of water on stone, or the swaying of a tree in a strong wind, surrender embodies the peace and comfort of *no resistance*. It summons a willingness to stay with what is difficult—not necessarily agreeing to or approving of the challenge, but softening our judgments and notions that what is happening is anything other than exactly the right experience for our development.

Surrendering fully lets in whatever is arising—physical discomfort, turbulent mind, or strong emotions. None of this is easy, and we will often feel the impulsive urge to succumb to our favorite addictive escape hatch rather than remain with the demon. We know where those choices have led us in the past. Surrender is *not* giving up the desire to overcome; rather, it is giving into what is actually happening, even as we welcome the sharp precision of disappointment.

When surrendering, we call upon the healing powers of the natural world in all its diverse beauty. We request the assistance of supportive allies, and we trust in the flow of the life force. As we do this, we are reminded that even in the most difficult circumstances, there are beautiful moments.

When surrendering, I can find the ease within the effort.

How do we approach each day with a sense of enjoyment rather than sorrow? No matter what is happening, we can appreciate what *is*. When things are going well, we can be grateful; when things are challenging, we can be thankful for the learning opportunities—the chance to rise to be our best amidst difficult conditions. We can use every experience as a vehicle for waking up and for greater healing.

No matter how bad things may seem, they could always be worse. The ever-changing nature of our thoughts and emotions reminds us that we need to call upon our inner healer to keep developing our steady inner core of acceptance and appreciation. We have learned the importance of this throughout our recovery process. There is a Tibetan practice called *tonglen,* in which we breathe in the suffering of the world, transform it in our heart, and breathe out comforting light and happiness. We can modify this practice to breathe in appreciation and breathe out compassion for specific people, or all beings.

Starting and ending each day with this awareness deepens our connection to our wellspring of gratitude and reminds us that our own universe of problems mirrors others' struggles.

*Today is a gift for which I am grateful, no matter what arises. I **breathe in** gratitude and **breathe out** compassion.*

There is always, *always* something for which to be grateful. Within the mysterious flow of this very moment, obstacles can be viewed as invitations to temporarily traverse and explore an alternate path. The creative surprise of being grateful releases us and opens us up, allowing something else to spontaneously arise. An attitude of gratitude is an essential cornerstone for happiness. Practicing gratitude can become habitual. While it takes time—as all good things do—with practice and commitment, gratitude can become our default response to a difficult moment. It becomes a very useful tool in our healing bag of tricks.

Gratitude reconnects us to our inner healer—the spirit that animates all of life. It expands who we are, and who we are capable of becoming. In the process of cultivating it in our everyday lives, we realize that, despite more pain and suffering in the future, there will also be more of *us*—a larger competent self—to soften those hardships.

It is interesting to keep a "notes of gratitude" journal in which we spend a few moments before bed writing down everything for which we were grateful that day. Just as journaling has been a useful tool in various ways throughout our recovery, creating daily pages of thankfulness brings surprising benefits.

When challenged, I can always rest in gratitude for what is still working well in my life.

Lovingkindness is an inherent natural human capacity, a fundamental instinct that balances our survival-oriented, common fears of the unknown or strangers. The Pali word *metta* is often translated as loving kindness or lovingkindness, a boundless friendliness joined with an all-encompassing sense of being amiable, benevolent, and affectionate. It is a dynamic and transformative force that changes—even heals—the whole experience of life.

Beginning each day with the thought "May all beings be happy, healthy, and free" effortlessly generates a feeling of connection, rather than isolation, with all those we encounter. Most of us have varying levels of intimacy with others in our circles. The continuum ranges from family and good buddies, to the larger field of acquaintances, then to those with whom we have a temporary affinity—an airplane seatmate, someone also waiting in line at the market, another driver who smiles at us in a traffic jam. Finally, there is the larger universe of total strangers—those people the American humorist Will Rogers spoke of when he said, "A stranger is just a friend I haven't met yet."

As recovery teaches me to live more out of love than fear, I generate loving kindness or lovingkindness toward all beings, no matter their level of closeness to me.

Our "small-self" ego mind is designed to create and achieve goals, a function necessary for survival and life enhancement. It is the ultimate event planner.

The ego is the metal between the hammer of life experience and the anvil of our essential nature. Because it is programmed for survival, it tenaciously holds on to self-serving behaviors and does not easily give up old patterns, even those we must shift in order to heal. We know how this aspect of ourselves—with its pride, stubbornness, and independence—contributed to our resistance to getting help, even when we were hitting bottom.

Our minds are also capable of perceiving the oneness thread that connects us to all of life. Most of us have had moments where we felt joined with everyone and everything—a temporary suspension of our ego mind along the ego-to-oneness continuum. Both are necessary; the ego keeps us rooted in our ordinary life and is important to survival, yet those instances of being one with the cosmos are transformative. When we experience this connectedness, we feel a tender opening toward all that is, filled with a depth of kindness beyond ordinary reality.

Instances when I feel at one with all of life are healing and filled with lovingkindness.

Imagine that the ego sits on top of a coach in command of the horses, with the higher self within. The ego thinks it is totally in charge, yet gradually, as our inner true nature exerts itself, the ego changes and begins to live in service to the greater good. We then relax into harmony with all that is, rather than staying stuck in our insatiable need to control.

Releasing whatever keeps us trapped in a prison of our making, we embrace those inner qualities that serve to expand our consciousness. Our higher self softens the ego so it becomes more peaceful and capable of expressing benevolence. We use the "horsepower" of our precious time and energy to guide ourselves into service work, assisting others and helping to make the planet a better place. And we find this love also directed at our own being, with all its faults.

In recovery, most of us realized that to get better, we had to love ourselves more, in the myriad ways in which that might be expressed. We learn to lavish on ourselves all those qualities we associate with heart—kindness, forgiveness, patience, generosity, acceptance, gentleness, and compassion.

Lovingkindness fills my own being, even as it radiates out to others.

Compassion naturally arises as we begin to see the unique beauty in each being, even with their faults, difficulties, and challenges. It is a quivering or tenderness of the heart, a strong feeling of wanting to alleviate pain and suffering—our inner healer at its best. Such an impulse seems to be wired in, and essential for, individual, family, and community survival. Compassion is a feeling of closeness with an attendant sense of responsibility, based on the realization that we all have similar desires to be happy and to overcome suffering. It is complete generosity without the relative notions of giving and receiving, a fearless openness without territorial limitations.

Compassion helps develop the capacity for enormous patience and persistence of a positive mind-set in the face of prolonged adversity. It flows from the desire to use our state of conscious awareness for the benefit of life itself rather than for personal gain. We begin to see how our own recovery brought lessons that might be helpful to others. Compassion honors not only the people who help us survive, but also the animal, insect, and plant kingdoms, without which our precious life could not exist.

May I be happy, peaceful, and free. May all beings be happy, peaceful, and free.

Our inner healer awakens our empathy, which at its most basic helps us understand how someone else feels—how their particular circumstances or experiences might feel for us. Empathy helps us recognize the pain and struggle common to all of humanity, and it is a welcome healing salve when we feel empathy from others. It also awakens our capacity to feel grief—our own and that of others.

Because we have loved, grief walks by our side. Relationships, physical breakdowns, and deep disappointments can all lead to pain. We even create agony by doing what is expected rather than following inner guidance; to the extent that our inner and outer lives are incongruent, we may experience hopelessness, helplessness, futility, and loss of the authentic self—part of the collateral damage from any addiction. Life sometimes seems a tragedy in endless acts. Pain, however, is stuck energy. Once shared, it can begin to dissipate. When we utter the Swedish term *uffda* to people, we simultaneously acknowledge their pain and express empathy, joining them in their suffering, if only for a moment. Grieving with others manifests in unique rhythms and is an occasion for healthy dependency—for not "going it alone." When we are there for another, despite the confusion and devastation, we become more of who *we* are.

In being present with another's pain, I expand my capacity for compassion.

Empathy opens the door for compassion to enter the living room of our consciousness. Compassion is empathy made visible in skillful action. Our happiness and suffering are seemingly dependent on the happiness and suffering of others, especially those with whom we feel intense connections.

When a friend or family member is struggling with an illness or disappointment, we have a natural impulse to want to do something to fix things, to somehow relieve the person's burden. Different from pity or sympathy, compassionate action arises when we *empower* others, rather than merely seek to impose *our own* perceptions upon the world.

Compassion is open, spacious, and generous—a fine-tuning of hearts to find some harmony in the midst of confusion and chaotic discomfort. Many of us benefited from this energetic quality in others as we began our journey in recovery. They were the people who "got it," no audience, no me/you separation, just a fearless openness without territorial limitations—while maintaining healthy boundaries. We felt not only their caring, but also their active support and encouragement. They held and accepted us because they related to our suffering. Compassion unites heart, mind, and body to alleviate the suffering of others.

Each day, I deepen my capacity for compassion.

We create a harmonious life when we consistently practice all that our inner healer promotes: forgiveness, surrender, appreciation, loving kindness or lovingkindness, compassion, and empathy. We can, ourselves, become a healing presence for others, a light on a dark path, calm within a storm. We may even decide to redirect our life path to include a profession that is focused on service.

Of necessity, when we were at our worst in the clutches of our addictive behaviors, we had to receive support from others. With recovery, it may be payback time, not in any narrow sense of "tit for tat," but rather out of the generosity of spirit we experience as we heal. From health care workers to frontline emergency personnel, massage and physical therapists to social workers, many diverse individuals comprise the helping, healing community.

Maybe our toolbox of healing should include some first aid, CPR, knowledge of nutritional supplements, and basic counseling skills. Volunteering with a nonprofit or working for the common good can also help us extend beyond what is needed for our own personal healing, widening the circle of helping hands and hearts while we grow our own well-being.

The more I feel in harmony with myself, the greater my capacity to assist others.

When things are going well, it is easy to forget. We forget the half-full, half-empty glass metaphor. Blessings suddenly seem everywhere if only we pause to appreciate them. Tune into any of our senses, and the marvels are nonstop: listening to music, watching a sunset, feeling rain on our skin; experiencing the nourishing warmth of a fire or the aroma and taste of a good meal. The sudden fullness of our cup leads us to forget the days that were half full or empty, because we have a new understanding of well-being.

Even with the ups and downs of living and the roller-coaster ride of our own recovery, we can be our own best medicine, creating harmony in our lives each day by filling it with love, laughter, and song, no matter the circumstances. Lighthearted cheerfulness sometimes heals as much as the heavy lifting of emotional processing.

We can summon ancient healing arts, in their many traditional and diverse forms, to expand the menu we partake of each day. For example, yoga, tai chi, qigong, and many martial arts practices offer a holistic system of coordinated, meditative breathing and body posture and movements, all of which enhance the healthy balancing of all our systems.

The world—and my life—is full of healing blessings.

The journey to wholeness is lifelong. The *I Ching* says that pain breaks the shell of understanding. Whatever within us needs healing, when we engage in the process wholeheartedly, using every modality available to us, our entire being is reinvigorated. We learn whatever lessons we need and harvest the gifts hidden within the apparent problem or difficult challenge. Bowing down to the altar of receiving support and blessings from others, we value and honor all those who lent an outstretched hand to us along the way.

To heal is not only to repair, but also to grow beyond what we were before. The more we feel our sadness and allow our grief to enter, the more spontaneity and aliveness we will have. The more we tend to our own wounds, the less likely we are to inflict them on others. We just keep moving forward: from an attitude of resentment to responsibility, from pushing pain away to curiosity, from coping to creating, from self-doubt to self-discovery, from inaction to playfulness, from feelings of shame to self-acceptance. Our shining allows others to do the same, and as a result, the world is constantly blessed by the presence of healing and healed people.

I am finding my place in the world as a healing and healthy human being.

Strength, endurance, and flexibility are a reigning triad in the physical realm. Combined with good nutrition and rejuvenating, refreshing sleep patterns, they comprise the major guideposts of honoring the temple of our body.

Emotional fluency—including learning to both grieve and forgive—also keeps us centered in our path of mastering intimacy. On the *mental* plane, we can harvest healing through visualization and shifting our *thought-stream* as we learn to ride the wild horse of our mind's constant output of wandering thoughts and impressions. Finally, the healing power of our *spirituality* can guide us to solutions based on prayer, meditation, time in nature, or engaging in various religious rituals and ceremonies.

At any given moment, each of these aspects of our being may be in need of assistance, and we are learning what resources to marshal to be most effective in creating a healing shift in the moment. The whole process of recovery strengthens our healing prowess, because we are constantly creating new, empowering habits and discarding destructive patterns. We finally begin to feel we are living in the center of our life, riding a wave of well-being to the shore of body, mind, spirit wholeness.

Each day, I restore my brokenness and enhance my capacity to continue to heal.

We stand in the gateway to ending the shame of our own imperfections. At this doorway, blessings sleep next to our wounds. Our inner healer reminds us that our brokenness can be transformative, that absolutely everything that occurs within us can be used to support the process of awakening and healing. Once we realize that we can stop labeling any given experience as "good" or "bad," we begin to embody a greater sense of inner peace, harmony, and freedom.

Whatever is happening *is*. Quite simply, that's what is happening. Our inner healer asks us to just go with the flow, trusting that we will marshal or develop whatever resources we need to cope with things as they unfold. It assures us that assistance—inner and outer—will arrive in many unexpected forms. We may not like or enjoy what we are being asked to face and embrace, but as long as we accept it and surrender to it in the most empowering sense of the word, then we are already healing. We get out of our own way, shift to a larger perspective, and rest in the spaciousness of gratitude rather than the constriction of fear. And when we fall off the horse of our higher awareness, we just humbly get back on again.

Everything contributes, and can be welcomed, as part of my healing journey.

AUGUST

The Hero

The inner Hero invokes your hidden potential, fills you with faith and hope, and teaches you about the sweetness of justice, right action, and mindfulness. He functions by making requests, asking you to confront your arrogance and the shadow side of being a savior.

True heroes do exist. They are the inspired beings who act with integrity in the pursuit of justice and who have the capacity to channel the support of others into positive outcomes for the greater whole. Everyone is hero material.

Heroes are engaged by some inciting event that propels them into action. With the help of our own inner hero, we are able to transform—first ourselves and then any challenging situation we may face.

The ordinary world of our own self-doubt, and what we perceive as our deficits, is the starting point for our own personal hero's journey. In order to overcome our addiction, we tapped into an inner capacity, a dormant potential for positive change. Like the warrior, we become boldly visible to self—to both our strengths and our weaknesses. We do not hide from unpleasant truths, but strive to live with integrity—meaning we tell the truth, keep agreements, honor our commitments, and respect and value the contributions of others.

Our inner hero is ever vigilant and ruthless in cutting through our own negative *mindtalk* and self-defeating behaviors. He knows we have much to learn, even as we stretch ourselves to assist others.

My inner hero constantly guides me on my path of self-discovery.

Take a moment to think about your favorite comic book heroes. What qualities did they have that made them so admired and respected? Beyond their superhuman capabilities, what *inner* characteristics made them so appealing? Perhaps they possessed an inner fire, a fierce determination to right wrongs, an endless willingness to sacrifice for their higher ideals and principles. Maybe it was their curiosity, their innate sense of finding a creative solution in the moment, a rare capacity to grasp both detail and the larger picture. Many embodied the best of the crusader spirit, a leadership talent for bringing together different voices to sing the same righteous song.

When we were at our most powerless, lost within the labyrinth of our addictive process, many of us sought such role models. We were often disappointed in the real-world versions, but something kept us hoping that a hero would appear in some form. A part of us kept faith and hope alive, until we realized *we* were the ones we were waiting for. We had to step into becoming the hero of our own journey. While we might leverage the support of others, *we* ultimately did the heavy lifting.

I can emulate daily the hero qualities that most inspire me.

Our inner hero knows the value of the Tenth Step: "Continued to take personal inventory and when we were wrong promptly admitted it." We cannot lead and be inspiring—to ourselves or to or others—without the ongoing assessment of our own strengths and weaknesses, arenas where we have honed our skills and those areas in which we still need to grow and improve.

The hero's story is always in flux. Sometimes he is riding high on victories—inner and outer—and other moments, he must grasp the lessons offered by any defeat. We know from our own recovery that progress often illustrates the clichéd two steps forward, one step back. We believe we have finally stabilized a positive behavior, only to find ourselves slipping into old, destructive habits. It takes time to unwind maladaptive and faulty connections, both in our brain and in our heart. But if we keep moving toward that which is good, beautiful, harmonious, and true in our lives, we will be rewarded with a measure of good fortune, as the universe occasionally winks and nods at us, in recognition that our journey is the perfect one for us—with all its imperfections.

I can rest in the reality that I am constantly evolving, and resolve to keep on keeping on.

The classic hero's journey always involves a number of stages in which he moves from ordinary reality to an elevated, special world, with the hopefully triumphant return as a transformed man, ready to live in the everyday.

This journey begins with a call to adventure, which he initially resists and refuses, until he receives the guidance of a mysterious force—a mentor, elder, or human or animal spirit. He then makes a wholehearted commitment and, in that very moment, crosses a threshold into new territory, where he undergoes tests, finds allies, and encounters enemies before approaching his most sacred inner cave to prepare him for his greatest ordeal.

He is rewarded, and then he begins the journey home. This is a *resurrection* of sorts—a rebirth, complete with the generative gifts and secret knowledge from his passage that are to be shared with his tribe for the benefit of all. Beyond the stuff of fairy tales, this overall framework often proves true in the gritty reality of our own lives. If we were to draw the course of the river of our own unfolding, marking it with critical events, we can see the parallels with our journeys more clearly.

I reflect upon my own hero's journey and what stage I may be in right now.

We will not be broken. We will find a way. Our inner hero will survive and thrive. Every cataclysmic event in our life temporarily destroys our security, but also plants the seeds of determination and hope. Faith, hope, love, and magic may be all that remain, but they are often strong enough to carry the day.

All our previous medals, awards, degrees, and diplomas will not serve us as well as the scars of experience we gain through the gradual conquest of our own inner demons. There can be no hero without adversity. While we may believe we have had enough challenges already, especially in terms of our addiction and its fallout, a part of us knows that more obstacles will eventually arrive at our door.

Hope implies expectation, desire, aspiration, and anticipation. *Faith* suggests complete trust and confidence in someone, or in a Higher Power. These twin energetic powers have their sublime purpose and can be most useful in times of duress. Their shadow side manifests when we do not get into action ourselves because we're waiting to be saved by forces other than our own initiative and right actions.

I honor the power of hope and faith, and I understand I must do my part as well.

When we leap, suspended in midair with no obvious place to land, the wings of faith and hope can begin to unfold and allow the winds to carry us. Even though we may be unsure of where we are going, we are buoyed by these twin forces that call us to a positive future. We may feel more often lost than found, yet the dance of exploring our edge continues, and that itself is a precious gift.

We have survived to this point—sometimes barely, depending on our particular addiction—and we are ready for the next steps, hurdles, or jumps. Faith and hope can help us rise above our own feelings of inadequacy and lift us to a more empowering perspective in dark times. We can become so fixated on our current problem that we fail to see the blessings still falling down upon us. While hope encourages us to stay the course, faith assures us that the light at the end of this particular tunnel is just that—and not another train speeding toward us. These inner resources remind us that all we can ever do is take the next obvious step and surrender to uncertainty.

Belief and optimism support my onward progress, especially in dark moments.

It is easy to lose faith in either humanity or in God—whatever we conceive God to be. Discouragement can be found in regular doses every time we tune into any source of news. Despair seems commonplace in the modern world. Part of the definition of faith is that it arises without any evidence. It is a strong belief in an internal force that is not necessarily supported by current facts.

Optimism is another word to describe the hero's confidence about a positive future and successful outcome. Depending on how much our own religious beliefs have supported us in our recovery and sobriety, we might be more comfortable with the idea of faith. Each of us has to determine how important religious doctrine and practices are to our recovery—and to who we are. We must make use of every support possible—our church or spiritual community, our tribe, our recovery group, our supportive family, and our healthy and supportive friends. When we utter, "Keep the faith," we must distinguish whether it is some form of prayer or a general call to hold a positive mind-set. The greatest benefit is attained when our intention is clear.

I honor God as I conceive God, and I surround myself with people who are positive and hopeful and who have faith in themselves and others.

Similar to love, forgiveness, and trust, respect is not something we can really engender from others until we have, ourselves, consumed from this special wellspring. What are the most important elements involved in respecting ourselves? We look up to, and think highly of, who we are inside and how our positive qualities manifest in the outer world. We honor our own esteem and treat with reverence our very existence. We admire our being, because of—and in spite of—our imperfections.

Respect permeates thoughts, feelings, and actions toward oneself or another. And most important, it is the foundation of us walking our talk. When we live a life that embraces respect, we keep our word to ourselves. In order for a hero to inspire the respect of others, he must be worthy, possess a certain dignity, and consistently act in ways that are in line with his values. Respect conjures images of politeness, civility, courtesy, being well mannered and friendly—all qualities worthy of cultivation. But this social veneer is less important than the more essential essence of being thoughtful, sensitive, and considerate. More than the demands of a polite society, respect speaks to a genuine, open-hearted caring for other humans.

I fill the well of self-respect when I do what I say I will do.

Assertiveness consists of effectively expressing one's own needs and feelings and defending one's own rights while respecting the rights and feelings of others. *Aggression* disregards the rights of others, while *submission* disregards one's own rights.

We may have lost some of our own self-respect by behaving aggressively or even violently while we were in our addictive haze. We can reclaim more positive feelings for ourselves with each act of sober centering—whenever we keep ourselves calm rather than reacting blindly with old habitual patterns of anger when triggered. We hold ourselves in high regard. Even when we make mistakes, we know we are worthy within.

Deep in the jungles of the Amazon, one uses the term *enlaki*—"I'm another you"—when another is heard nearby in the rainforest. The response offered to the unseen greeter is simply *"alakim,"* which translates roughly to "you're another me." There is such inherent respect and caring in this salutation because it is an acknowledgment of the universal lifeblood we all share. Beyond the practical aspect of not being mistaken for a form of edible game moving through the dense growth, this interaction offers the simple joy of recognizing the presence of another human being and seeing that person as a reflection of ourselves.

Respect helps me surrender to the mystery of our shared journey in this lifetime.

Respect for another does not necessarily mean we want to be like them. We may not agree with their choices or opinions, yet we honor the reality that they are a human being who deserves our kindness and caring. We may admire some of their qualities, abilities, or achievements but dislike other aspects of who they are in the world.

If all people inherently deserves our respect simply because they are sentient human beings, what do we do when we find ourselves full of negative judgments about them? We can begin by observing whenever we are engaging in good-bad or black-white assessments. We can, in such a moment, simply take a deep breath and say to ourselves, "That, too, is within me" or "Just like me, this person is trying to find happiness and avoid suffering."

Whenever we feel the pull of our judging mind that wants to put others down, we can remember this basic commonality that transcends all differences. This levels the playing field and sidesteps the dangerous precipice of feelings of superiority or inferiority. We acknowledge our common human bonds and our need to uplift each other, more than putting each other down.

Respect guides me to drop harsh judgments of others or myself.

Humans have what has been termed a *triune brain*. We have a midbrain that controls the most primitive survival functions; a limbic system that is the seat of our emotions; and—most recent in evolutionary terms—the cortex, which is connected with thinking. Thinking is the intellectual function of reasoning and forming logical conclusions, while feelings provide more personal valuation and determine what we do about what we know.

Brain development seeks to establish the greatest possible integration between thinking and feeling. The smooth, unified functioning of the three systems leads to harmony.

Our brain demonstrates enormous *neuroplasticity*, which allows its development to be responsive to the stimuli it is receiving. This means we can develop new brain connections. Just thinking about something differently, or rehearsing a series of body movements in our mind, actually creates and strengthens the relevant neural pathways. Counseling helps us develop new ways of perceiving our situation, and this, too, changes how our brain functions.

I can use the incredible power of my mind to change my brain.

Our brain is really the command center that ensures our survival. The mind is the part of the brain that generates thoughts and organizes information by integrating past memories and future possibilities into something that might be useful in the present. Our mind likes to recall, plan, and anticipate, and it very much enjoys wandering.

Terms like *monkey mind* or *wild horse of mind* are attempts to describe such meandering tendencies when our mind processes jump from one focus to another, or simply run away. While its data collection, rational ordering, and synthesizing qualities are admirable, our mind's greatest potential unfolds when it undergoes training. Because we are born knowing how to think, we assume it is a natural function that just happens, like walking or using our hands to manipulate things.

The process of recovery has asked us in different ways to learn new skills and abandon old, destructive mind habits. How we use our intelligence to create a good life for ourselves is part of this equation. We take to heart the bumper sticker wisdom "Don't believe everything you think." We appreciate more and more how our perceptions influence our reality.

It is never too late to develop my mind and improve how I think.

When certain muscle groups learn a specific skill through practice, they become more efficient. We can easily imagine this if we think of what it's like to play a favorite sport or learn a musical instrument. The same is true for our mind. If we consistently work on our ability to concentrate, visualize, imagine, or logically analyze, the functioning of these faculties will improve, which increases our sense of well-being and capability to live confidently in the world.

One of the most damaging aspects of addiction is that it often interferes with our normal development. We experience an enormous brain growth spurt between the ages of fourteen and eighteen, and if our substance use began in earnest at an early age, we suffered some setbacks in the normal progression of our brain's faculties. This is often especially true in terms of the frontal lobe, which is the center for planning and problem solving, judgment, and impulse control.

With time and attention, sobriety allows us to overcome these deficits. With practice, we can again become masters of our own thinking and processing. We can learn to observe the flow of our own thinking and to transform it with more empowering thoughts.

I honor the reparative functions of my brain and work diligently to improve my mind.

Most storybook heroes take a time-out from their battles at some point. They go off by themselves, not only to clarify what needs doing, but also to gather the energy required for the tasks and trials ahead. They calm their bodies and minds in order to receive intuitive guidance. They contemplate what effects their present actions may have on the future. They observe the flows of their own negative thinking in order to shift everything so that mind, body, heart, and spirit are aligned with their sacred purpose.

Our inner hero deeply understands that our mind functions best when it is calm and relaxed. In some ways, recovery offers us the chance to take a break from our routine ways of thinking and being. We can use counseling sessions to stimulate shifting old patterns, and we can give ourselves the gift of some quiet time every day to integrate the changes we are creating. We learn each day what practices are good and helpful for us. We take time to celebrate the progress we have made—and continue to reach for. We trust, more and more, that our innate intelligence is finally blossoming.

The disciplined practice of regular daily prayer, meditation, or contemplative quiet time in some form helps me stay centered and focused.

The hero knows that there can be no lasting peace without social justice. Many beloved historical figures fought for what they believed was correct and true in terms of the basic rights of human beings. From the end of slavery to the flowering of women's rights, the ongoing struggles for LGBTQIA rights, and emerging issues around the right to die with dignity, the quest for justice continues to bear fruit.

Once we free ourselves from our necessary but intense personal involvement with getting clean and sober, we see many injustices in the world that require our talents and committed action. We may begin to feel the pull of wanting to be part of a larger movement like #metoo or Black Lives Matter—of joining our unique voice and skills with others to make a positive difference.

Seeking fairness in the protection of basic rights and appropriate consequences for wrongdoing, we can carry some of the wisdom of the Twelve Steps into current social struggles for equality and ethical behavior. Because of our own suffering, we are more sensitive to the mistreatment others experience.

The wrongs I experienced when younger, and during my addictive times, help me see the larger injustices in the world that I can be part of changing.

It sometimes takes heroic efforts to right a wrong. There is an interesting distinction between the notion of *restorative* justice and the more prevalent idea of *retributive* justice. Unlike retributive justice—which focuses on punishment—restorative justice focuses on reconciliation.

In restorative justice, victims of crimes take an active role in the judicial process. Offenders attempt to take meaningful responsibility by righting their wrongs, which is based on the same principles as making amends. The offender has the chance to redeem himself and avoid future offenses, but the paramount focus of the interaction is on the needs of the victim. The goal is *healing* rather than *punishing*, though we know from our own experience that reaching out with the intent to make amends may sometimes result in rejection and disappointment.

Victim-offender mediation requires a hero's skill, determination, and willingness to be vulnerable. Both parties can talk about how the event affected their lives, victims get to ask questions about the incident, and offenders can tell their story of how they came to act in such a manner. Repairing broken relationships through active listening and mutual empathy is ongoing important work, and both our successes and failures serve to make us better human beings.

I make amends because doing so is right and just.

True humility is another essential character trait of the hero. It is really part of intelligent self-respect, in that it keeps us from thinking too highly of ourselves. As humble human beings, we are modestly reminded of how we can still fall short of our potential. It is not a subtle form of put-down, nor is it a belief that we are inadequate. Rather, humility is about a shift in perspective when we are becoming too enamored with our own talents and sense of being special. Like other humans, we have limitations—aspects of ourselves that are perfect just as they are in this moment—with lots of room for improvement.

Humility allows us to say "no" to ourselves, to honor restraint, and to see the value of acknowledging our shortcomings—the first step to transforming them, and the First Step in recovery. The powerlessness we experienced in trying to control our addiction made most of us eat a large dose of humble pie. The idea of humility as a desirable trait evolves slowly. We need not seek superiority over others, but rather only over our former self—our addictive self that was less aware, less conscious, less in touch with the deep flows of our precious existence.

Humility serves me because it helps me to be more aware.

Difficult people can be our greatest teachers. Certain individuals can be a seemingly endless black hole of need and negativity, stuck in criticizing, demanding, blaming, labeling, and pronouncing judgments, rather than being in touch with what they are needing and feeling. They are often trapped in defending, attacking, or withdrawing, constantly determining levels of wrongness with others or the world, rather than focusing on what they'd like that they are not getting.

During our most destructive addictive times, others may have viewed us as difficult, full of arrogance and self-centeredness. Remembering how we used to be and employing a few other basic principles can make it easier to interact with difficult individuals. We can connect first, then redirect their focus. This helps soften our judgments of them. Offering empathy before trying to educate or change them gets better results. They usually listen to us because we listen to them. They are more apt to let us in because we let them in. Instead of asking them how they feel, we concentrate on what we might do for them to make their situation better. This encourages them to focus on needs rather than perpetuating the victim role.

I honor difficult people as teachers and can learn to assist them, while keeping healthy boundaries.

Our inner hero reminds us to be humble—not haughty. Arrogance generally pushes others away rather than inviting them into our world. The know-it-all, always-needing-to-be-right, my-way-or-the-highway attitude can quickly undermine the collaborative nature of any interaction. When combined with a big-headed sense of superiority, it can be a deathblow to building meaningful partnerships, not to mention friendships.

Our external bravado is often an ineffective cover for our deep insecurities. Others usually see right through our pushy disguise, quickly bursting our balloon of overinflated greatness. During recovery, we no doubt encountered many such people in group counseling sessions—they were often the ones with their arms protectively folded in front of them, the ones with a condescending sneer on their faces.

As we progress in recovery, we discover we can rest in the center point of quiet competence on the humility-arrogance continuum. We know our capabilities, and we need not constantly seek external approval for doing what we know to be right and true. We do the best job we can under the circumstances, and we are open to feedback and learning. We are not so proud as to reject a good idea just because someone else thought of it or to admit when we screwed up despite our best intentions.

I am always learning from others how, and how not, to behave skillfully in the world.

Mindfulness is an essential component of the hero's journey *and* our journey in recovery. The essence of mindfulness is letting our experience be what it is and simply observing it from moment to moment. We might experiment by placing our hands in prayer position on our chest and then noting what happens to our thoughts, feelings, and bodily sensations.

To be mindful, we trust what is and accept what is happening, as we simultaneously let go of striving for things to be different or judging how they are somehow wrong. Just as a slowed-down TV sports replay allows us to see more clearly what was happening, so mindfulness creates spaciousness by combining awareness with acceptance. It is thus an enhancement of sensory experience, giving attention to life processes we normally take for granted—like breathing, walking, eating, or bathing—and attending to each experience as it arises, giving it its due, rather than clinging to it or pushing it away.

Such body-based attention is different from thinking, where we easily get caught in our nonstop flow of changing thoughts. Hands on our chest, we sense everything there is to experience with our different senses, both external and internal, but without falling into just thinking about it.

Mindfulness supports my recovery because it allows me to experience all sensations without pushing any away.

Mindfulness is helpful because it reminds us how often we are *not* present and that a larger field of awareness beyond the small self exists. It also teaches us to skillfully be with that which is unpleasant, to experience these things without feeling the need to construct a story around the pain to justify, explain, or deny it.

As with many other important life skills, *practice* is the breakfast of champions. Small moments of such awareness gradually stitch themselves together so we begin to experience a seamless state of actively participating in the *now*—without getting lost in the jungle of just thinking about life rather than living it. When we are eating mindfully, we are fully doing just that, reveling in all the sensory and pleasurable aspects of that everyday activity. When we are feeling sadness deeply and mindfully, we become capable of also being fully present to that, even when the sensations that are arising are not so pleasant.

Planning, intending, and using our brain to imagine and make useful distinctions and decisions are all important survival functions. Mindfulness brings us back into our bodies right here and now, avoiding the seductive, often addictive pull to "future tripping." It grounds us, over and over, to the power to change lives—a power that exists in the present.

Being mindful opens up new levels of awareness around habitual activities.

Daily meditation helps build our "mindfulness muscles." Meditation can be instinctive and spontaneous, but can also be enhanced through training. Breath provides an always available and easy point of focus. Slow, deep breaths let our brain know we are in a safe place, far away from predators. We simply allow our attention to gravitate toward the sensory experience of breathing, the texture of air, the ongoing wonder of breath.

What is most interesting about the process of breathing right now? As we explore the in breath and out breath, what is pleasurable, terrifying, restful, ecstatic, providing relief? We can just savor the breath as we might good food, since it is the primary nourishment for the body. And as the natural tendency of our mind to wander takes over again and again, we simply return to the breath. With time and repetition and a few calming breaths, we can enter a peaceful inner courtyard where we can quickly and easily find deep relaxation and renewal, no matter the external circumstances.

Without drugs, we can reduce anxiety and maintain sobriety. Breathing in, we feel calm and centered. Breathing out, we let go of any impulses to relapse into old destructive habits.

I am willing to harvest the many benefits of regular meditation.

With practice, as we regularly become more mindful of our thoughts, feelings, and bodily sensations, we start to view the world differently. However, there is a strength in always staying a beginner. With a beginner's mind, we grasp the extraordinariness of the ordinary.

Zen master Shunryu Suzuki insightfully said, "In the beginner's mind there are many possibilities; in the expert's mind there are few." Beyond brainstorming and out-of-the-box or sideways thinking, this quality of perception enlarges our view and reveals to us what is often hidden by habit. The freshness and eagerness implied in being a beginner serves the hero well as he confronts new dilemmas, even as he must continually reinvent meaning in the old.

With open beginner minds, we become willing to examine previously held beliefs, drop preconceptions, honor our intuition, and expand what we consider possible. In the depths of our addictive process, the world seemed very limited—to the point where we could not even imagine a better way. Instead of potential and possibility, escape and denial were our companions. Mired in our own prison, we had to start somewhere, and from that place of beginning, we created a larger field of being, one step at a time.

I embrace the openness of being a heroic beginner, over and over.

Beginner's mind is that quality of attention that allows us to walk around our old neighborhood and notice many new things. We appreciate the novelty in the commonplace. We examine an old familiar object and discover new details previously unnoticed. We can do the same with someone's face when we really look, as if it were the first time we were seeing them.

There is an inner spaciousness that gets created whenever we put on these "fresh mind" spectacles, observing everything about us. It deepens our gratitude as we perceive in new ways the beauty that has always been there. Beginner's mind supports our inherent curiosity and sense of wonder, beyond the mystical and into the ordinary, practical fabric of daily life.

The entire process of our ongoing recovery is a miracle of beginnings, wherein we see people and circumstances in the new light of transformed awareness. Even our own shortcomings are perceived differently, as stepping-stones to a new reality. We realize that "I don't know" can be a very empowering summons and that the questions of beginner's mind may be more important than the first obvious answers.

In the midst of confusion and despair, I can be curious about what might be next.

We all treasure our brilliant opinions and cherished beliefs. Beginner's mind recognizes that our thinking mind comes with its own preconceptions and distortions. Whenever we temporarily set aside our notions of *how it is*, we open to the large possibility of what we don't even know we don't know. We enter a dimension that can renew our sense of miraculous unfolding, our commitment to evolving in spite of ourselves. We get out of our own way to sample a separate reality—one in which the very surrender of admitting to not knowing all the answers is highly empowering. Expectations, judgments, and prejudices all go on vacation.

Childlike fascination with a simple spoon is a fine example of the newness that comes with looking through the eyes of a beginner. The young one may use the spoon as a noisemaker, a catapult, or a shiny mirror that catches and plays with light—all beyond the limited view of an implement used to put soup in one's mouth.

As we enter the expansive space of our own recovery, beginner's mind is an ally in our quest to redefine ourselves. It is a mind free to just be awake, to experience the present without grasping or fleeing what is with us in the here and now.

Just now, just this, I embrace the vast boundless gift of the present moment.

The inner hero embodies many positive qualities. His double-edged sword of conscious awareness comprises *right action* and *right speech*, tools he uses in every endeavor.

In his quest for justice, the hero is mindful of his positive actions as well as what he refrains from doing. He does whatever he can to avoid injury to living things, since all life is sacred. This starts with himself, by avoiding lying, stealing, killing, or abusing himself—or others—sexually or through drugs. He fosters and inspires connectedness through thoughts, words, and deeds. His inner moral compass is grounded in the hardships of his own transformative journey.

Comfortable with uncertainty, the hero knows when to wait, and when to act. He fully expects that he will lose his way, make mistakes, and grapple with his own insecurities. Few in the world take the time to really clarify and write down their own personal code of conduct. But this can be an incredibly useful exercise that merits re-examining as we continue to evolve. Asking ourselves often if we are engaging in positive actions, true to self and our code, keeps us firmly on our path of self-discovery.

In my everyday interactions, I am learning to marry positive intent with skillful action.

The hero is skillful in terms of using *right speech*. He does not engage in lies, gossip, harsh or malicious words, or idle demeaning chatter. He understands the enormous power of words to inspire and to cut through the deceitfulness of others.

A hero utilizes the **THINK** grid—especially with important communications, asking himself, "Is what I am about to say **t**rue, **h**elpful, **i**nsightful, **n**ecessary, and **k**ind?"

The "right" part of right speech is *not* about good/bad, moralistic judgments, but about the skillful use of words to enhance the well-being of oneself and others. Right speech ultimately gives rise to happiness and peace in ourselves and others. This does not mean we avoid speaking hard truths that may cause temporary feelings of sadness, turmoil, or disappointment, or that we sugarcoat our perceptions. Rather, right speech is when we speak mindfully with purpose, with a kind and gentle tone of voice.

We each benefited from such skillful use of language during our own recovery. Right speech requires great self-awareness as well as sensitivity to the other. The challenge is often how to frame things in a way that the other person can "get."

I can choose to use right speech in all my daily interactions—especially in moments of anger, confusion, or hostility.

We see evidence every day of how different actions and forms of speech create different results. Certain behaviors and forms of communicating invariably create more suffering, which we can observe within ourselves as tension in the body, remorse in the heart, and turbulence in the mind.

In recovery, we realize how right actions and speech create less turmoil, and instead foster a greater sense of peace and well-being within us. Whenever we lie, steal, speak, or act aggressively, we push ourselves further away from what we most seek: acceptance, love, and happiness. The times during our addiction when all we knew was how to lash out and blame others for our predicament are long gone. We now understand—more deeply than ever—that our words and deeds have direct consequences.

Do we prefer to foster respect, mutuality, and patience with others in our communications, or do we increase the possibility of mistrust and defensiveness? Sometimes simply sharing with another *what* we want to discuss— especially when discussing a difficult topic—and inquiring *when* would be a good time for them to talk with us, go a long way to setting the stage for meaningful communication and its counterpart of generously listening from the heart.

I am willing to constantly improve the skillfulness of my speech and actions.

The shadow side of our inner hero often manifests in two different forms. One embodies the big-screen tough guy who consistently chooses violence and aggression over inner development. In this world, everything is painted in black-and-white, right and wrong, no shades of gray to confuse the righteous application of power. This type of hero is more about trying to be a rugged individual rather than learning to stand shoulder to shoulder with others in pursuit of the same goal. This shadow energy does not permit us to make mistakes, to acknowledge our own blind spots.

The other common distorted image of the hero is that of the savior, always trying to take charge of everything and save every person in distress. Whenever shit happens, this "hero" blames others and immediately believes he has to compulsively fix it or save others from stepping in it.

Either path—big-screen tough guy or savior—does not lead us to our authentic hero and actually prevents us from accessing all his positive qualities. Part of our hero journey is to confront and make peace with our shadow aspects, which if ignored or denied will only contribute to our downfall.

I am aware of the shadow sides of my hero energies.

Just as the magnificence of an oak tree's leaves and branches lie hidden in the acorn, so the source of many different possibilities rests within us. What seeds of greatness are still within us, untouched by the world, dormant, unattended, never surfacing? Do we still believe in ourselves enough to reach for our dreams and offer our unique contributions to the world?

It is never too late to honor our own sacred path, to love ourselves more freely and openly, to risk all we are capable of being, by walking the hero's path of transformation. As we relax into recovery, we can awaken the treasury of seeds within us—all those potentials that have only been waiting for the right time and conditions to emerge. The full-time school of life continues to offer lessons, and we are finally in a position to receive new teachings. Some of us will feel cumbersome and burdened, but we can experience the vitality of our new life wherever we are, under any circumstances. Our sobriety will continue to open up new realms of self-discovery, and our commitment to the wholeness and wellness that recovery can bring will see us through the challenges that still lie ahead.

I embrace all my inner hero still has to teach me.

Becoming the hero of our own life is our birthright. It has taken us a long time to be ready for this immensely satisfying journey, but here we are. We have survived the trials of our addictive fire, and now we are freer than ever before to pursue the quest for a good life.

Every hardship up to this point has prepared us for what is next. We have found guides and teachers and support along the way, and we know we can call on them again when necessary. Our inner senses of faith, hope, respect, intelligence, and mindfulness continue to grow and create an increasingly positive spiral of competent, skillful actions and speech.

Heroism is ordinary people empowering themselves. Suspended between the great deeds we yearn to perform and the small tasks we dislike doing lies the realization that we can be heroic in the ordinary, commonplace situations of our daily lives. At its core, being a hero is not about passing tests or successfully completing quests. It is less about external rewards for achievement or performance than it is about the beauty of the transformative journey we are on, the preciousness of every moment of our own evolution.

I embrace the hero within, with all his teachings.

SEPTEMBER

The Artist

The inner Artist invites you to free your creative imagination, to discover your unique, inspired, authentic, artful mode of expression. The magic of mentors and the mystery of mastery await you, beckoning you to embrace this timeless, energetic part of you.

The archetype of the artist calls to every one of us. From the depths of our being, the universal urge to create may sing softly at first, but ultimately will fill our hearts with the sweet music of artistic expression. From the earliest humans, who scratched stick figure symbols on cave walls to share their experiences, artists have always embodied the struggle to express externally in some form the impressions and feelings from their inner world.

This is the crux of the artistic process, this translation from the inside depths of our being to an outer manifestation that then touches others, evoking feelings and memories from their own journeys. We simply must embrace these longings. At times, we may resist as life's demands pull us in different directions, yet the fountain of our imagination, our traditions, and our authentic self will eventually summon expression—even if only in the form of doodling on a scrap of paper or humming a tune in the shower.

Recovery offers us a palette of possibilities to bring forth and transform some of our deepest yearnings and most painful episodes into artistic symbolism. It's part of our healing journey to wholeness.

I honor the artist within as a guide to finding my deepest self.

Our inner artist reminds us of the Seventh Step: "Humbly asked [God] to remove our shortcomings." For most of us, the whole process of artistic expression brings up all the conversations about what we are *not*. Art can magnify our defects by placing them front and center into clear focus, whether they be lack of discipline, fear of risking, or somehow negating or not developing our specific talents.

There is always a huge serving of humble pie whenever we begin any artistic endeavor, so much so that many of us suppress our creative impulses in order to avoid looking bad or risking failure. Fearing rejection, we might not follow through with what we start—if we start at all.

But recovery has taught us that we must face head-on whatever we perceive as shortcomings and ask for assistance from others as well as from our Higher Power to strengthen what is already good. Just as our capacity to express ourselves artistically develops over time, so does our ability to move through and improve upon our more challenging characteristics. We're learning that this is a lifelong process. Facing our inner demons often provides some of the passionate juice that stimulates and informs our creative expressions.

My life as an artist—however undeveloped at this moment—is full of potential to help me grow.

We are all artists in the sense that we are crafting our individual life. We use our creativity, imagination, time, energy, and rich cultural and ethnic traditions to find our authentic voice and offer our unique gifts to the world.

In response to the query, "Can you sing, dance, draw, and write?" almost every child will enthusiastically respond "yes," while only a small percentage of young adults will answer affirmatively. Somewhere between the vast playground of childhood's creative innocence and the adult strictness of classroom rules, we stop believing in our own magic. Having our sensitivities, feelings, and initial artistry crushed or ridiculed rather than affirmed by the adults in our world may have contributed to our descent into substance use. This is not about blaming others for our choices, but about understanding that their blindness to our goodness created a void we thought we could fill with our addiction.

We are now in a very different place where we can rediscover some of what we buried in order to survive. The treasures of our own inner creative storehouse are more available than ever, just waiting for our curiosity and attention.

Once I feel safe, my inner artist allows all my sensibilities and imagination to blossom.

A great lie we have been fed is that if we don't immediately show a knack or inherent talent for something, we should just give up. When this happens, the extravagant, playful creativity of childhood is soon crushed by demands of parents, education, and society. Most people then become only consumers of art rather than actually crafting something themselves that can be appreciated by others or taking the risk to explore creation as a vehicle for awakening the beauty and mystery of life.

However, artistic talent is not a finite substance doled out to just a few. The craftsmanship of long ago can still reveal its secrets to those who invest the energy to explore its intricacies. From making baskets and pottery to creating exquisite jewelry or handmade clothing, crafting fine furniture with noble tools of the trade, or making beautiful musical instruments and *objets d'art*, humans in every culture have married beauty to functionality to enrich the human spirit.

For the creative artist, life is abundant and nothing is insignificant or unimportant. When we open ourselves to the artist within, we can break the spell of "I can't!" and discover our unique brilliance in an arena where we experience deep creative fulfillment and satisfaction.

I can use the energy freed through my recovery to find my creative voice.

Creativity is a natural human phenomenon, an expansive state, a flowering of our basic needs to imagine, express, and manifest. Highly creative people possess certain characteristics that we can cultivate within ourselves. Inventive individuals trust their intuition and are comfortable with uncertainty and doubt. They are willing to take risks and make mistakes, and they actually enjoy pushing the boundaries of their abilities. They find pleasure in the problem itself and in playfully experimenting with new connections that go beyond traditional assumptions and solutions. They tend to have a great ability to fully engage their concentration. They are open to new and different creative approaches and have a significant capacity for visual imagery and imaginative leaps.

Any artistic medium or scientific inquiry can open the doors to exploring these qualities. The ability to see the big picture while meticulously attending to numerous specific details is itself highly creative. Some of these characteristics have been stimulated through our process of recovery where we've found a new willingness to risk, to trust our inner voice, and to expand our own levels of competency. We are finally emerging, like butterflies, after a long period of inner development.

I can spend time with creative people who inspire me.

Any creative process unfolds through a number of phases, whether the endpoint is a new mousetrap, a painting, a sculpture, a choreographed piece, or a song. It begins with some insight into formulating and defining the project, followed by an information-gathering time in which we might review techniques or assemble needed supplies.

Next comes the incubation stage, the realm of big ideas where imagination is given free rein. Illumination provides a bit of the *aha* experience as different puzzle pieces come together, followed by implementation where we begin to see what works and what does not. Next comes a frustrating period where we may have to change course and open ourselves to new possibilities. Finally, we release our creation to the world, which can inspire others to do the same.

Knowing where we are in the process helps us understand what we need to do in that particular phase, which reminds us that the whole enterprise has its own rhythm of unfolding. We might even play with the notion of our recovery as a creative process. What phase are we currently exploring?

Understanding the creative process fosters patience and persistence, two valuable qualities needed in my ongoing recovery.

If necessity is the mother of invention, then imagination is the father of creative endeavor. It is critically important not to let our inner editor get ahead of our inner artist. So many of us have developed patterns of self-criticism and judgment that can quash our creative imagination before it even begins to find its flow. We know how destructive such tendencies can be and how they have sometimes thwarted our attempts at sobriety.

Imagination exercises our intelligence. It is a vast playground that is the foundation of all innovation and invention. It is where additional possibilities are allowed to incubate, to marinate in our mind, to arise from subterranean and unconscious outposts we don't normally visit.

What can we imagine for ourselves now that we are in recovery? What lives might we live that are now just flights of fancy, preludes to what might be created? Think about what singing or poetry does to words. We can do that to our own destiny—we just have to start by conceiving it. Those who most inspire us to imagine ourselves at our best are often those who have been through the fire and survived bleak circumstances. We can call upon them to help our inner artist emerge.

I use my imagination to envision a spectacular future for myself.

There are many different ways to cultivate a rich imagination. We are familiar with the notion of brainstorming, wherein the goal is not to worry about quality but to initially generate as many ideas as possible. Brainstorming frees our mind to explore new and unfamiliar areas. Then we play with combining ideas and novel notions, gradually sifting through the pile of possibilities to find what might be workable and useful.

We might take a few moments each day to astonish ourselves. We can let ourselves be filled with whatever artistic quality we most need as we go about our daily routines. We can imagine the secret messages offered to us by animals and plants. As we develop this oft-neglected capacity, we may find ourselves living the reality that more gets done when we are having fun. As we let our artist within come forth, we form images, ideas, and sensations within our mind without the direct input of our senses. This "stirs the creative pot" within us, expanding our resourcefulness. Imagination carries us to worlds that may never be, but also to ones that are just forming.

My creative imagination is a magical muscle I can strengthen over time.

Our inner artist is one of the inspirational muses of Greek and Roman mythology. This creative force reminds us that daydreaming is an important part of the artistic process. The multitude of rich and pleasurable thoughts, images, and sensations that come to us when we daydream can be a rejuvenating relief from the frequent boredom of everyday life. Such short-term detachment can be a wellspring for creative imagination.

Drifting off into la-la land creates a dialogue that occurs when our daydreaming mind communicates with different parts of our brain as it accesses information that was previously out of reach. In this way, daydreaming can be a fount of insights, solutions, and wisdom otherwise hidden from our awareness. Allowing ourselves to be idle once in a while can generate novel, "sideways" perspectives.

How often in the midst of our addictive hell did we fantasize about a heavenly life free from our most destructive compulsions? Rather than labeling daydreaming as being lazy or inattentive, zoning out into a "mind wander" may actually plant the seeds for positive future actions. It is perhaps no accident that the frontal lobes of our brain—the seat of planning, logical thinking, and impulse control—are where the mind-wandering action is!

I tune into what insights my daydreaming might offer.

One of the beautiful aspects of surrendering to the artist within is the gift of timelessness that often comes along for the ride. The artist's sensibilities remind us that we can shift to a greater sense of spaciousness at will. We can—in any given moment—go off "clock time" and practice pausing, taking even a dawdling, purposefully strategic break, where mind wandering or stepping outside helps build a more relaxed time sense into our nervous system.

The Indonesians have a term, *jam karet*, which roughly translates as "rubber time." Rubber time acknowledges and allows flexibility in how we interpret a meeting time or how long a ceremony might take. Our inner artist invites us to practice "power lounging" and creative idleness when we aren't engaged in what the Taoists call the "ten thousand things."

When we give off nothing but busy signals, the deep inner knowing can't get through to us. Normally there are no hallelujahs for idleness because it doesn't sync with our society's misplaced value of workaholism. But the pressure to always have nose to the grindstone and do nothing but work for long periods of time doesn't seem like the healthiest way to live our lives.

I can find a good balance each day between being and doing, all in service to my continued recovery.

Time can shift according to how we choose to experience it. Do we sense time differently when we are waiting for someone who is late than when *we* are the one who is late? Time also often seems to slow down when things are harder in winter or with the experience of pain.

Time has very little to do with clocks and everything to do with thought and perception. Yet most people are in a 24/7 competition against the timepiece, obeying the orders of their calendars, their completely charted days, or their clock-crazy, appointment-driven, dizzying time-table of overscheduled duties. The weight of overwhelming demands, commitments, and options and the endless list of responsibilities can easily pull us off balance.

Our collective obsession with clock time creates a magnetic pull toward overcommitment and speed. In our mad dash to get things done, we often bow down to the tyranny of the urgent, forgetting that multitasking is *not* a normal human state, even if our idea of it is holding a remote control and eating chips simultaneously.

Our inner artist allows us to break out of this hour-glass prison and enter a world where each moment is unfolding just so—no matter whether the vehicle for such unfolding is song, dance, painting, sculpting, or writing.

With recovery, I need not be afraid that boredom will lead me to destructive choices. I enjoy the timelessness found in practicing my art form.

Organic *timeflow* is the opposite of *hurrying*, which can cause damage because we burden ourselves with expectations and try to compress one or more actions into too small an increment of time. The desire to just get something done, to get it over with, tosses away the gifts of the present for some illusory better future. And it tends to trample anyone standing in our way, whether that translates into road rage or just plain rudeness. Rushing can violate our innate desire to connect by arrogantly declaring that whatever *we* are about is more important than everyone else's agenda.

When faced with those trapped moments of "time compression," we can choose to sing, hum, or whistle more, sauntering rather than careening through the tasks in front of us. We can turn obstacles into ornaments by slowing down and tuning into the natural world and summoning its gifts of the moment.

Look at the big sky, which does not hinder white clouds coming and going. Tune into the soft, flexible strength of the trees swaying in the wind. Rest in the peacefulness of sun on faces.

I enjoy catching myself rushing and then shifting in that moment to slowing down the speed of life.

Every artist must become aware of their optimal rhythms for creative flow. Beyond the basics of whether we are a morning lark or a night owl, our circadian rhythm is an internal biological clock that sets itself to daylight conditions and gives us many physical signals that tell us when it is time to be active and when it is time for sleep.

There are also certain periods throughout the day and night when we experience temporary peaks and valleys of energy, and these are very helpful for us to identify. For instance, the middle-of-the-night call to create is not an uncommon phenomenon.

How we start and end our day significantly affects our well-being as well as our creative impulses. We can play with our threshold consciousness, that non-dreaming drowsy interval between waking and sleeping that is often filled with sensory images, unusual thought processes, and word messages. We can learn to take advantage of those moments when our peak performance is more likely, and we can respect the times when frustration and low energy are likely to hinder our progress.

When we were caught in the web of our addictive process, many of our natural rhythms were significantly disrupted. Recovery and our inner artist offer us the opportunity to discover our most creative periods of the day.

I commit to discovering my own best rhythms.

Learning to take our "energy pulse" can be a very useful skill. Right now, in this moment, how might we describe our energy flow? One way is to check in physically, mentally, emotionally, and spiritually. Anything seem "off" in our body? Are we feeling good, anxious, sad, or irritated? Are our minds turbulent, confused, or mostly calm? Are we sensing a connection to self and the wonder of the world, or walking the edge of being isolated and lonely?

When we regularly ask ourselves, "How am I?" we open the door to understanding our own unique energy flows. Then we can make adjustments, depending on what needs to be optimized. Sometimes this is just a matter of altered physiology—asking ourselves if we are hot, cold, hungry, or tired. Attending to those physical needs can improve our general sense of well-being.

Our overall energy state is affected by all of these physical factors, and most are possible to quickly satisfy once we develop the tools to do so. We all have periods when we can be more productive and creative. Honoring those times is important to our artistic growth, our well-being, and our recovery.

Checking in with the state of my being by regularly taking my "energy pulse" is helpful on many levels.

Most of us fall far short of the sage and ancient imperative to "know thyself." We don't even understand the basics of how things work in our body. Here are some key concepts to consider:

Change our posture and breathing, and our physiology changes. Change physiology, and our thought patterns change. Change thoughts, and our emotional state shifts. Change emotions, and our communication and actions change. Change behaviors, and our overall energy state changes.

We have all had the experience of feeling bored or restless and then starting to do something interesting—changing the "boredom channel" in some way by going outside, starting to draw, dancing, or playing music. When we change channels by getting in touch with our inner artist and letting our creativity flow, we set up a cascade of different possibilities.

So, too, with our basic energy flow. We can alter what is happening at any given moment and shift our energy to a more empowering state. This is discovery work that most of us neglected when we were too busy trying to satisfy our addictive cravings. Each day we have the opportunity to better understand ourselves at the most basic levels of how our thoughts, emotions, and bodies interact to produce high, calm, positive energy—or the opposite.

I am learning how to quickly get myself into an optimal state of well-being.

One of the most challenging energy states is being "wired and tired." This is when our energy is apparently high, but so is our anxiety level. We may actually need sleep, but we can't stop our mind from churning. This is one of the worst states in which to try to accomplish anything—especially creative artistic expression.

Many of us spent a lot of time feeling wired and tired during some of the most arduous moments of our addictions, when nothing was working to reduce our anxiety or restlessness. The truth is that there's no way out but through.

So how do we shift out of this state? A simple check-in will tell us if our energy is high or low, and whether our tension is high or low. We always need to downgrade our tension before we try to change the energy part of the equation. We can do this by exploring tried-and-tested techniques: taking centering breaths, slowing down our thought stream, and visualizing ourselves taking in calm with each in breath and releasing tension with every out breath.

I will add a few simple techniques to my toolbox for shifting anxiety and restless energy, both of which can threaten my sobriety.

To find our authentic voice is one of the most satisfying moments on our journey, an essential milestone for the artist's way. The triad that supports authenticity is honesty, integrity, and transparency. In order to be authentic—real and genuine, without falsehood or misrepresentation—we must be self-reflective, delving into our innermost chambers, willing to take a fearless and honest inventory of who we really are at the core.

We also need good ego boundaries, the willingness to be open and consistent, and the desire to let go of needing others' approval to feel good about ourselves. When we are authentic, we can choose to be a team player, but not blindly follow the crowd and get lost in it.

Anytime we tap into our artistry, we affirm and state out loud, "*This* is who I really am!" The vulnerability that arises when we courageously share our talents and let our light shine enhances our sense of freedom and honors the journey that has brought us to this point. Our addiction is *not* who we *are*, but it has been a part of our authentic experience.

My quest for authentic artistic expression is a marvelous undertaking that enriches me on many levels.

What does "radical honesty" really mean, and what does it have to teach us? As we know all too well from our using days, the web of lies that seems so easy to spin often hijacks us into impulsive, reactive, avoidant, or otherwise unsound behaviors.

Trust develops over time when we are open, vulnerable, and honest—with ourselves and with others. We observe carefully what feelings and information we tend to withhold, and we find the healthy boundary balance between what we conceal and what we reveal. We don't withhold just to avoid conflict.

For many of us, our childhood wounds made us especially sensitive to lying, and we are aware how our lack of healthy boundaries brought us into turbulent waters in the past. Recovery finally allows us to have faith in ourselves—to stop lying to ourselves. Our thoughts, words, and body language are all on the same page because we are able to be real, to genuinely express what we have kept hidden.

Art is a great vehicle for practicing radical honesty on a regular basis. More than words, dance, music, visual, and sculptural forms speak a universal language of understanding, of *radical truth telling*.

I continue to tell the truth, one day at a time, through my art and in my life as a recovering person.

Our artist within calls upon us to live in integrity. When we live in integrity, our word is golden, and we do what we say, which is what we actually want. *We walk our talk.* The coherence and solidarity of living in integrity translates into doing the right thing and adhering to our cherished values, even though this may not be convenient or approved by others.

Trustworthy, reliable, and consistent, we experience the harmony that comes when our inner and outer lives are in balance. These different spheres are integrated, and profoundly connected. Whatever our artistic medium, this sense of wholeness influences and infuses what we create.

Experience tells us that when we access and bring forth whatever is challenging, we grow. Not all art arises in suffering, but there is no doubt that expressing what is difficult on the inside can create stupendous beauty on the outside. Integrity is a *choice*, and it eventually becomes a habit. We recognize it in others, and we understand its value, especially in supporting our continued sobriety. Technically and conceptually, our art can remain aligned with its deepest purpose, and we can remain at peace.

Today, I walk in beauty and live my life with integrity.

Yaaaass! So what if someone else thinks your style is useless and is intent on putting you down? If your artistic expression comes from a place of authenticity, then you have found the groove in the daily grind of artistic struggle. Your mindless risk-taking days of YOLO—you only live once—have matured into constructive activities that you love. Language evolves and morphs over time as we do, and every generation has its own versions of both doublespeak and *truespeak*.

Only the artist, the genuine voice of a generation, can determine which is which. In recovery, we have the chance to connect to our inner artist and to discover that each of us can have moments serving as a poet-at-large. Excited to be alive, we are blessed to craft messages capturing the gratitude we feel for our sober lives.

Creating poetry is profoundly possible for everyone. We need only suspend our warped perspective that ours is not good enough. The form—rap, sonnet, haiku, or poetry slam material—is less important than pouring forth a genuine utterance of what we feel inside. Say it out loud! With our words, we become purveyors of sound and light, tone and vision, creating sparkling life rafts for the ocean of our daily experiences.

Recovery affirms my commitment to the art of truespeak, *finding a way to create empowering lingo.*

Throughout history, no problem has ever been resolved by keeping silent about it. Using art for social change is a time-honored tradition, with many diverse dimensions that have contributed to positive shifts, both large and small. While many videos that have gone viral are silly, some have had a significant impact in altering our perceptions. Song lyrics have spawned entire movements, and documentary films have broadened the base of those concerned about an issue.

Poets and artists have used their art to expose adverse conditions and address needed change. Art can be a formidable mirror held up to societal norms and injustices, and it can also be a sledgehammer that helps reshape those problems into more humane forms.

We might reflect on how various forms of art—films, songs, images, or words—influenced our own recovery. Perhaps we were inspired by a simple truth clearly set forth in a piece of art, or we were driven to change by exorcising some of our own demons through the practice of a medium with which we resonated: recovery deepens through finding a medium to express what cannot be brought forth with only words. Maybe there was a particular line or poem in our recovery literature that struck a chord. Art has within it the power to change, to become a force for good and beauty in the world. Art transforms.

I honor the part that art, in all its forms, has contributed to my recovery.

To keep our creative edge, we need a regular and diverse flow of ideas, materials, and inspiration. Some of these can unexpectedly arise from our own roots. Our ethnic origin, our extended family history, and the novel perspectives and influences of our ancestors can be a source of inspiration for our creative selves. Communing with other artists, or visiting museums, performances, and exhibits can also serve to stimulate our own artistic explorations.

Experimenting with different materials and artistic approaches can bring refreshing insights. We might explore different tunings and amp effects for guitar. We might try our hand at line drawings, charcoal, watercolors, and collages or playing with rap, sonnets, limericks, or haiku. We might take up photography.

Although such shifts have their own learning curve, the richness of switching gears can break us out of same old, same old ruts. We can try a hundred-day project—doing one thing every day for one hundred days straight—related to our art. Some people record their hundred-day journey in a blog or on a social networking site like Instagram as a way to ensure that they are actually following through. Even with our sobriety, we can improvise with new and different ways to stay on the path, calling forth new forms of support.

My creative edge is always worth exploring.

Throughout history, people have gathered in *salons* for conversation, inspiration, expansion, and deepening of knowledge. Establishing such a creative get-together that meets regularly can stimulate and nurture our own creative explorations.

Salons are places where people can find their voices and become familiar with different aspects of art and creativity. The evening can be focused on a single discipline such as writing or drama, performance art, poetry, music, or dance or on arts that use a physical medium like film or photography. Or a salon might center on a combination of diverse art forms, evolving as the time together unfolds, which opens the door to a number of communal artistic possibilities. The only ground rule is that there is no criticism or complimenting, a stipulation that fosters an atmosphere of free expression, where the high comes from sharing our inventiveness with others. The process is often chaotic, but can also be playful, pulling us out of the solitary cocoon of artistic exploration we usually inhabit and into a communal, joyful collaboration with other artistic beings.

Creating or finding a salon-like atmosphere can stretch me in delightful ways and remind me how good it feels to enjoy life while remaining sober.

In an age of effortless access to videos, images, and material of every imaginable type, it seems possible to learn anything faster than ever. The idea of doing a real apprenticeship or finding a mentor may seem like an old-fashioned concept lost in the dust of newfangled technological progress.

Although many good books can be found on any subject that can help us learn the basics, there is no substitute for the ongoing presence of another human being who wants us to succeed. What are some qualities of a good teacher? The best mentor is someone who provides positive reinforcement in at least equal measure to critical corrections, who pays attention to even the slowest learners while encouraging maximum performance from all, and who has a commitment to actively engage students in their own learning process.

The "sage on the stage," know-it-all teacher who preaches about a given subject certainly does not embody these essential qualities. Learning is best achieved through personal connection and active engagement, where feedback is freely given and richly appreciated. Like the best sponsors in recovery, artistic mentors bring with them a specific expertise as well as the ability to communicate and interact with their mentee in intense, productive ways.

Finding good teachers can help me progress along my artistic path, no matter what subject I am attempting to master.

The mentor-mentee relationship is a much more intense student-teacher interaction than working with a coach or instructor. Mentors are individuals who actively push us to enhance our capabilities and are willing to share their skills, knowledge, or expertise and enthusiastically value our ongoing growth and learning. They may use their influence to further our advancement or offer counsel in discouraging times.

Mentors inspire our inner dream by modeling who they are, how they live, or what they have accomplished. Most elders are honored to have a chance to pass on their wisdom, to share their expertise, and to contribute to the unfolding of a younger man's potential. We lose nothing by sincerely asking someone to be our mentor, and have much to gain when the response is a resounding "yes." Maybe we have to knock on a dozen different doors, starting with connections we already have, in order to find that one person who opens it and begins to illuminate and expand our view of the universe. Tapping into successful people's ideas and connections is just being smart, and doing so can dramatically accelerate our own progress as well as contribute to theirs.

I honor those who have mentored me in the past, even if we never officially declared that relationship.

When it comes down to it, there are no experts, only learners sharing the lifelong path of mastery. Many cultures value the concept of oral tradition, where those mysterious teachings that are never written down are passed from person to person through private conversations, whispered transmissions, and the modeling of revered elders. These teachings are gifts from a master who guides us, provides counsel in discouraging times, and offers new learning opportunities.

As much as we appreciate these kernels of wisdom—known and revered in Japan as *kuden*—that encourage us to consciously explore just beyond our limits, there comes a time when conflict with our mentor or guide is inevitable. Indeed, mentor-mentee relationships often go through many stormy periods. We may have experienced similar discord during our recovery when our ideas of the best next steps clashed with those who were trying to assist us.

And there comes a surprising moment when we know it is time to set out on our own, to leave the protection of our mentor and go forward to teach others.

We are charged with the joys and responsibilities of teaching those who walk behind us, just as we learned from those whose steps have already passed our way.

The curve of mastery always involves brief spurts of progress—often not regular—followed by plateaus in which forward motion seems elusive. Just as with learning sports, any new artistic "muscle memory" takes time and attention to stabilize. The reality is that most of the time we inhabit a long, uninspiring plateau rather than an exciting upward trend. We must somehow learn to love the practice itself, find satisfaction in making baby steps, and rest in appreciation that we are still on the path.

In such times, we can call upon our inner artist to help us surrender to the demands of daily discipline and to the requests of those who are teaching or supporting us. We can look within for the strength to find the balance between reinforcement of what is going well and correction of what needs improving. In doing so, we find the energy to keep on keeping on, honoring our prioritized commitments during both low moments and high ones.

The parallels with recovery from our addiction are obvious. Courage, persistence, mediocrity, resistance, edge, intentionality—pick any single word related to the idea of mastery and live it fully for that day. Our brain can organize around the concept, and interesting insights will emerge.

Betwixt and between, wherever I am on the path is a good day.

Rather than immediate gratification, quick rewards, and instant success, the path of mastery involves a willingness to repeatedly go where edges meet and inventive impulses flourish—the frontier of possibility worth celebrating, which always involves the unknown and risk. We don't need to be super-talented or fortunate enough to have gotten an early start at whatever ingenious endeavor we are attempting. As is true with our recovery, we just need to persevere, to muster patience, to love the eternal *now* of consistent, persistent practice.

We learn to embrace the inevitable plateaus and continue to play at the edge of our own incompetence. We try not to get stuck in the small stuff.

Progress on the path—in life *and* in our artistic expression—always involves acceptance of our apparent limits, and then moving beyond them. We move forward by surrendering to the unique demands of our chosen artistic path—and to our teacher if we have chosen one. We resolve to always be a beginner, even as we embrace mastery.

There are no quick fixes or shortcuts on the road to recovery or the journey to mastery.

Our inner artist reminds us that we are each unique, different from any other being on the planet. We are indeed special, and our potential and actual gifts to the world are also one of a kind. Yet the chorus of the "not good enough" voices within our head can still be overwhelming at times.

The long stretches on the creative plateau where little progress is evident, despite our diligent practice and efforts, can be particularly frustrating. Inevitably, doubts about our sobriety or our artistry creep in and establish a foothold. The slump in energy and focus, driven by the sense that we are getting nowhere, can lead us to believe that our innovative initiative has run dry and our inner artist has abandoned us.

But amazingly, this movement is actually helpful. It pushes us to reaffirm our commitment, to seek out teachers and guides who can assist us, and to dig even deeper into the amazing wellspring of creative impulses that lie within us. It is always difficult to feel that we have to begin anew. But we can choose to hold the larger perspective that previous efforts have not been wasted but are part of creating a more solid foundation for further progress.

Every setback is a setup for a comeback.

At some point, we realize that even if we have never declared ourselves to be an artist, our life is infused with creativity and imagination. We know that our time and energy are limited, and we want to make the most of these gifts. Our authentic self longs to be expressed, and various mentors may have reinforced that we *do* have something to contribute to making the world a better place.

Grounded in our recovery and sobriety, we may finally take the leap to pursue a path of mastery in a given artistic field. But even if that is not our goal, we still express our artistic sensibilities in how we dress, fashion meals, create a home living environment, and engage in pleasurable activities and interests. When we get stuck in our problems rather than in manifesting solutions, we tend to focus on what we don't have, what we still need, and what isn't working. Art pulls us out of such conundrums, beckons us to come out and play and to experience the joys of creative flow. It summons us to satisfy our deep hunger to discover who we really are.

Through my inner artist, I learn more about myself, which in turn deepens my ability to create and live fully.

OCTOBER

The Trickster

Waking you up—not always enjoyably but often with illuminating accuracy—the inner Trickster laughs at your mistakes and invites you to do the same. He beckons you to play, to trust everything is okay, to not take yourself—or your endless dilemmas—too seriously.

The trickster is also known as the fool, joker, or comic. Often taking an animal form—such as Anansi the spider in Africa; the coyote, hare, or raven in Native American lore; or the fox in many parts of the world—the trickster holds a place in the community of revered spirit guides that is legendary. This rascal, this mischief-maker and lovable creature who frequently triumphs in spite of his antics, often brings profound gifts. Wittingly or not, these anthropomorphic beings bring with them stories full of wisdom and usually offer knowledge, food, clothing, medicines, or specific customs.

The trickster reminds us, often in humorous ways, that the key to surviving—and thriving—is to just keep trying. A trickster's zaniness inspires us to examine the beauty of our own faults, even as he lifts our spirits.

When we reflect on our younger years, how many stories were shared with us to help us along with our growth or to demonstrate right and wrong? How many such stories do we know and can retell? The world of the trickster overflows with tales that both instruct and entertain, an essential evolutionary aspect that contributes to the ongoing lifting of humankind's conscious awareness. We see how the trickster's humor, playfulness, well-being, simplicity, and sense of trust in life itself can teach us lessons in the face of adversity.

I welcome the wisdom of the trickster's stories into my life.

Trickster energy reminds us not to take ourselves too seriously. It is like a carwash for our ego, cleansing away the accumulated dirt of thinking we are so special and the illusive dust of our believing that *we* are actually in control.

We often receive a wake-up call from our inner trickster that puts us back on track. Sometimes this is a gentle tap on our shoulder, but more often it's a rude "You've got to be kidding" shove that reminds us we are fallible, vulnerable, and just as imperfect as everyone else.

Sometimes our trickster's job is to keep us on guard. If we're getting overconfident about our good fortune or our sobriety, for example, our trickster reminds us that situations we may *not* enjoy are usually just around the corner. This is not some subtle form of sabotage or self-destruction. We might lock the keys in the car, leave important papers at home when going for a job interview, or watch the toilet flood in dismay as we are rushing to get somewhere. *S**t happens,* and whenever it does, our trickster is often lurking in the shadows having a good laugh at our irritation and annoyance.

These minor calamities keep us just a little off balance and cause us to reframe things in a more positive light, right in that moment when things are not going our way. This is excellent practice for dealing with the inevitable ups and downs of our daily life as recovering human beings doing the best we can on this planet!

I honor my inner trickster for lessons in flexibility.

Trickster reminds us of the Sixth Step: we're "entirely ready to have God remove all these defects of character." When we work this Step, we get to eat some humble pie and realize that—despite excellent progress on our path to awakening in recovery—we still have a long way to go in terms of self-acceptance and love. We might be clean and sober, but we still have cravings. We may have escaped the horrors of bottoming out, but not the daily grind of fashioning a meaningful life.

We have learned some things about surrendering to a Higher Power, and we understand more clearly how the choices we make each day contribute to creating our own reality. Whenever we think we know all there is to know about life and recovery, trickster invites us to go spend time with our family, so we can realize how easily the progress we think we have made can dissolve and how quickly we can again turn into a struggling child when triggered by our old, as-yet-unhealed wounds.

Often the mirror that trickster holds up to us does not have a happy face staring back. We are reminded of our still oh-so-present limitations. But when we begin to laugh at and accept them rather than retreating to a place of shame or anger, we are making some progress in *really* accepting ourselves.

Trickster encourages me to smile at my own imperfections.

Trickster often operates at the margins of social morality and "normal" behavior. He may exhibit strong appetites for food or sex, may seem footloose and spurn traditional responsibility, and sometimes may even seem a little mean-spirited. The good news is that we are on the cusp of realizing that this "cosmic flyswatter" is there not to cause more suffering, but to invite us to lighten up, even when the darkness seems so deep.

When we do lighten up, we often begin to see that we will never achieve a life free of obstacles—existence is just brimming with unexpected twists and turns. The situations we desperately want to avoid are simply part of the fabric of being alive. What we seek to "get through"— all those unpleasant moments, large and small—are necessary and normal aspects of life's vicissitudes, not to be taken personally! This is an incredibly important insight in terms of maintaining our sobriety.

Sympathetic, lovable, and irrepressibly curious, while also being confused and befuddled, tricksters speak to this daily reality of light and shadow. As both a player of tricks and a victim of tricks, we can see our own tendencies as being sometimes foolish, sometimes a little stupid, often laughable, but *always* human. In recognizing the trickster, we learn to transcend the roadblocks and restrictions we encounter.

Trickster energy informs me that my life always holds both obstacles and the overcoming of them.

Ridiculous, extreme behaviors, ludicrous situations, and silly actions often bring a smile to our face, or even an outright belly laugh. Part of the draw of substance use was that it took us out of ourselves, lightened our load, and helped us feel good—at least initially.

Sobriety teaches us that we can laugh and have fun *without* the crutch of using a substance, with all of its downsides and dangers. The trickster teaches us that we can change the channel of our reality in other ways—without substances—and laughter is one of the most pleasurable. Laughing at our own troubles and foolishness is especially liberating.

More than the mere recitation of entertaining jokes, having a sense of humor—a key part of social skills that reflects high emotional intelligence and cheerfulness—is also highly connected with resiliency. A sense of humor involves the capacity to step out of our current dilemma to embrace a larger, more empowering perspective. Forms of laughter that cause tears to stream down our face may not appear all that often. But our ability to laugh at ourselves with others can be uplifting and ease the tension of even the most challenging of situations.

Developing a sense of humor is possible, desirable, and fun.

Humor can also have a dark side and may be used as a weapon in social situations. Making fun of another's physical traits or personality characteristics is often a part of a bully's armor.

Our "shadow trickster" has an antagonistic, aggressive humor style that can inflict serious wounds, especially on the most vulnerable and troubled. Publicly making fun of someone in a mean way is really not humor at all—even though it may provoke some bystander laughter. It is *cruelty*, plain and simple, and is often used as an expression of power over others in order to feel better about ourselves.

We each need to distinguish between being funny and being mean. How would we feel if we were the butt of a sexist, racial, or ethnic joke? How would we feel if we had a handicap that others made fun of? By putting ourselves in another person's place, we can begin to sort out what is humor from what is just nasty trash—and choose not to participate in making mean "fun" of others.

I will root out any remnants within me of meanness disguised as humor.

Human feelings are an interconnected, complex, emotional ecosystem. Many people are confused when they try to sort out the basics of intense emotions such as mad, sad, glad, and afraid. Sometimes there is no dominant emotional chord, just a free-floating "symphony" of emotional sensations. People may cry when they are happy, because the predominant sentiment is one of release, like the relief they feel when a loved one has come through a difficult time or arrived safely after a dangerous journey.

At the opposite end of the spectrum, life's difficulties may seem so overwhelming that we realize how absurd it is to even try to maintain control. In the midst of sinking deeper into despair, this awareness allows us to see the humor in the situation and appreciate any small impulse that briefly lightens the load. Someone makes a joke or a lighthearted statement about what will go wrong next, and suddenly we all erupt in laughter.

Current hardships remind us of the great resiliency that resides in the human spirit. We recall our own experiences in treatment and might remember the welcome gift of a sudden chuckle. We remember the temporary lifting of all the dark drama, an invitation to share our common humanity. This is our inner trickster at his best.

Humor can be a healing balm, available anytime, anywhere.

Studies show how the great emotional release of laughter can actually reduce stress hormones and boost our immune system. Pain reduction, lowered blood pressure, reduced risk of heart attack, and faster recovery from medical procedures are additional benefits of humor. Laughing, being silly, jesting, participating in slapstick antics, and telling jokes are all part of the comic's repertoire. We can call upon our inner trickster to help us cultivate more of this in our own daily life.

The commonplace wisdom of "more gets done when we're having fun" applies to many situations. Bathed in natural endorphins—chemicals that reduce pain—our body and brain relax, and creative solutions flow more easily. When we make a humorous approach to life our default habit, we strengthen our inherent resiliency. We step into a rarified realm where life's little annoyances and frustrations dissolve in a lightness of being, the sweet nectar of appreciating what is easy in a hard moment.

Laughing at our missteps is *not* a form of denial or minimizing, but an empowering shift. We are reminded that our quest for perfection is absurd! As we wind our way through the ongoing trials and demands of remaining clean and sober, our sense of humor can function as a little booster rocket, instantly propelling us into a lighter and larger perspective.

I enjoy immediate and longer-term benefits of laughter.

Our natural capacity for curiosity, imagination, and creative engagement has helped us survive. As we watch a father play with his child, we see evolution in action. The physical flexibility, endurance, and strength being developed occur in parallel with building the muscle of imagination in the "let's pretend" world. Social communication, rules, roles, and teamwork are also explored in games.

Civilization did not arise only out of work; it also grew out of free time and play. We shortchange ourselves by thinking of human beings only within the context of the species *Homo sapiens;* theorists suggest that while we've evolved to be wise beings (*sapiens*), our playful nature is a crucial part of our sense of self and what defines us as *Homo ludens.* By nature, we are playful beings and must embrace both of these aspects of ourselves.

When we engage in play, we foster friendships while we fulfill our needs for novelty and pleasure. Play is like oxygen—it is found everywhere. Now on the positive path of sobriety rather than continuing the descent into our own personal hell of addiction, we can embrace play as an essential component of the good and full life. We have many chances each day to rediscover the simple joys of wonder and curiosity, focusing on the actual experience rather than on a goal.

Play may boost my productivity, health, and happiness, but I do it for its own sake—not because I'm high on substances.

Whenever we engage in playful activities, our body is active and energized, and our mind is alert. Our emotions tend to be spacious and elevated, our spirit open and accepting. This is a prime example of the flow state, in which we get lost in an eternal present where heart, mind, and body are aligned with action and intent.

Free from the suffering and drama of our addictions, we can now embrace the best of trickster's playfulness without concern about how others might judge us. We can take time to walk in the rain, jump in mud puddles, collect images of rainbows, smell wild flowers, blow bubbles, build sandcastles, watch the moon and stars come out, read children's books, act silly, take a bubble bath, fly kites, say the magic words, talk with animals, climb trees, have pillow fights, tell stories, and do anything else that brings more happiness, celebration, and a sense of freedom to our life.

While we honor the ongoing work necessary to heal old wounds and develop positive habits, our guiding mantra for today is to just have fun. We embody the primal and youthful purity of the free, rambunctious, joyful play energy.

I enjoy finding different ways of being outrageously playful.

The mysterious paradox of play is that it can be done for no reason at all, and yet it is vital to our continuance as a species. The inner trickster hereby gives us permission to frequent amusement parks, beaches, meadows, mountaintops, oceans, forests, playgrounds, picnic areas, birthday parties, festivals, toy stores, and anywhere children of *all* ages come to play. We are on an official mission to rediscover the joy, freedom, and abandon of childhood innocence.

Some of us had few times of bliss during our childhood because we were too busy surviving the violence, substance use, and mental illness present in our households. But there were also those precious moments—if only a few—in which we tasted freedom and happiness through the divine chariot of creative play. Now that we are sober, we can grant ourselves full permission to wonder and wander, to pass idle moments in creative fantasy, to fulfill our healthy desires for playful exploration. From video games to paintball adventures, from sports we could never engage in as a child, to card and board games we missed, our inner trickster hereby empowers us to just enjoy merrymaking for its own sake.

I welcome the joys of free-flowing play into my life again.

Some observers see human beings as grounded in our love of play, and view all of the natural world as the creative activity of the divine—a Higher Power who is sportive, frolicsome, and joyful.

It is part of our higher nature to marry raw, uninhibited energy with emerging skills, to bring forward a spark of our unique creative passion. Playful artistry dances between the conscious and unconscious, calling forth deep memories within us. When we cook a good meal, dance spontaneously around the living room, make love under the stars, or allow music to bring us to tears, we are immersed in the language of sacred play—the parlance of *lila,* which is a Sanskrit word that depicts cosmic vitality and the free play of the gods in creative expression.

The business of recovery is serious business, and there are so many goals to move toward as we make up for years lost in addictive haze. Our innate craving to reach beyond ourselves and playfully explore, even as we work hard in recovery, is often obscured by the demands of our new "adult" life as recovering individuals. Yet we must remember how exquisite it is to be swept away by creative amusement and passionate living.

I welcome the magnificent sense of play that still flows within me as I do the serious work of recovery.

The trickster characters found in different world cultures are most often loved and seen as attractive, despite their comical flaws. Trickster energy, so often engaged in stepping beyond social norms, asks us to examine the question of what being attractive *really* means. At the same time, much of the trickster's power is rooted in an ever-changing *image*.

Internet stories abound of people putting up one face on social media or dating websites while their "in-person" reality looks quite different. Why is there this need to pretend to be someone other than who we are? Usually it is based on some aspect of ourselves that we deem unacceptable, whether this is physical appearance or a specific character quality that does not quite measure up to some mysterious standard.

Much of the language of the Twelve Steps is about defects of character, and even though we stand firm in recovery, we may still view ourselves as somehow broken and unworthy. The first step in generating the energy of being attractive to others is *to accept ourselves as we are*, right now, this moment. Not some new and improved version we think we need to be, but the authentic being we see staring back at us in the mirror. We are all works in progress, learning to love who we are each step of our recovery journey.

I am whole right now, and ever changing, evolving into my amazing greatness!

Attractiveness is more than a state of mind. It is also about projecting certain qualities—an image—into the world. We can play with picking seven features that we find appealing in others, one to live out each day of this week. What could they be? What possibly attracts others? Perhaps we might choose confidence, a sense of humor, courage, kindness, gentleness, curiosity, and strength.

For an entire day, we can examine what it really means to live through the lens that focuses on the quality of the day, to center ourselves in its essence, to keep coming back to it, to guide us, as we would seek a lighthouse in a storm. We can even write the particular attribute on the fridge each morning to remind us of the quality we are striving for on that day. Part of the scheme is to also observe when others we encounter during the day exhibit our chosen characteristic.

What form did it take? How did we feel when we experienced it emanating from another? This is very much *not* about being competitive, but just remaining neutral as we notice when someone is demonstrating what we are striving to embody. It can be an amusing experiment in "attractive consciousness."

Recovery offers me the opportunity to expand who I am in the world in terms of attractiveness to both myself and others.

How do we show ourselves to the outside world? Some of the most basic ways might include grooming, clothes, temporary adornments such as jewelry, or the more permanent ones of piercings or tats. Each of these elements contributes to the energy we project into our daily life.

As men, we are often conditioned not to pay much attention to these personal aspects, and we certainly get less destructive programming about their importance than women do. But we *do* receive other messages about how our bodies are *supposed* to be. We think we need to be tough, for the athletic field *or* the battlefield.

Since we now have some energy and intent to put into something other than satisfying our addiction, we can experiment with look we want to project as a healthy and confident recovering person. Thrift stores are great places to begin trying on a different look, buying something to wear that is a stretch for us—whether this means ripped-up jeans, a business suit, or brightly colored clothing. Part of determining what makes us feel attractive is to experiment with the "art of costume." We might feel comfortable growing a handlebar moustache and wearing a cowboy hat—even if we live in a city, or sporting a long beard, or shaving our head, with personal poetry at the ready.

Clothes do not make the man, but they do influence how others perceive me, an avenue for playing with who I am.

What do we look for when seeking a mate? Is it just "chemistry" that makes someone sexually attractive? The path to love varies so much from one person to the next that the answer seems more mystery than science.

For generations, our culture has held on to the old-fashioned notion that a man seeks a "sex object," while a woman desires a "success object." Many more factors and lifestyles quickly enter into play in these social and economic times. What we do know is that attractiveness is *not* about haircuts, cologne, muscles, cars, money, or penis size. It's more about confidence and how one thinks, behaves, and acts. How we truly carry ourselves—not just the image of ourselves we project—reflects the mind-set of how we feel about ourselves, and our body.

During our dark addictive days, we may have neglected many aspects of self-care. We can now learn to relish caring for our exterior with the same authentic, loving attention we are giving to our inner development; this can be done without feeling we have to hide behind our exteriors.

I am more sexually attractive when I am kind, confident, and authentic.

Our trickster heroes seem to have an abundance of *poise*. Even when things are falling apart all around them, many can still come across as dignified and self-confident.

Poise might seem like an old-fashioned concept that summons images of waistcoats and top hats, but it still has relevance in current times. A person with poise usually receives the respect of others. Beyond his good grooming, dress, and manners, he conducts himself with an open, willing attitude to be of service. No matter how difficult the circumstances, he maintains an aura of reliability, a sense of calm reassurance that, in the end, things will turn out okay.

A person with poise doesn't come across as arrogant or superior—he is genuinely friendly, with a "we are all in this together" attitude. We may have witnessed such admirable qualities in a favorite counselor during our addiction treatment.

Because a person with poise is so comfortable in his own skin, he models that capability for others. People feel relaxed and at ease around him. Such individuals seem to have found a place in the world. This gentle power of social intelligence is worth cultivating.

Poise takes away the noise and reveals a solid human being.

Poise is built upon these five characteristics: projected confidence, a positive perspective, patience, presentation, and presence.

The *confidence* of poise is one of self-assurance, built upon life experience rather than on "book knowledge"— something we can relate to from our addiction challenges. Having a *positive perspective* enables us to develop a calm composure, because no matter what is coming down, we have probably encountered worse. *Patience* is often difficult to get our heads around, but kindness and compassion often travel with it by way of support. Poise implies that we offer all three of these characteristics to those we encounter, no matter their status or need.

Presentation calls on us to pay attention to details of our appearance, which shows that we respect others as well as ourselves. When we strive to embrace these qualities, we become fully *present* and available so we can respond to whatever arises. We have no agenda, just a desire to live passionately in the now.

I will pay attention to practicing the art of poise.

With the help of our inner trickster, smiles and laughter can flow freely. People seem open, receptive, and friendly. This can create an "intentional" community for enjoying the company of friends and acquaintances.

Creating community in this way is a training ground for the practice of *craic,* an Irish form of communication that has universal appeal. While often associated with bars and sports, the *craic* arena extends beyond these realms. It is a slow, gentle, social exchange that is evident in the verbal play and good-spirited teasing between close friends or between parents and their children.

Depending on our addictive and family history, we may have trouble with this concept and might suspect there is malicious intent in such teasing. But the craic/trickster energy here is light and lovely. The reciprocal joking generates an energy that is sweet and endearing for all who are present.

I will cultivate the art of easygoing and lighthearted conversation.

Tricksters "keep their cool." Coolness reflects our personal taste in style, appearance, attitude, behaviors, and how we generally conduct ourselves in the world. Our conception of cool also reflects what we value.

When we "keep our cool," we maintain a peaceful calm. When we "are cool with that," we show respect and acceptance. When we say "that's cool" about an object or activity, we taste a bit of wonder and amazement. By further example, winning is cool, but doing anything to win is not.

The stuff of *cool* is always something positive, desirable, and acceptable—even as its form shifts. Because it is always evolving, it is often an elusive quality to cultivate. *Cool* is an elevated, inspirational state that most of us inhabit intermittently. Yet it can also point us to those values we most cherish, reminding us to find a way to embody them as we "walk our talk" each day.

Being *cool* is really being true to the highest and deepest version of ourselves that we can imagine at any moment. Beyond rules and standards imposed by others, we honor our inner guidance, creating positive change from the inside out.

I embrace the cool aesthetic of my inner trickster when I honor my own commitment to sobriety.

When we were younger, we might have admired a set of "cool kids" who were the risk takers. At times, they came across as a little crazy or different because they were consistently thumbing their noses at society in unique and authentic ways. However, what we admire, or even covet to a degree, follows an interesting developmental curve.

As we got older, we may have begun to admire those who exhibited outrageous behavior with a clear sense of purpose: people who were willing to stand by their ideals and get out on the streets to protest. Perhaps our admiration further morphed to include those who were always exploring interesting things, willing to test the edge of their own creative engagement with the world.

People who are centered and grounded in their own being epitomize the energy of the trickster, because their sense of self radiates what it means to be cool. We admire someone who does not give into peer pressure nor puts pressure on others. We cannot claim our *own* cool—it is just recognized by others. We don't have to ooze mystery and intrigue or become trendsetters. But it is important to be an integrated and kind human being.

We now have a chance to embody our own sense of *cool* by remaining sober and holding to the lifeline we have been granted. We are growing and evolving. What took us off balance in the past no longer has a hold on us.

I embrace my current path of increasing awareness and understanding my sense of self.

Often, the people we admire—who seem intrinsically *cool*—have an abundance of will. That's what catches our attention. Will is like a muscle that is strengthened with every use, not depleted the way sand runs through an hourglass. When a person's worldview is not just blind optimism that denies reality, nor a false, sunny, "everything is okay" attitude, we wonder what propels them forward. We are learning that their motivation stems from an embrace of the unknown, a call to meaningful action. This view is *beyond* optimism or pessimism—it is a belief that what we do has meaning and impact.

When we adopt this perspective ourselves, we have no need to misdirect and manipulate, lie, or withhold. We may have used those survival techniques in our darkest days of addiction, but we no longer need them in recovery.

Coyote, raven, fox, and other trickster figures possess an element of being cool: they do not confuse right and wrong with being smart or stupid. And their persistence in the face of things falling apart is always inspiring. They are aligned with the highest good for the community, even if that means they take a winding path to that truth. The quality of *cool* is a subtle display of maturity. Our actions are not dependent on approval from others, and we have the will to live with integrity.

I can impress others without trying to be impressive, simply by inhabiting my best self.

Almost every religion has three or four virtues that are central to bringing about both inner and outer peace. Equanimity is considered one of the four virtues in Buddhist thought, along with lovingkindness, compassion, and joy.

Equanimity is freedom from the cravings of self-serving desire, as well as freedom from hostility and hatred. It opens our heart, dissolving prejudice, anger, and indifference, especially as we extend it beyond our immediate circle, in order to embrace strangers and enemies alike. Equanimity teaches us the importance of staying at the center of the wheel. If we are only concerned about the worldly pursuits that make up the rim, we will sometimes be at the top of our game, but other times we'll be in the bottom mud in terms of health, wealth, and well-being. The center is the realm of our most cherished values, where we can always rest in living our life with purpose and meaning.

We know all too well the dangers of the deep valleys in our life, when things go awry and fall apart, and the pull to escape via old, familiar yet destructive coping strategies is strong. Equanimity reminds us there is another strategy available.

Equanimity keeps me on the path of sobriety.

Is inner peace a goal worthy of pursuit? Can we actually attain it directly, or does it only arise when we somehow trick it into appearing? If we close our eyes and go inside, is it clear, or is it lost in the currents of anxiety, anger, and sadness?

We can visualize inner peace as an inner well we can always drink from, realizing that it needs regular replenishing in order to continue to offer us its goodness when needed. Trickster has figured out that the peace that arises from practicing equanimity is both wide and deep, nourishing us through difficult moments, quenching our thirst to understand why these challenging circumstances are happening to us.

In recovery, we are comforted by the realization that pain—emotional and physical—just *is*. It is an unavoidable part of being alive. Rather than feeling victimized by this stark reality, we can choose, in this very moment, to surrender to what is actually happening, to shift our awareness to gratitude for what life is offering—even though it may be quite different from our expectations.

Equanimity means I temporarily give up my personal agenda to find peace in what is, which leads to greater equanimity, creating a very positive, uplifting spiral.

We have all encountered individuals who seem to radiate a sense of serenity, a welcoming abundance of calm and equanimity. We feel good in their presence because we intuitively sense the absence of a war within them. Like our inner trickster, they have come to terms with who they are and entered into the deep silence of accepting themselves—warts and all.

Serene individuals are not without trials and tribulations, but they find freedom in how they react to them. Perhaps our recovery has allowed us to taste some moments of this deep tranquility, and we know more is available, if we are willing to consistently strengthen this muscle in the gym of self-awareness.

How easy it is to close our hearts—as we may have often done in the past—with finger pointing and blaming and putting down another person. Why can't *they* be different, see the light, change their harmful behaviors?

From wish, to aspiration, to resolve, we can continue to deepen *our* intent to embody equanimity—even under the most difficult of circumstances and in our most challenging relationship moments. The mental and emotional stability involved in this endeavor eventually becomes habitual, and more and more unshakable.

I replenish my well of inner peace every time I am aware of, accept, and take full responsibility for my experiences.

Life provides, but for it to do so, we must actively and wholeheartedly participate. The old joke about a man trapped on the roof of his house during a flood is instructive. A neighbor offers him a ride as the floodwaters are beginning to rise. He refuses, stating that God will save him. After some time, a boat comes along, and again he states the same as he climbs a bit higher on the house. Finally, a helicopter arrives, lowering a rope ladder, which he again declines, placing his trust in God, until he finally drowns and dies. At the pearly gates, he asks why God abandoned him. God's response is, "Who abandoned you? I sent a car, a boat, and a helicopter!"

Other stories from diverse cultures offer the same message: trust in our version of a Higher Power, but pay attention to the details. They are the lifelines that are being tossed to us. We are never in this alone, though it may certainly appear that way at times. Like faith and hope, trust is not blind waiting, but a call to action, a belief that what we do and what we choose matters, and can positively influence the outcome.

I trust, and I also act.

The trickster mirrors the wisdom of the Twelve Steps to constantly remind us that life is not under our control. We learn to accept that when we are present, open, and trusting, a way through—rather than out—always appears. With time and experience, we also begin to trust the wisdom that when we carry burdens heavier than we think we can bear, we become stronger.

The essence of this kind of trust is acknowledging that we are vulnerable. Although we naturally seek predictability in others and in life itself, we can't control the outcome. So we risk. We trust, and we work together, because we deeply understand that more can be accomplished—socially, physically, and financially—when we join forces with others.

We also learn to trust ourselves. As with other important qualities, such as self-respect, self-discipline, and self-forgiveness, self-trust is an inside job. We appreciate over time the progress we have made to deal with our addiction and to become more aware of the consequences of our actions. We settle down into taking care of our needs and our safety day by day, creating a firm foundation for future growth and development. We practice kindness—not perfection—with ourselves and with others, and we refuse to give up on our own evolution.

I trust myself, more and more, to make skillful, positive choices.

The voices of consumerism whisper from the airwaves and cyberspace, constantly urging us, "Trust me, I have what you need." Their seductive pleas try to convince us to purchase the newest, latest, and greatest product of the moment to cure all our ills and ailments.

Why do we believe certain people to be trustworthy in their pitch, and others not? Chat rooms, social networking sites, and texting can also create a false sense of intimacy, even though we really know very little about the persons involved. Apparently trustworthy people can lie and manipulate more easily in cyberspace.

Issues of trust flood our days, not just at the big moments when we're signing contracts, making a big purchase, or acting on a big decision. Sometimes we might feel "double-crossed" in the process, which can make it difficult for us to trust again. As a result, our deep desire to connect with others and create close-knit bonds can be destroyed by betrayal.

Early family childhood experiences helped set our "trust barometer" at a basic level, which gradually extended to others. Along the way we learned that *genuine* trust always has to be earned.

My recovery process informs me that trust develops over time, through honest, open, and vulnerable communication.

In the early 1900s, Rudolf Steiner founded the first Waldorf school, which taught that we have twelve senses—not just the five that most of us are familiar with. Steiner maintained that the *sensation* senses, which support a consciousness of our body, include touch, movement, balance, and a sense of life—how we experience our own sense of well-being. He said the *perception* senses include sight, smell, taste, and warm/cold. The *cognitive* senses comprise hearing, speech, thought, and ego (the ability to be sensitive to one's individuality).

On a scale of one to ten, where are we in terms of our own well-being today? In the physical, mental, emotional, and spiritual realms, where are we most feeling off and in need of improvement? Trickster invites us to regularly ask the simple question "How am I?" which begins to hone our sensitivity to our own being. We check in and quickly scan to see where we might want to make adjustments, so we can function in the world with minimum energy output, yet maximum positive effect. This core query actually enhances all of our other senses, as we learn to keep them tuned up to serve us in the best ways possible.

I am in frequent touch with my own sense of well-being—an important habit that helps me move forward on my path.

As we work toward enhancing our well-being, we learn not to fight the old, but rather to create new habits that make the old dissolve from disuse. We place our focus, energy, and intention on moving forward instead of looking back. We view the past as instructive for the lessons it has offered us, which is very different from staying stuck in the same old disempowering stories.

Recovery begins to show us that we are worthy and lovable enough to be taken care of at the highest levels. Who can we really rely, depend, and count on in this life? It is up to *us* to make choices every day that enhance our well-being, rather than accepting the self-destructive options that always seem to be readily available.

Of course, we won't always make the right choices—hence the importance of having ready doses of self-forgiveness in our wellness toolbox. More than just the absence of disease or infirmity, well-being embraces a new and engaged vitality; a connectedness to self, others, and the planet; an excitement and sense of gratitude about the gift of another day. It is a conscious, self-directed, affirming process of achieving our full potential.

My well-being permeates everything—all the being and doing I will experience today.

Trickster energy admonishes us to bless everything that is, just for being. It is generous and expansive, forgiving of faults and shortcomings, and endlessly entertaining, especially on All Hallows' Eve, or Samhain. This energy invites us to be an audience to our own theater, to marvel at our own crazy antics in pursuit of happiness. It is the wind, rustling all around us, encouraging us to not take ourselves too seriously. It is the rain, gently falling down, surrounding us with blessings, if we only pause to see them. It is the shining moon, its image reflected on water.

The moon never says, "If you are open to me, I will do you a favor and shine on you." We need not prove anything or get something from someone—trick or treat—in order to feel connected as human beings. So many others have walked a path similar to ours. They have struggled with addiction, hit bottom in some fashion, and begun to pull themselves—with love and support from others—up and out of that deep hole of suffering. Like us, they have, and are, finding their way to becoming healthy, happy, and contributing members of their world. Celebrate! We are growing, loving, and evolving.

Today, with the help of my inner trickster, I will smile, laugh, and live life to its fullest.

NOVEMBER

The Wildman

The Wildman dances his way into your consciousness, sparkling with wonder and curiosity. His vitality takes you by surprise, and his silence stuns you, while his freedom and connection point you to what might still be possible in your healing and recovery.

The wildman knows. He is raw energy in motion, risk, spontaneity, and unfettered gusto. He lives deep within the wilderness of our passions and desires, the untamed parts of who we really are. Even though we may prefer to keep him chained, buried, or simply unacknowledged, his persuasive, persistent call will eventually overcome our resistance. He will scare us for sure, but only to the extent that we need to be shaken out of our self-satisfaction, woken up from our deadening routines and habits.

To make the wildman our ally and find beneficial use for his power in our life, we must be willing to face our fear of his seemingly unpredictable impulses. When we set him free in our mind, he will not bring chaos and injurious calamity; he will rattle the cages we have constructed around us that protect, but also limit us. Interacting with him is not to be taken lightly. He will question everything we have constructed in our lives—even our sobriety—and mock our adherence to the societal rules that hold us back from being our true selves. Topsy-turvy may start to feel normal, but his teachings are *exactly* what we need.

Entering the realms of my wildman, I begin by asking him what he needs.

"Long live the wildman. Let him be! Long live the wild-man. Set him free!" One hundred men repeatedly shout out the chant as they explore together in small groups what this archetypal energy might have in store for each of them personally. Images of men dancing and drum-ming around a fire at a men's conference are actually accurate. Yet such celebration and connectedness is only part of the story. What is also found in such conclaves is a safe space in which to share both the joys and pain of being a man in the modern world, to discover and voice insights about the journey to conscious manhood.

Such gatherings are places where we can risk vulner-ability, expose our darkest secrets, and be held in a com-munity of caring men who aspire to a different version of masculinity than the ones so often fostered in us by society. Recovery and sobriety give us the gift of examin-ing deeply who we are as men, the possibility of dropping some of the negative baggage we have been carrying, and the responsibility to determine how we might contribute to making the world a better place.

I will find a men's gathering where I might explore what the wildman means to me.

In the sparkling stillness of a deep forest lies a clear mountain lake. Our inner wildman gazes at his reflection from the shore. He sees fierceness and a willingness to break not only whatever rules he deems unreasonable, but also weaknesses.

Our wildman remembers the Fifth Step: "Admitted to God, to ourselves, and to another human being the exact nature of our wrongs." He is no stranger to his own destructive nature, for he has lived through some of the consequences of those actions. He has survived and learned from past lessons—as have many of us who are recovering from addiction and a lifestyle that supported it. Yet he still honors his wild, restless yearning and longing, the energies he devotes to the sensation of being fully and passionately alive. He knows how to make fire, survive harsh conditions, be comfortable sleeping under the stars, and draw upon an intense inner determination to keep exploring his edge. He can look himself in the eyes and see *both* his wrongs and his rights, and all the in-between spaces that are not quite so tidy or black-and-white. And he accepts and loves who he is, and who he is becoming.

When my wildman calls, I listen with my full attention.

Richard Louv, the author who coined the term *nature deficit disorder*, embraces the following ancient wisdom: "We cannot protect something we do not love, we cannot love what we do not know, and we cannot know what we do not see. Or hear. Or sense."

Reverence is born from our intimate connection with not only nature, but all of life. Whatever we cherish, what touches our core and inspires us, must be protected. If we believe in a Divinity, Higher Power, or Cosmic Force, then it follows that we will honor all creation as the manifestation of that mysterious power. Even agnostics and atheists can find reason to bow before the altar of the beauty and bounty of life that surrounds us.

Since we now walk the path of sobriety, we are more awake than ever to this reality. We don't need religion to guide us in this endeavor; we have our own experience in the world that speaks to us of the complex fabric of life, which supports and nourishes our being on many levels.

The reverence I feel for nature is strengthened every time I enter directly into its embrace.

If we have never encountered a wolf in the wild, a whale breaching, a herd of elk, a rambling bear, an eagle hunting, an underwater forest of coral brimming with fish, or tropical growth so thick we can barely find our next step, then perhaps it is time to do so.

So many of us have been raised in cities, where we witness the marvels of human ingenuity every day but miss out on the dynamic vitality of a day in the life of a forest, seashore, or jungle. In nature, adoration and worship can be woven throughout our day, simply by paying attention and being grateful for the abundance of beauty in the sky, sea, and landscapes we inhabit. We enter a world where we can collect profound experiences that continue to inspire, rather than collecting or purchasing things that soon lose their luster.

To live with reverence is to support that quiet inner space that *really* sees the incredible complexities of life's web and relishes the simplicity of how available such a comforting connection is. Reverence is a mind-set that heals, a spacious embrace of all that is, reminding us of the preciousness of this very moment.

I need not go far to experience the closeness of reverence.

From the perspective of organized religion, reverence encompasses many behaviors, which may include prayer, studying sacred texts, fasting, and payment of tithes and offerings. Many religions come with lots of rules and regulations, all designed to enhance our experience and contact with the Divine.

Many of us have participated for years in such religious practices, sometimes with minimal gain because we were just going through the routine motions. In recovery, we may have already discovered the highly spiritual—but not religious—reverence in seeing another's pain and wanting to alleviate it, in planting a tree whose shade we might never enjoy, in the simple acts of kindness we both give and receive on any given day.

As we attune ourselves to the song of reverence, we vibrate with kindness and gratitude. During our counseling sessions or group meetings in recovery, we probably encountered many beings who gave freely of themselves, who shared their journey so that all of us might benefit—embodying the best of the wildman. At the time we may not have given such actions the reverence they deserved, but later came to realize their positive effects upon us. It is never too late to acknowledge another, to speak reverently with them about the uplifting influence they had on our life.

Saying thank you is an act of reverence.

Grounded in gratitude, we bear witness to the marvels that surround us—we are connected to the wild, and we *are* the wild. To have a highly developed sense of wonder is to allow ourselves delight in the world around us, with its myriad living and mineral forms. No matter the circumstances of our lives, wonder is possible. While we can do without constant pleasure and may experience lean times when money or jobs are scarce, we can still summon a sense of awe at the magic and mystery that surrounds us each day. Such gladness must be welcomed and warmly accepted, as we would embrace a starving child, despite all the suffering on the planet.

The world needs our astonishment and amazement, whether its origins lie in the miracle of a snowflake, the power of a summer storm, or the subtle invitation of a stranger's smile. If we deny our admiration for all the goodness that surrounds us, keeping our attention only on what is wrong on Earth, we mock those who are less fortunate. Now that we are sober, each day really is a new beginning, and all around us is incredible loveliness to be embraced, treasured, and cherished.

Life's miseries—those claimed by me and by others—need never stop me from singing my joyous wonder out loud.

Sometimes we appear to be unwitting beggars at an expansive feast. We begrudge ourselves the slightest morsel of satisfaction because we are so focused on what we do not have. But life's abundance is literally everywhere. When we make the time to just walk around and find ourselves smiling at how vibrant everything is, we are happy in the realization that we don't need substances to experience this wonder. At these moments, we have embraced the wildman.

To reclaim our childhood innocence and belief in awesomeness can be uplifting—a gateway to the immense satisfaction and happiness that awaits us. Whatever we're viewing—from everyday objects we use to survive to those crafted for beauty alone, we can marvel at the process that turned a tree or parts of the Earth's crust into *that*. Whether we're growing food or cooking and eating it, we can see and appreciate how each small act contributes to our well-being.

When we pay deep attention to the mysteries that abound, we might see beautiful patterns in rotting wood or the destructive magnificence of a hurricane. Even the amazing odors that emanate from spoiled food can awaken our brain.

My addiction blinded me to many wonderful aspects of life. Now my eyes are open to being alive.

Our inner wildman reminds us how special it is to be a human being who has the capacity to wonder. No other species cares about fossils, mimics nature's mathematical patterns in designs, or imagines living on another planet.

Curiosity is essential to our collective survival. What shows up on our radar screen each day, cloaked in wonder, is dependent on how often we work out in our mind's "curiosity gym." Every display of inspiring mastery and genius started with a dash of curiosity and passion for living. Getting out in nature, seeing the world through the magnifying lens of curiosity as we amble about at a snail-like pace, can quickly sharpen our discovery talents.

Curiosity is an awakening into our highest potentials. Our penchant to explore and investigate—our bizarre unique thoughts, our inquisitiveness about the natural world or even ourselves—is the foundation for our own learning and personal evolution.

I give thanks for the beauty and bounty of the world around and within me. Being bored or disinterested is not really a sensible option.

It is a natural human tendency to want to change the channels of consciousness. Drugs and alcohol are an easy way to do that, which is why they are so prevalent. Besides being used to self-medicate, a variety of substances offer the promise of a quick escape from an oppressive reality. Unfortunately, as we know from our own experience, people like us are not able to maintain a good relationship to drugs or alcohol. We made them our best friend. We used them as escape whenever we felt the need to celebrate *or* commiserate, to amp up our good times and soften the blows of the bad ones.

Addiction then took over and ruled our lives. For some of us, this progression from occasional, experimental dabbling to daily use was a rapid descent. Because of our genes or the help of those who saw we were in trouble, others of us seemed to manage to escape the clutches of full-blown addiction. But all of us discovered the dangerous power and life-damaging consequences of addiction—not just to substances, but to gambling, pornography, or even work or exercise

I can find healthy ways to alter my perceptions of reality and relieve stress.

Various researchers have identified characteristics of the addictive personality. These include a tendency toward impulsive behavior and seeking a rush of excitement that, at the moment, seems irresistible—to hell with our stated goals and commitments. Another trait is a high level of stress and anxiety, part of the drive to find something—*anything*—that will help relieve this uncomfortable state.

Social alienation and loneliness can also be significant factors in addiction, the sense of "not fitting in" that many of us experienced growing up. Frequent, intense mood swings and issues of self-worth comprise the final element that puts us at greater risk for substance use disorders.

We are not static beings—we are capable of change and of using our intentionality to break out of destructive patterns. While each of these addictive personality traits may continue to have some hold over us, we need not allow them to direct our behaviors. We can notice when they arise, embrace them as we might an unruly child, and then make a different choice in the moment. Eventually, we find more skillful ways to cope with our loneliness, stress, low moods, or impulsive desires.

I am learning how to manage myself and my personality traits.

How are we to find our sober way in a substance-obsessed world? Our inner wildman might provide some useful guidance. He is the master of vitality, of being high without relying on addictive behaviors, of dissolving stress and anxiety through his contact with the natural world and rapid, empowering, substance-free awareness shifts.

For those of us who have hit bottom with a trail of destruction in our wake, abstinence is the only course of action. But many friends, acquaintances, and family members have a different relationship to alcohol and other drugs. Our society seems to have such an entwined affiliation with substances that "just say no" may not be possible or desirable for many people.

The growing relaxation of cannabis laws across the country exemplifies this reality. Traditional indigenous cultures have used substances like peyote or psilocybin mushrooms in ceremonial rituals for generations, and the extensive ethnobiology of psychedelic substances worldwide reveals experimentation across the planet. Western medicine pushes opioid painkillers to the extent that this addictive force is destroying both pain and patient.

Turning to the wildman at this time can show us what's real. His vivacious, spirited, dynamic energy and engagement generate the sense of being fully alive that substances often promise, but ultimately fail to deliver.

I choose to tap into my wildman energy rather than use substances to alter my reality.

Many people live very fulfilled lives without ever experimenting with substances. They see through the advertising illusions, dispense with the peer clamor that "everyone is doing it," and avoid alcohol and tobacco because the health trade-offs are just not worth it. Maybe they have seen too much addictive destruction in their own families. But mostly they have learned to develop other ways of shifting their reality, altering their awareness, and expanding their consciousness.

Again, this tendency for humans to seek release from stress or boredom is natural and normal. We might make a list for ourselves of ways we already do this and other things we'd enjoy experimenting with. We could try dancing in the moonlight, drumming around a fire in the middle of the woods, skiing, practicing martial arts, running, or playing other sports we enjoy—any activity that invites flow and gets our endorphins pumping. Cooking a great meal, sharing sexual pleasures, playing or listening to music, meditating, or taking a walk in the woods are other options. Each holds the potential to radically shift our perspective and mind-set, opening the gates to an altered reality. We can envision many creative and healthy ways of modifying our neurochemistry in life-enhancing, community-building, and creative ways.

I commit to becoming a master of altering and shifting my reality without addictive behaviors.

Silence is at such a premium in our world. It's sometimes impossible to find it even within the sanctuary of our home, and even harder to embrace if intruding city sirens and neighbor's noise offer no solace. Yet, we must find a way to enter the silence, where we can experience relaxed body, clear mind, and open heart. To do so is to feel the spaciousness within, the vast universe between our ears, the immeasurable cellular distance between our thumb and big toe.

In serene silence, our breath rises gently like morning mist, expels with the softness of a sunset, filling and emptying us at the same time. Waves upon the shore, it carries us to the ocean of our own stillness, the beating heart of our being. The banks of the river of our life open wide as the depth of the life force within us flows onward. Taking a break from the hustling, rushing busyness of daily life, we settle into a quieter pace and space— we return to the purity of the wild.

In the past we may have avoided such states because all too often, tremendous grief would arise to engulf us and bring us down. Recovery allows us to savor the silent emptiness of this moment, to find tranquility there instead of turmoil.

Playing with breath and silence, I am at peace and yet energized.

Choosing to spend a day in silence can be quite illuminating, especially if we can do so in a wild place, where only natural sounds fill our heart and mind. The incessant, rambling, rumbling, loud volume of our own thoughts still has space to breathe and eventually calm down. We can enter the zone—a serene yet very alive space where we realize how little is necessary for us to feel happy and content.

Sitting by a fire, or under a tree, or next to a body of water for hours, with nothing to do and no "should" about how to be, we can just observe the world—inner and outer—and see what life is offering us in this very moment. We simply commune with existence rather than endlessly trying to communicate our parade of desires, wishes, ambitions, and goals. We can put all our questions to the universe and have them answered, without speaking a syllable.

Experiencing the flurry of words and superficial sharing that can occur during recovery group meetings, we might have begun to appreciate the mantra "Do not speak unless it is a real improvement on silence."

The emptiness of just sitting, doing nothing, being present is full of life and teachings.

The wildman knows we were raised with the great lie of our own independence. When we are conditioned to believe that we alone control our destiny, it is easy to deny or minimize the contributions that others have had in our lives. Too often, we mistakenly attribute most of our success to ourselves and the bulk of our failures to others.

Who made the chair that we sit upon as we read? Who manufactured or mined all the materials used to build the structure that encloses us, or produced the print and pages of this book, or sewed the clothes we wear? Modern technology and corporate structures usually blind us to the supply chain that provides us with the goods and services we use every day.

Every time we pay a bill, use a smartphone, surf the net, or eat a meal, we can appreciate the incredible human effort and contributions of the many hands it took to make that moment possible. The web of our interdependence is vast and seemingly endless—and that is just speaking about the physical plane.

Although we are ultimately the ones who make ourselves whole, we also know that standing shoulder-to-shoulder, face-to-face and relying on each other is what makes life worth living—this is the only way to survive the wild.

I celebrate both my independence and my interdependence.

We walk upon the shoulders of our *mancestors*. Their sacrifices, in part, made possible the world we inhabit today. They provided the momentum for each generation to forge a better life. Many cultures believe that our ancestors play an active, positive role in our lives, that they are a palpable presence that must be honored and respected.

Even if our ancestors were hard, mean, and unsuccessful at times, we owe them. Both the gifts *and* the wounds we received make our progress on the path of recovery and growth possible. Their choices—good *and* bad—reverberate into our own lives.

Constellation therapy suggests that many of us unconsciously take on destructive familial patterns, including violence, substance use, anxiety, and depression. Such underlying forces and invisible bonds continue to wreak havoc through generations, until we become aware and healthy enough to cast aside what hurts us and embrace the qualities that help us in our journey. We may have never met our great-grandfather who was a violent alcoholic, yet his influence within our clan may still be felt through stories and the damage he inflicted along the way. In recovery, we discover that we can liberate ourselves from the trauma experienced long ago by creating healthier dynamics in the present.

I can break free of the shadows that have existed in my family for a long time.

At times, the strands of love that connect us to each other are so delicate. Certain friendships fade away as individuals move or as our work together is completed. Other people seem destined to remain in our circle of caring until death calls. We may share only occasional conversation with some of them but have deeper bonds with others, sharing experiences and confidences throughout the years. "Forever friends" are always welcome in our hearts, and there is comfort in just knowing they still walk the planet.

There is another special group of people who hold for us an *utang na loob*—a Tagalog term originating in the Philippines that refers to a debt of the heart. These are the people who were truly there for us at a time of crisis, and there is no way to ever fully repay the "heart debt" we owe them. Perhaps they became a supportive companion when we lost someone we loved. Maybe they took us in when we needed shelter, lent us money, or helped us through the worst of an addiction or illness. It is possible they saved our lives by helping us reconnect to the wildness that led to peace. Whatever actions they took, they are etched forever within the deepest recesses of our being.

I honor and acknowledge that which has been given to me that can never be repaid.

Different cultures use a variety of terms for vital force—*qi* in China, *ki* in Japan, *bayu* in Bali, *prana* in India, and *ha* in Hawaii. These words all describe the three elements of vitality—the times when we are *energetic, alert,* and *fully alive.* We recognize this life force when we see it in others, and the traces of it also linger within our own being. It isn't just a by-product of peak experiences—those things that give us a "peek" into a heightened, blissful way of being in the world. Rather, this dynamic energy is available to us each day.

Neuroplasticity is a medical word that means our brains are capable of change—proof that old dogs and humans can learn new tricks. Pessimists *can* become optimists, depression *can* morph into a renewed zest for life, and calm *can* replace anxiety.

As we progress through our recovery, we see how positive, persistent, consistent behaviors can change the habitual responses of our brain to more empowered states of being. As we grow stronger in recovery, the wildman's passion for living permeates everything we do with the impulse to achieve our maximum potential. We enhance our physical and psychological well-being as we focus on being enthusiastically, wholeheartedly present to whatever is occurring. As we rewire our brains, we rewrite the story of our lives.

I amp up my vitality through the potent choices and momentum I generate today.

In the Yoruba culture, stories and drumming serve as portals to another dimension, a crossroads where the spirit world and this reality intersect. The art of making a drum and learning to listen to its voice require special initiations and rituals.

Since ancient times, humans have had an inherent impulse to make sounds—beat out rhythms on tree trunks, bang sticks together, or shake bundles of shells—and to dance with surrender and abandonment in joyous celebration. Such a buildup of intensity, climaxing in heavy breathing and the flow of sweaty bodies, still exists in modern-day tribal settings where we can lose ourselves to the untamed parts of who we are. The rhythmic energy of using our own body as a drum, singing in the shower, or shucking off our clothes and dancing in our living room speaks to the freedom of the ongoing flow of the uninhibited primitive that we still relish. Music and dance bring out our wildman within, inviting us to remember the ancient pulses that even now course through our body and uplift our psyche.

I can sing. I can dance. I can drum and express joy in many unfettered ways.

Along with curiosity, optimism, gratitude, and the ability to give and receive love, vitality is a foundational pillar in building a meaningful, happy life. We can learn to summon and visualize an immediate, intense infusion of the wildman's vital energy. Imagine swallowing a star, summoning zip and zing in the form of light infusing our body, or dipping our hand into an ocean of dynamic potency.

Using our breath as a bridge from malaise or laziness to increased vim and vigor, we focus on drawing in whatever we need and then exhaling what does not serve us in the moment. We align mind, body, and heart into a laser-like beam of uplifting positive presence. We let our light shine, giving permission to others to do the same.

Our vibrant lightness of being illuminates our little corner of the world, and just as lighting one candle with another does not diminish either, we spread the exuberant positive energy around. We have spent enough time in the dark dungeon of our addictive process. It is the moment—if only temporary—to shine and express our joy of living a great adventure, infused with passion.

Using my breath and visualization, I can "state shift" to a higher sense of vitality at will.

During a three-hour airplane ride, I once sat next to a man who played a video game on his phone the entire time. I felt a deep sadness that there was no openness there, no willingness to look beyond his own narrow focus to see what the world might be offering him during his travels. All he seemed to care about was getting to another level of his game. Not that I am any great repository of wisdom, but we might have had a meaningful exchange that may have affected our lives in unseen ways.

We have all had similar times when the person we were with was busy texting, surfing cyberland, flipping through camera images of the past, or tuned into their headphones, while the creative possibilities for connecting in the present moment vanished.

If we want to be open to the world best embodied by the wildman, we have to get our heads out of our screens and pay attention to our surroundings. Addicted to distraction, we miss quite a bit of life.

I will examine how technology closes off certain forms of genuine connection, even as it enhances my life in other ways.

In the circus of our daily life, how many moments are we receptive and vulnerable, present to whatever possibility might arise? Journaling is a wonderful way to expand our capacity for authenticity, so we can cultivate an openness to the world. The miracle of an empty piece of paper before us is that it both summons from deep within whatever needs to be expressed and invites us to ask important questions that are essential for our growth and well-being. All the divergent voices within us can have their chance upon the stage of a blank page.

We are "as sick as our secrets." The wildman confronts them all. He is a living repository of events and reveals all. In a journal we can do the same—we need not edit or hide from ourselves. We can tell the truth and ascend to new heights of self-realization within its safe sanctity. It is a place to be completely real—to whine, rage, and celebrate with wild abandon.

Therapeutic, contemplative, purging, creative, or inspiring, our journal entries fully support the process of healing—from childhood wounds, addiction traumas, and relationships gone south. We can practice *handstorming*, where we surrender to the flow of ink on page, creating a no-holds-barred, free, uninhibited, streaming state of relaxed awareness. Doodling, drawing, diagraming, sketching, scribbling, random musings, and poetic outpourings are all welcome to the party.

Journaling regularly frees and opens me.

The truths of love and openness are bigger than our individual small mind, which can never entirely capture their secrets. Like the inflow and release of breath, the endless cycle of giving and receiving kindness is the portal to the greater appreciation of the mysteries of relationships.

Terima kasih is an Indonesian form of saying thank you that signifies that something is given and accepted with love. Uttering this phrase is a manifestation of enlightened wisdom. To be able to offer—and to accept—the blessings of love and infuse all of our daily encounters with that awareness is to participate in the most basic form of openness to life itself.

Said with a smile, and a sparkle in the eyes, a simple expression of gratitude acknowledges the most essential aspect of our lives. It reminds us that we are luminous beings of goodness. Each moment of our relatedness with others is part of a consecrated dance whose rhythms we will never fully comprehend, but whose music we can effortlessly enjoy. Open to the world and to each other, we live and walk a sacred path. What we seek healing for is already whole, already free, and alive in the core of our being.

Today, the many blessings raining down have my name on them.

Our inner wildman knows how to connect deeply to himself, to others, and to the planet. This sense of being in relationship with all of life is what sustains him through challenging times. He grasps the immense significance of his own part in the evolution of consciousness, and he does whatever it takes—including breaking down some social norms—to create a more empowered vision of being human.

When wildman spends contemplative time in a natural setting, he enhances his power to enter into intimacy with others because he is so grounded in his own being and in the beauty and bounty of the world we all inhabit.

Recovery offers us the opportunity each day to deepen our bond with ourselves, because we are finally able to release some of the shame and negative conditioning that has imprisoned us. We can see ourselves in a clear, fresh, powerful light. This new lens expands our perspectives on making allies and forming partnerships. Because we trust more in our ability to make good choices, we are able to risk and trust other humans in deeper ways than before.

The more I connect to my truest self, the greater my capacity for intimacy with others.

Many of us have experienced the supreme gifts inherent in being in close relationship with animals—domesticated or untamed. Dogs, cats, horses, and pet birds can bring no end of joy and loving acceptance into our lives. They teach us many positive lessons about being in the world, including how to deal with pain. Those of us privileged to have had contact with elephants, dolphins, whales, bears, wolves, or herds of elk or caribou are also forever changed by such encounters.

The call of the wild satisfies some primitive longing within each of us. For millennia, humans lived in close contact with the planet, attuned to seasonal survival rhythms and the migration of birds and beasts. Then, in the United States, the light bulb entered widespread use in the early 1900s, and indoor plumbing became a reality for most in the 1930s. With these advances, we lost some of our connection with nature. In this technological age, our genes still hunger for virgin lands, desolate seas, and uninhabited primitive expanses of wilderness where our wiles, will, and wisdom can be tested. Our innate intelligence is stimulated and refined by such contact with the wild. Connecting to source in this way enlivens our whole being.

I endeavor to spend more of my life outside and in contact with other creatures.

Human connections are based on many different biological factors. Our brains are very involved with neurochemical **CODES.** Cortisol levels—elevated by stress—remind us that when we are relaxed with others, we can be more present. **O**xytocin—the cuddle hormone—is released when we hug or touch people, or when we make love. It is the biological basis of attachment, trusting, and bonding. **D**opamine is part of the brain's reward pathway, triggered by novelty and change. **E**ndorphins help us feel good, especially through physical activity. **S**erotonin is elevated when we feel more united and linked together—through sharing emotional intimacies or being kind to one another.

Put it all together and we have the "CODES" for the unseen magic behind feeling good in another's presence: reduced stress, touch, doing something interesting, moving our bodies, and expressing caring while sharing meaningful emotional stories.

Because all of these neural proteins get out of balance with any form of chemical addiction, we may have had great difficulty with human connections in the past. Recovery grants us the promise of expanded possibilities for intimacy as our nervous system rewires itself into greater openness, trust, and receptivity.

I honor the healing my heart and brain continue to experience through sobriety.

As we heal, we begin to experience more joy and freedom, which is very much an *inside* job. Although freedom may flow more easily when outer conditions support it, what we observe is not determined solely by external circumstances. It also depends on what lies within us.

The lens is as important as the light. Freedom *from* and freedom *to* are two sides of the consciousness coin. Such freedoms always exist within limits: no yelling a false alarm of fire in a crowded movie theater; our fist is not allowed to occupy the space where someone else's nose is; we can't just take what we want from a supermarket—at least not without unpleasant consequences.

Freedom is *not* a lack of responsibilities; rather, it is having a choice between them. As we contemplate our failures (which, sadly, can be significant and frequent), it may appear that any notions of free will went out the window with our compulsive, pleasure-seeking behaviors. We believed deeply in the illusion of freedom that our addiction of choice offered. However, the harsh reality is that we gave up our liberty in pursuit of a seductive, false, deceptive way of being, ignoring the life-damaging consequences.

I must cultivate my own garden of freedom each and every day.

Our individual sense of freedom is always affected by the factors that influence behavior: reward, punishment, restraint, and constraint. Reward may be as simple as a smile or as complex as a financial bonus. Punishment might be a disapproving frown or being thrown in jail. A locked fence around a building may physically restrain us from entering; we are compelled to show a picture ID before boarding an airplane. The severity of these limitations on our freedom determines how onerous we find them.

As we navigate the rules and regulations of "civilized" society, we must make choices about which rules we follow and which we ignore. Within the *terra incognita* of our own beings where the unexplored aspects of our deepest selves exist, we are dealing with similar constraints, and the more conscious we are of those patterns that bind, the freer we can be. When we create healthy boundaries and then move beyond the self-imposed limits we have constructed, we expand our freedom. Personal borders allow us to feel at home in ourselves, a place of healing and wholeness from which we can then emerge into a new way of being in the world.

How exhilarating it is to break out of oneself!

The inner wildman asks us to examine our face in the mirror to see what it has cost us to not be living fully. What happened? Where did we lose our way? Have we lost contact with deep desire, forgotten the bliss of wonder and curiosity, the importance of reverence, the power of our own vitality?

It is not too late to unlock the inner gates that hold us back from experiencing a passionate sense of aliveness. It is not too late to discover and manifest our truth in the world, to dance with delight at our freedom. We can drum, sing, leap, run, paint, ride horses, sleep under the stars, and make animal sounds around a fire in the middle of nowhere. Let's do something outrageous—not stupid, crazy, or totally unsafe—to explore our edge.

We might attend a nudist gathering, go on an extended wilderness travel adventure, start learning a martial art, or find a regular drumming circle—whatever fully engages our mind, heart, and body in new, untamed, unexpected ways. Our addiction, as well as our ongoing recovery from addiction, has made us stronger. Our wildman within seems less intimidating and ready to share his gifts with us—now more than ever.

I am ready to explore living passionately and wholeheartedly, in radical freedom.

DECEMBER

The Sage

The inner Sage cautions you to question everything, as well as to learn patience and practice stewardship in all things—large and small. He is the truth teller who shares his wisdom, peace, perspective, and resolve freely, even as he approaches the final frontier of death.

The sage's inner and outer lives are in total harmony. This wise archetype intuitively knows and understands the lessons of the universe. He has also come to appreciate how problems arise when he thinks *only* of himself, as well as how dilemmas can be solved and wisdom can be gained when he expands his thinking to include others.

The sage knows, deep in his bones, that trying to control himself, others, or life itself only leads to sadness, frustration, and disappointment. He accepts the uncertainty that relationships often bring and knows that we receive from the world what we give to the world.

Our addictions have already begun to teach us some of these same painful lessons. Perhaps we have had contact with older men who provided uplifting guidance during our most turbulent times. Our inner sage—sometimes through an entire male chorus of elders—counsels us to be mindful that such guidance is always available. Elder grandfathers don't protect us with their bodies; they support us with their indomitable spirit. They remind us that mortality rides on our back as well. We have no time to waste in our quest to be more integrated, healed, and whole. Winter is coming, sooner than we think.

My inner sage reminds me that every step of the way is the way.

The sage is not immune to making mistakes. In fact, he has learned that errors are to be expected, even welcomed. The faster he can identify them, the sooner he finds the solution he was seeking. He refines his message continually as he shares his insights with others in his role as mentor, teacher, advisor, or confidant.

Our inner sage reminds us of the importance of the Twelfth Step: "Having had a spiritual awakening as the result of these steps, we tried to carry this message to alcoholics [or addicts], and to practice these principles in all our affairs." We need not wait until our elder years to speak out about our passage through the fire of addictions. No matter our age, we can contribute right now by sharing what we have learned that might be helpful to others. And the elders among us can also be inspiring—in support groups, in a public format, and in their social circles. They have survived much and thrived through agonizing defeats and accumulated victories. Their scars of experience contain truths that are unavailable in a "regular" library. Their stories can uplift us, even as they instruct us in both how to be and how *not* to be in the world.

I commit to assisting others as I age, as others have supported me.

The shadow side of our inner sage is that we can become so hopelessly overwhelmed by details that we never act. We spend too much time seeking the ultimate truth, and we forget to water the garden. Or we live in our heads, constantly hunting and sifting through more information and ignoring the demands and pleasures of the body.

When we focus so much on the intelligence of the mind, we ignore the insights and lessons of our bodies. The love of learning creates a wondrous repository of possibility, and we need to include some body-based practices in our emerging library of talents. Yoga, qigong, tai chi, or any martial art offers the depth and breadth to engage us for more than one lifetime in harmonizing body, heart, mind, and spirit into a powerful force for good.

The other shadow aspect of the wise one is that we become convinced of our own superiority. A lifetime of study has finally and truly enlightened us—except, perhaps, when it comes to seeing our *own* arrogance and sense of superiority. We are blinded by our own piercing intellect, unable to read social cues and essential feedback that tell us we still have much to learn. We remain unaware of our ever-present limitations.

I aspire to balancing intellect and insight in my life.

A single candle is lit, and we sit quietly and comfortably within the circle of its illumination. Perhaps we hold in our hands an object of special significance, a ritual token or animal fetish—some sort of charm that represents our most cherished and yet unanswered questions. We empty our mind and open our heart, letting go of any expectations or desires.

In this meditative state, we may sense the presence of another. It is our own being, our inner sage in the form of an older, insightful man. He steps behind us silently, bends over and whispers in our ear, affirming our goodness, alerting us to very specific obstacles still to be encountered on our life journey. We feel safe and comforted by both his words and demeanor. We can sense his caring, concern, and warm heart as he invites us to be patient with all that remains confused in our heart. Rather than offering specific counsel, he reminds us to trust deeply in our own inner guidance, to stay true and authentic to our path of becoming a conscious, empowered man.

Whether through guided visualization, random contemplative insights, or messages from the dreamtime, we can access the kindness and wisdom of our inner sage.

I open the channels of communication with my inner sage— my older, wiser self.

Who, why, whence, and whither? Perhaps we have been blessed to have an elder ask us some important questions about what we are *really* up to in life. These inquiries planted seeds of awareness by turning on our inner "house lights," illuminating queries we had never even considered.

Essential questions can serve us throughout our lives in empowering ways. Like stone cairns that show us the path on a wandering trail, they keep us on the course of awakening. Such questions serve as a chariot that carries us across the breadth of our life and draws us to what we most need to experience on our journey. Stimulating both curiosity and skepticism, they invite us to dig deeper into what we are *really* about. They help us get clearer about what we intend to manifest in both our outer and inner planes.

Such musings were beyond us for a long time when our focus was on surviving the perils of our addictive process. Now that sobriety has a foothold, we can climb to higher peaks of awareness and begin to question everything. All we can ever do is take the next obvious step and keep asking a few essential questions that keep us pointed in the right direction.

Often, holding the right question is more important than finding an immediate answer.

The quality of our lives is dependent on the empowering conversations we have within ourselves. Not only the endless, often repetitive *thoughtstream* of our mind's daily musings, but also the difficult questions we hold in our hearts that cannot be responded to immediately, but that rather beckon us to gradually live along into the answers.

When we ask ourselves penetrating queries, ones that strike to the core of what ails and inspires us, then we really begin to plumb our own depths. The light of conscious awareness always grows brighter and clearer. Such contemplations were not possible during the fog of our addictive process, when we possessed neither energy nor capacity to unravel the barriers that separated us from our true self. The very idea of asking ourselves about our inner workings—or journaling about them—might have seemed absurd at the time.

Now, we can discover some of the introspective joys we have been missing and kneel down in praise for the riddles that both beguile and enlighten us, because they teach us to listen to our own knowing. Insights bubble from the darkness of our unconscious realms at unexpected moments once we have opened a channel and put in a request.

By asking essential questions, I open myself to receiving vital messages.

Essential questions can prod us into new territory, upset old belief systems, and ask us to go deeper in our contemplation of what is *really* important right now. What is the primary cause of our own suffering? What inspires us? What feelings and thoughts arise when we gaze at ourselves in the mirror? What would we be doing differently with our lives if we had no fear? For what do we most need to forgive ourselves? What values have we lost touch with that remain very important to our philosophy of life? What habits and perspectives do we cling to that no longer serve us? What still needs to be healed from our struggle with addictions and the collateral damage we created? How do we honor, care for, and love ourselves on a regular basis?

When we actively and regularly engage with such critical queries, we activate hidden resources within us, give voice to repressed impulses, and invite some of our inner demons to take a walk with us down a different pathway.

Today, I will ask myself an essential question and trust that I have the answers deep within myself.

One need not be Spock, the brilliant Vulcan from the Starship *Enterprise,* to appreciate the value of logic. Every day we are bombarded with information, and we must discern what is true and sift out what is useful from the information stream.

Our intelligence is influenced by many factors, including past perceptions, experience, and what we would like to believe is real in a particular situation. Objective analysis and evaluation often leave when our emotions are in the driver's seat. Critical thinking is an important faculty of mind, but is only one of a host of abilities.

We have all had occasion to wrestle with a problem and try to make a decision that turns into a mindless repetition of what we already know. When this happens, our ability to "figure it out" becomes a less-than-helpful obsession. If it were as simple as "A leads to B, which produces C," we would get in less trouble. We have gotten into a mess by using this kind of simple logic before. Have pain? These pills relieve pain, so take these pills. Equations like this have obvious shortfalls, as evidenced by the current opioid epidemic.

The sage understands the limits of logic, which is why he distinguishes intuition, insights, and information from feelings in his approach to decisions.

Critical thinking becomes more powerful when combined with my other faculties.

Detecting common mistakes and inconsistencies in our own reasoning is not always an easy task. Using information to solve our personal problems requires that we trust the source of the data, facts, or advice and that we constantly evaluate and improve our own arguments.

We can see how good friends—those in whom we have developed confidence—can serve as excellent mirrors for us. Friends like this are able to really listen, with their hearts and minds as well as their ears, and then reflect back to us their understanding of the issue as we have stated it. This is different from giving advice. A deep and respectful listener does not directly show us the way through, but offers us a better chance to find the answer for ourselves.

As we may have experienced in counseling during recovery, we discover our own truth, stumble upon our own insights, and make the solution more our own when we are guided to find our own way. We have more solutions-oriented skin in the game, so to speak. Receiving guidance is very different from just being told what to do or what is "best" for us.

I appreciate those who lend an ear and reflect back to me my own thinking about something important.

Analyzing information and integrating diverse sources of knowledge are important skills in a constantly changing global economy. If we are to find a place within this new world, we must also develop language and presentation abilities. How well we express ourselves is one of the first hurdles in building our lives. And the more languages we can do it in, the better.

Unless we have developed a highly specialized talent, interpersonal skills are an essential ingredient for success. Growing up in poverty or spending years lost in substance use or addictive behaviors may have taught us how to quickly read people and situations, to see through the BS, since we became so good at spinning it ourselves and have the "street smarts" to survive.

Now we need to hone those abilities to serve us in our current endeavors. We can reach out to those we encounter—perhaps other Twelve Step members—who already embody the talents we seek to strengthen and get some inspiring assistance. We build on what is already positive and helpful within us rather than putting ourselves down.

I can take a risk and learn another language or find other ways to improve my interpersonal skills.

The sage honors and supports *all* forms of intelligence. Howard Gardner, a developmental psychologist, described nine types of intelligence: naturalist, musical, logical-mathematical, existential, interpersonal, bodily-kinesthetic, linguistic-verbal, intrapersonal, and visual-spatial. How we wish our school systems and every teacher had understood this and did their best to support our own unique forms of learning!

Too often, if we were a fabulous visual artist or really good with our hands in terms of fixing things, we were discouraged by the predominant expectations of schools that focused more on linguistic, mathematical, or scientific achievements. We may have been pushed out, more than dropped out, of an institution that was not honoring or serving us.

Now is the time to reclaim our inherent talents, which may also have gone underground during our addiction struggles. Whether it is our easy flow with nature, music, art, or sports, we can find a way to leverage these forms of intelligence into moving us forward. We need not stay stuck, and we can let go of some of the negative feedback we received in school settings. Learning is lifelong and something to be embraced, not feared or pushed away.

Today, I begin to really appreciate the different forms of intelligence I possess.

What are the optimal conditions for us to learn something? Of course, it depends on *what* we are learning, but discovering *how* our unique learning style preference manifests is also very important. Do we prefer audio, visual, or kinesthetic-tactile ways of approaching something new? When setting up a piece of new technology or furniture, do we just get in there with our hands, or read the manual and look at the diagram, or do we have someone read it to us while we work?

Some of us make lists and notes because we do better remembering tasks and responsibilities through the act of writing them down. We may enjoy standing back and just observing people in different situations. Others remember things better through verbally repeating the information. They prefer radio or podcasts to reading a paper or news online. Still others prefer moving around and feel trapped when they have to be at a desk, in a meeting, or listening to a lecture. While we all use all these methods at different times, knowing which fits us best can help us use our energy and attention most effectively when learning something new.

My learning style preferences also apply to maintaining my sobriety in terms of developing habits that make my commitment even stronger.

What are we most curious about exploring at this point in our life? What draws us, sparks our interest, keeps surfacing at unexpected moments? Now that we are addiction free, an enormous well of energy has been liberated in our life.

Often, as we build the first part of a bridge to a new reality, to the universal life force or the divine, we are presented with unexpected opportunities and chance encounters. Things "fall into place" as information or critical people show up at the right time. The old saying "When the student is ready, the master will appear" still holds relevance in the modern world. It doesn't matter if we are learning banjo, singing in a chorus, playing with robotics, or writing some poetry. Once we just begin, all manner of unseen assistance will appear. Our passion drives the outer wheel of change, and that in turn shifts who we are on the inside.

More than one person has found that what started as an interesting hobby became a lucrative and very satisfying business. Yet not everything need be goal oriented. We can do just for the pleasure of doing. The ability to keep learning is a hallmark of empowered, conscious manhood.

Today, I will begin in earnest to delve into something that has been calling me.

Choosing situations that call for us to be *present* allows us to connect with the sage. It is possible to connect with the sacred during the most average moments. When making a cup of tea and waiting for the water to boil, we can practice patience and observe the gradual movement of time and energy. Gathering the aromatic leaves of culinary herbs from which we will make a tea or infusion, we can diligently prepare them, knowing the real transformation will occur when we allow the leaves to dry slowly in the sun. We welcome each step that requires us to wait, to be, to trust.

In the same way, we practice allowing the outer events of our day to work their way within us, brewing some lessons learned, which we can then sip slowly as we experience the heat of our mistakes mingling with our victories, warming our hearts. Soothing, gentle, and calming, what might have been bitter on its own becomes sweet.

Patience redefines what is important in the moment. Whether the challenge is a traffic jam, a long line at the market, or a person who drones on without ever getting to the point, we have the power to transform what is happening by reframing it. We can consciously redirect our attention to something for which we are grateful rather than focusing on something we want to be different.

Patience in small things leads to wisdom in larger ones.

Impatience is a cousin of fear. The more we hurry, the more likely we are to stumble. Life unfolds in its own manner, and waiting simply means not being driven to action by desire or fear. If we're patient, we'll have more peace of mind, and we might even occasionally feel happy. We'll begin to see that rushing, impatience, and control are really forms of violence against ourselves and others.

Even as we long for the new, desiring to get through whatever challenge is currently engulfing us as quickly as possible, we can sense the edges of not wanting to do what is needed. We can simply observe our resistance without judgment and honor it as a very important teacher. We can choose "yes" to what nurtures us, drop the "shoulds," embrace our willingness to tolerate frustration, and postpone some gratifications because of our commitment to moving forward in our life. We keep coming back to patience by engaging positively every day with our desired change or intention. When we summon patience, we honor life's flow *and* ourselves. Certain changes cannot appear, because we are not yet able to fully live them.

I trust that my progress on the path to awareness continues, even when impatience is pounding on my door.

We must be patient with both our weaknesses *and* our strengths. When we are in pain or feeling stressed, we can regain some balance by taking deep breaths and remembering that what we are experiencing is uncomfortable, but *not* intolerable. We need not succumb to the "hurry sickness" that is so prevalent in our multitasking, digital, instant-everything age.

An old adage advises, "One should sit in meditation for twenty minutes every day, unless one is too busy—then one should sit for an hour." This is a perfect reminder for how patience transforms and is most necessary to summon when we are least desirous of its influence. Rushing has its own energy and momentum, and slowing down may sometimes seem an impediment rather than a useful strategy.

As we move through stages of recovery and sobriety, the temptation exists to get ahead of ourselves, to not "waste" any more time in counseling, because we want to get on with our real life. But that is *exactly* the time when patience needs to be our daily mantra. Patience is harnessing the power of the present—harvesting the gifts right in front of us—rather than yearning for those yet to come.

Patience is a useful attribute to cultivate, anytime and anywhere.

An old person in a fairy tale often provides a needed magical talisman—some unlikely, unexpected, and mysterious power to help others overcome a difficulty. Such a sage often urges people to "sleep on it" when dealing with a dilemma as a way to solidify self-reflection. In this way our inner sage serves as a patient, visionary guide to what needs to be done.

The Yanomami tribe of Brazil utilizes the wisdom of such an approach. Community decisions are made by an informal council, which includes older tribal members. The elderly, imbued with respect, manifest diplomatic and leadership qualities in their moral authority as they urge persistent, determined consideration of an issue—which requires taking time for *all* viewpoints to be voiced. After listening intently, the elder has the responsibility to deliver a *patamou*—a verbal lecture. This public, passionate speech attempts to convince others of the necessity to support those in need, or gives specific initiatives for young people. Sometimes this is a way to just state an otherwise hidden point of view, to evoke thought in community members. Without any real power of coercion, elders lead by word and by example.

The truth-telling wisdom of elders can sometimes shift my own confusion.

The sage understands suffering, the origin of suffering, the cessation of suffering, and how to remove it. His right view is composed of a number of empowering perspectives that assist him in his work of reflecting truths born of hard experience to others on the path and offering counsel to those who wish to receive it.

We often hear the saying in recovery groups that "Pain is inevitable, while suffering is optional." Pain is rooted in not accepting what is. Resistance is futile, because what we resist persists. Grieving and forgiveness can lift us above the most trying circumstances.

Whatever we dislike or reject in another usually mirrors what we disdain or push away within ourselves. As long as we cling to our painful past, we cannot reach for a benevolent future. The protective walls around our hearts are dissolved, one loving feeling at a time. Responsibility is ours to take, not assign to another. We have suffered long and deep in our addiction, and our inner sage can be a source of not only compassion, but of guidance about how to not fall into the same hole again. We begin when we embrace right views and endeavor each day to live them.

I am learning. Let me succeed by holding uplifting perspectives rather than being held down by limiting beliefs.

The human race has evolved in consciousness because of protest, because people have been willing to speak out against ignorance and injustice, to speak up for human rights and dignity. Right resolve is evident in how the sage moves in the world. He leans into being an open discoverer of truth rather than a closed keeper of secrets. He models for us the willingness to examine, over and over, the beliefs that serve neither him nor his brothers and sisters on the planet.

The sage is not afraid of his tears, nor is he intimidated by his fears, for he understands that—even with the best of intentions and strong resolve—we are all falling apart and coming together at the same time. Two steps forward and one back is often the way our journey unfolds. What the heart knows beyond all words becomes accessible only with vulnerability. When we make amends, we not only look injustice in the eye, we increase our own ability to see and be seen as we are. We intend to relieve the suffering of another, and in that openness, relieve our own. The few who dare to do this right the wrongs of the many.

Every instance of breakdown only strengthens my resolve to keep on the path of waking up.

We want to be wise like our sage who guides us. Instead of leaping tall buildings in a single bound, we'd prefer to be able to dispense pearls to reduce suffering and assist those most in need. To find compassion for another's anger, lovingly penetrate their fear, hold serenity in the depths of our heart, and timeless awareness near. Blake said it differently, but it is the same: "To see a world in a grain of sand, and heaven in a wild flower, hold infinity in the palm of your hand, and eternity in an hour."

We want to be intelligent and see beyond the narrowness of our own perspectives, release the illusion of separateness, and yet stay centered in our own truth. We want to be awake to the beauty of the planet, the precious gifts of this moment, and the edge of our growth. Lost for too long in the maze of our addiction, we are now just beginning to taste the freedom—and responsibility—that making discerning, insightful decisions entails. It is said that the path is formed by walking on it, but what if there is no path because we all can fly and are already home?

Wisdom grows within me even now; it is an acorn developing into a mighty oak.

There is a noble tradition of crazy wisdom, an eccentric holiness, in which practitioners, often *skyclad* (dressed only in their birthday suit), probe untruths and dispel ignorance through actions that are as pure as heaven's rain. They focus their powers on debunking hypocrisy and frauds that hold up a tower of illusions and false hopes. Their intent is to do whatever is necessary to cut through conditioning, to break the ties that bind each of us. The spontaneous lifestyle of these seemingly crazy wanderers on the path of spiritual aspiration and wisdom realization was usually offensive to conventional religious authorities. Although some were persecuted, their complete renunciation and surrender was inspiring to many.

The choice to give up bitterness is simple but *not* easy. Do we prefer to hold peace, or poison, in our hearts? Expecting the best, these wild, apparently crazed beings just continued to let their light shine out. We can fully appreciate this aspect of their teachings, having had our share of resentments around people we blamed for our descent into addiction. They invite us to our edge, so that we might leap beyond our fears, listen to our own inner knowing, and taste freedom.

Crazy wisdom helps me discern deeper truths.

I had a friend who would spend time on busy street corners, holding a simple sign: "Will work for peace." So many people are killed in wars, and so many more returned damaged and struggle to regain a sense of themselves and their ability to forge a good life. The rain of hardship for vets and their families is stormy indeed. From suicides to PTSD, from domestic violence to mass shootings, the ripple effects of the original battle live on. For some, such gaping, unhealed emotional wounds are what initially led them into their addiction—but they discovered it was a false promise of some temporary relief.

The chaos of war—whether an inner battle or military-led engagement—leaves its mark on everyone, even if it is just some collateral sadness and sense of powerlessness from the screaming headlines. Each of us is bruised, and a part of us dies whenever conflict in some far-off locale results in more suffering and killing. Dove or hawk, surely the human needs for safety, security, and protection can be met in many creative ways. There can be no lasting peace without sincere, sage social justice.

I can reach out to people of all kinds—whether friend or stranger—to offer them a helping hand up from the wars we all fight.

Our mind can be our best friend or our worst enemy. Ending the war within—or at least calling a ceasefire—is an essential step in creating a more peaceful center. Imagine that a good buddy is looking in at our stream of negative, obsessing, self-deprecating thoughts. What objective advice might our friend give us to help challenge the predictable flow of those recurrent thoughts?

When we go to the gym, we don't start with hundred-pound weights. We practice with smaller challenges. Gradually, with regular practice, we build greater capacity. So it is as we turn our attention inward and focus our awareness on our own physical, mental, and emotional experiences. We relax, pay gentle attention, and maintain a neutral attitude toward our thoughts, feelings, and sensations. Cultivating a clear but even-keeled awareness can reduce stress, bringing us harmony and increased peace. The flow of competing desires pulling us in different directions gradually decreases.

What if most of the thoughts we had were peaceful and beautiful ones that focused on the goodness and natural beauty in the world, and we invited all the others to depart? We can practice each day just observing and letting go of the ones that do not serve us.

Peace begins with me, within my own heart and mind.

The stillness of a silent mind allows greater vulnerability and tenderness, allowing us to turn soft and lovely anytime we have a chance. When we "drop" our thinking, we can concentrate on only being. We move to a place of no worry, no fear, no anger, and are left feeling calm, peaceful, satisfied, and happy.

Sometimes the hardship or distress of those close to us can destroy our own sense of peace. But we can imagine the face of someone we know who is in pain or going through a difficult time, see their countenance in our mind, and send them blessings of support. We can offer a prayer or a simple "May you be free from suffering." This may not only assist them but can also alleviate some of our own concerns.

When we are feeling overwhelmed, we can imagine ourselves as a vast sky that does not hinder white clouds from coming and going. Cravings might arise, but we visualize them as being washed away by a gentle, purifying rain. We *are* peace and acceptance, our breath connecting us with all that is right with the world. We can regularly practice taking a sacred pulse in which we pause and focus on the energy of our heart, sending its spaciousness, love, and acceptance to radiate out to everyone.

There are hundreds of ways to create peace in my heart.

Expanded consciousness always involves a willingness to abandon the comfortable rung on the ladder of how we perceive the world and what is "really" happening. The sage calls on us to regularly re-evaluate and sometimes abandon our concepts and viewpoints to make room for better ideas and truer perceptions. We do not think ourselves into new ways of living. We live along into new levels of consciousness.

We know the truth of this from our own difficult times, when our addiction was front and center of our awareness, blotting out any other truths. The great teachers of the major religions—Jesus, Buddha, and Muhammad among many others—uplifted the awareness of their followers. Their timeless wisdom was focused on improving the lives of those they encountered, through delineating better principles for living—in effect, asking them to shift their consciousness. Today, Christmas offers us such an opportunity.

Viewing the world through a straw allows us to see only a tiny bit of it. Taking an eagle-eyed perspective on our life places temporary hard times in context and reminds us of all the goodness that continues to accumulate. True wisdom recognizes that, although conditions are always changing, awareness sifts through the distractions to concentrate on what is most important right now.

My wisdom grows with each skillful choice I make.

Kwanzaa is an African American holiday celebrated from December 26 to January 1. For each of seven days, a different core value of living is examined, guided by the perspective of past struggles and future visions. *Ujima* is the Kwanzaa principle of cooperatively working with each other, which emphasizes that the lives of family and community are intimately bound together. What if each of us really took to heart the idea that our own neighborhood is a temple, to be honored, preserved, and maintained in beauty?

When we know and interact with those who live near us for a common cause, we create a meaningful community that can make a real difference. The trouble with changing the world is that weeks can go by and nothing happens. Just look at all the lofty principles, frameworks, conventions, models, declarations, and revised dogmas. The change process at the scale required demands both patience and persistence. From developing alternative energy and electric cars, to revitalizing lands taken by deserts and paper-thin topsoil, to establishing habitat corridors for wild creatures, much work needs to be done. We can begin in our own little corner of the world.

I endeavor to practice stewardship of my immediate environs, as part of giving thanks for my sobriety.

When was the last time we directly expressed our affection for the land that nourishes and sustains us all? What did we do? Perhaps it was giving simple thanks as we ate something from the garden or when we were swept away by the majesty of old neighborhood trees. Or maybe we engaged in a more direct action by planting a tree or working to preserve a piece of land.

Aloha 'aina—love of the land—is a vital thread in the tapestry of daily Hawaiian life. In Hawaii, offerings, feasts, and flower leis all speak the language of gratefulness. To see the Earth more as part of sustaining one's heritage, rather than as a commodity to be bought and sold, is to invigorate and sanctify a unique bond. It is in our nature to become attached to special places—our inner sage knows this and encourages us to embrace what we can learn from living as part of such a tapestry. Perhaps it is a stretch of beach, a favorite forest grove, a plains rock outcropping, or just a city park or neighbor's garden that calls to us. Whatever it is, when we suffuse such a parcel with affection and care, we become a babe evolving inside a womb, growing together with the Earth in harmony and beauty.

Stewardship of the land is a natural expression of my love for it.

How we see the world determines how we act. The Western philosophy, at its roots, encourages competitive individuals, with society being a collective of self-interested people, each striving for a share of the survival pie. Humans represent the top of the food chain, often thinking they're entitled to whatever they want. This attitude of entitlement can bring about a scarcity of resources that becomes a self-fulfilling prophecy.

The Indigenous worldview suggests that we are all related: that all aspects of life on Earth are interdependent and that sustainability—with its inherent balance and harmony—is more important than endless consumption. This sense of interconnectedness extends to all living creatures, including our kinship with the animal and plant kingdoms. The web of life, with all of its interrelatedness, is simply astounding. It is what supports our fragile existence every day. Can we even imagine a world without birdsong, or wolves and coyotes howling at dusk, or magnificent elephants migrating toward water on the African plains?

Becoming more aware of how my food and water gets to the table is part of becoming a conscious man.

What constitutes a good death? For some, a good death might occur after a long life in relatively good health. It would find us awake and aware, as pain free as possible, surrounded by loved ones, with laughter, song, and stories, and graced with silence and the secret languages of sight and touch. The sage does not fear death; rather, he has concerns about living too long, after the quality of life is gone or he can no longer recognize or communicate with those he loves.

Recovery has taught us that we can gradually get unstuck from our notions of how life (or death) is *supposed* to be. Such liberation becomes more and more possible with the small stuff, and then with the larger challenges. If we can open our hearts and trust that whatever is unfolding is okay and that we can indeed handle whatever comes, then even fears of death evaporate like dew in the morning sun. We more fully embrace the life we have, knowing that—at any moment—our precious existence can be lost. Death becomes a kind teacher rather than a wrathful master.

Contemplating my own death can be liberating, providing more lessons in letting go.

Many of us grew up without ever participating directly in the dying process or witnessing a death. This has only contributed to our alienation from the subject. Instead of home birth and death, technological advances moved most of us in developed countries to a hospital beginning and ending. This is not the case for the majority of humans in the world.

Some of us have witnessed friends die on the battlefield or in the war zones of poverty and addiction-laden city streets. Perhaps we have lost family or acquaintances to suicide. So death may not be a complete stranger. Every encounter with dying is a "strip search" that asks us to fully examine the life we are living right now. Being ill is a wonderful opportunity to observe that death lurks just around the corner. Even while just being sick with the flu, we feel so fragile, so vulnerable, and so afraid of suffering. Death is the great equalizer, and no matter what our status in life, it is inescapable. Whether we're rich or poor, famous or unknown, powerful or oppressed, anything can happen at any time.

Greeting the possibility of death each morning, I can begin the day determined to create happiness and to be of service to others.

As this year closes its door, it is an opportune time to write a letter to our present self from our future self—an older, insightful, peaceful man. This interesting exercise lets us tap into our archetypal sage energy to bring forth some of his wisdom as it applies directly to our own unique, current circumstances. We might reflect upon the lessons learned, the risks taken, and the gratitude we hold for our continuing sobriety.

What is most troubling our minds and hearts right now? What might our best advice to ourselves, from an older, more discerning perspective, look like? Can we envision that someday those concerns will be put to rest, although other challenges will inevitably arise? Our daily issues have certainly shifted from when we were consumed by our addictive process. As we grow and evolve through our sobriety, the patience, truth telling, peace, and wisdom of our inner sage will continue to blossom within us. "One day at a time" holds many levels of meaning.

Our sage understands the struggles we have endured, the dead ends we have encountered, and the light of conscious awareness that burns ever more brightly. He promotes nothing short of a revolution of the heart, asking only that we open ourselves, each moment, to our precious existence in order to find our true place in the world.

My inner sage both inspires and guides me into full manhood and beyond.

Acknowledgments

No one writes a book alone. Special thanks to the wonderful team at Hazelden, especially Vanessa Torrado and Jean Cook, for believing in the vision and making it sparkle. My heart is filled with gratitude for all the support I continually receive from my daughters, Gina and Rosa, and my partner Carla. Any masculine wisdom I may have gained through the years was nurtured by the incredible bonding with other good men from my men's group and close circle of friends. You know who you are! Mille grazie! I bow down before the many teachers I have had over the years, who kept me on a good path when I might have gone sideways. Especially my dear Gram and Gramps, without whose love I would surely have been more lost than found.

About the Author

 Victor La Cerva is a retired medical doctor, board-certified in pediatrics. He spent much of his career in the realm of public health, while holding teaching positions with the University of New Mexico's medical school.

In 1984, he founded New Mexico Men's Wellness and has contributed to many publications, films, and activities addressing violence prevention and the mental health needs of young people. He cares deeply about social justice and violence prevention, and believes that solutions are found by strengthening what is already good within ourselves, our families, our communities, and our culture. He has delivered keynotes and workshops in every state and internationally.

A writer, speaker, and consultant, La Cerva is the founder of Direct Village Compassion (2008), which provides assistance to the Children's Hospital of Asmara and its outlying clinics in Eritrea, Africa. He is a member of the American Public Health Association and the New Mexico Pediatrics Society.

La Cerva is the author of several books, including *Pathways to Peace*, *Worldwords*, *Masculine Wisdom*, and *Letters to a Young Man in Search of Himself.* A few brief passages from these tomes are included by permission in this book. He lives in New Mexico. Connect with Victor at myheartsongs.org.

About Hazelden Publishing

As part of the Hazelden Betty Ford Foundation, Hazelden Publishing offers both cutting-edge educational resources and inspirational books. Our print and digital works help guide individuals in treatment and recovery, and their loved ones. Professionals who work to prevent and treat addiction also turn to Hazelden Publishing for evidence-based curricula, digital content solutions, and videos for use in schools, treatment programs, correctional programs, and electronic health records systems. We also offer training for implementation of our curricula.

Through published and digital works, Hazelden Publishing extends the reach of healing and hope to individuals, families, and communities affected by addiction and related issues.

For information about Hazelden publications,
please call **800-328-9000**
or visit us online at **hazelden.org/bookstore.**

Other Titles That May Interest You

Touchstones
A Book of Daily Meditations for Men

Speaking straight to men who are striving for serenity or trying to maintain emotionally and spiritually balanced lives, these daily touchstones begin with thought-provoking quotations and conclude with affirmations that underscore the lessons of intimacy, integrity, and spirituality.

Order No. 5029; ebook EB5029

Sober Dad
The Manual for Perfectly Imperfect Parenting
BY MICHAEL GRAUBART

You are a parent (or you're about to become one). A father! A sober dad. You aren't going to get everything right. Everything isn't going to be perfect. You'll soon see that perfection isn't the point. Perfectly imperfect is okay. Showing up, being present, getting up, and trying again with your eyes wide open and crystal clear—that's what counts. That's exactly what this "manual" will help you do!

Order No. 3017; ebook EB3017

A Man's Way through the Twelve Steps
BY DAN GRIFFIN, MA

Author Dan Griffin uses interviews with men in various stages of recovery, excerpts from relevant Twelve Step literature, and his own experience to offer the first holistic approach to sobriety for men. With guidance through each of the Twelve Steps, as well as practical advice and inspiration to help you define your own sense of masculinity, this groundbreaking book offers you the tools needed to work through issues we often face as men: admitting powerlessness, finding connection with a Higher Power, letting go of repressed anger and resentment, contending with sexual issues, and overcoming barriers to intimacy and meaningful relationships.

Order No. 4734; ebook EB4734

Step Up
Unpacking Steps One, Two, and Three with Someone Who's Been There
BY MICHAEL GRAUBART

Step up to your best life, alongside the millions of people who have embraced Twelve Step programs as a way to gratefully recover from their substance use, alcoholism, and addictions. Author Michael Graubart has been where you are today. With this book, he shows you what it's like to not only maintain sobriety, but to find a different way of life. With honest answers to your most common questions about being part of a Fellowship, this book provides straightforward explanations on working the first three Steps of a Twelve Step program.

Order No. 3411; ebook EB3411

Also of Interest

Find inspiration anywhere, at any time, with Hazelden Publishing's highly rated and well-reviewed mobile apps. Available for iPhone, iPad, iPod Touch, and Android devices.

Touchstones
Recovery Meditations for Men

Featuring all 366 daily meditations from the best-selling meditation book designed for men in recovery from addiction.

Day by Day
Meditations for Addicts in Recovery

Daily inspirational readings that reinforce the Twelve Steps and Narcotics Anonymous principles. Each message also includes a question, a prayer, and a "sentence starter" that help you relate the daily topics to your own life. Use these as inspirations for journal writing or discussions, or type your thoughts right into the app.

Twenty-Four Hours a Day
Recovery Meditations

One of Healthline's Best Alcoholism Apps of 2016 and 2017, featuring all 366 daily meditations from the classic best-selling meditation book for people in recovery from addiction.

For more information about Hazelden's mobile apps, visit us online at **Hazelden.org/mobileapps**.